The Middle Colonies

Inquiries into American History

Our Colonial Heritage: Plymouth and Jamestown
by William Gee White

The Middle Colonies: New York, New Jersey, Pennsylvania
by James I. Clark

The American Revolution
by D. Duane Cummins and William Gee White

The Federal Period: 1790–1800
by Lloyd K. Musselman

Andrew Jackson's America
by Thomas Koberna and Stanley Garfinkel

The American Frontier
by D. Duane Cummins and William Gee White

The Origins of the Civil War
by D. Duane Cummins and William Gee White

Reconstruction: 1865–1877
by James I. Clark

Industrialism: The American Experience
by James E. Bruner, Jr.

American Foreign Policy: 1789–1980
by Thomas A. Fitzgerald, Jr.

Contrasting Decades: The 1920's and 1930's
by D. Duane Cummins and William Gee White

Combat and Consensus: The 1940's and 1950's
by D. Duane Cummins and William Gee White

Conflict and Compromise: The 1960's and 1970's
by D. Duane Cummins

America at War: World War I and World War II
by Douglas Waitley

America at War: Korea and Vietnam
by Douglas Waitley

Women in American History
by William Jay Jacobs

The
Middle Colonies:
New York,
New Jersey,
Pennsylvania

James I. Clark

Glencoe Publishing Co., Inc.
Encino, California

FIRST EDITION

Glencoe Publishing Co., Inc.
17337 Ventura Boulevard
Encino, California 91316

Collier Macmillan Canada, Ltd.

Library of Congress Catalog Card Number: 79–54221

Printed in the United States of America

ISBN 0-02-652540-2

1 2 3 4 5   83 82 81 80

CONTENTS

An Iroquois warrior is memorialized in this statue in Canada. At the height of their power, the Five Nations of the Iroquois Confederacy controlled most of the territory from present-day Tennessee to the Saint Lawrence River in Canada, and from Maine across the Great Lakes into Michigan.

INTRODUCTION

Along the northeastern coast of the continent that
Europeans would later call North America, warfare was en-
demic. Much of the time people traveling singly or in small
bands knew no safety on forest trails.

Deeply distressed, Dekanawidah, born among the Huron
of the north, dwelling among the Mohawk, sought a code of
laws to abolish war. He wished to sit with tribal leaders beneath the great world-tree and seal eternal peace. A stranger,
he found no listeners.

Among the Onondaga lived Hiawatha, a man beset by
sorrow, his seven daughters lost to witchcraft and disease.
He too deplored the perpetual conflict. Despairing, Hiawatha set out to join his sister Dasio, living with the
Mohawk. At each village he came upon he sang of peace, to
no avail.

Learning of Hiawatha's coming, Dekanawidah took
heart. Here, it seemed, was a man like himself, longing for
peace—a man who, as a member of a tribe close to the
Mohawk, might aid his cause. Dekanawidah and Hiawatha
met near Cohoes Falls. There they worked out the laws,
established ceremonial chants, and laid plans. Then they set
out to persuade the tribes.

This time the Mohawk listened. But they insisted that the
code be accepted first by the Neutral nation—the "Mother of
Nations"—living near Niagara and remaining always aloof
from the quarrels of neighbors. In the Neutral town of
Cayanoga, Dekanawidah and Hiawatha consulted the peace
woman, Jikonsaseh. She praised them, and agreed to

A drawing of the Indian village of Sappokanican, which was built on the site later occupied by New York City's Gansevoort Market.

accompany them to the lands of the Mohawk, Oneida, Seneca, Cayuga, and Onondaga. And after five summer days—five years—of journeying, and much counseling, even the fierce Adodarhoh, an Onondaga chief whose hair resembled snakes, was overcome. He consented to head the first council. Representatives of the five nations sat down beneath the pine tree of Dekanawidah's vision and ratified the Law of the Great Peace of the People of the Longhouse.

So, according to legend, began the Iroquois Confederacy, known also as the Confederation of the Five Nations and the Great League of the Iroquois, in all American Indian history a unique achievement.

A central council house of the Iroquois, in a drawing made in 1881.

Member tribes of the numerous Algonkian language group, including the Delaware, Mahican, Manhaset, Mohegan, Montauk, Raritan, and Wappinger, had long occupied parts of the area that came to be known as the Middle Colonies. They were woodland Indians, most living in rounded wigwams of sapling framework covered with bark. They combined agriculture—the growing of such plants as maize, beans, and squash—with hunting, gathering, and fishing. There were powerful tribes among the Algonkian, but none was more powerful than the tribes of the other language group, the Iroquois.

Although evidence is scanty, some archaeologists believe that the Iroquois were relative newcomers to the region. They may have originated in the Mississippi Valley, moving north and east around 1300 A.D. until they reached the southern banks of the Saint Lawrence River. Unlike their neighbors, they were a longhouse people. They resided in sapling and bark structures measuring some hundred feet in length and about twenty feet in width. Each held forty to fifty families. The longhouse had one entrance, no windows, and smoke holes in the roof. The Iroquois palisaded their towns with upright logs, sometimes in double rows. They cleared the land nearby, and planted maize and vegetables. After several seasons, when the soil was exhausted at one site, they moved on to another.

And, legend aside, the Iroquois Confederacy was real. Formed around 1570, it was vital to Iroquois survival. Altogether the five nations numbered scarcely five thousand among enemies, real or potential, who numbered five times that many.

Each Iroquois nation was divided into clans—Turtle, Bear, Beaver, and so on. Each had its own council of sachems—elders, or chiefs—which governed the tribe with the consent of the members. In addition, each sent representatives to the council of forty-nine sachems which governed the confederacy. Each nation was free to decide whether to go along with a decision—for example, to make war—or to ignore it.

It has been argued that the Framers of the Constitution of the United States drew upon the Iroquois Confederacy for ideas and inspiration. Evidence on this point is inconclusive, but it is at least certain that some of the members of the Constitutional Convention—including Benjamin Franklin—were familiar with the League and respected it.

A general division of labor prevailed among the Iroquois. Both men and women worked to build longhouses. Men cleared the land of trees and brush; women tilled the soil and harvested the crops. Women also gathered berries and other wild food, cooked meals, made clothing, and reared children. Men hunted, fished, made weapons, constructed canoes, and made war.

Yet, despite their seemingly inferior position, women in fact ruled the Iroquois. The society was organized as a matriarchy, and men traced their ancestry through the female line. Women of each nation nominated sachems for the individual councils of elders and for the Great League. And the women could remove a sachem from power should he fail to perform well. The Iroquois, it is said, considered the word "squaw" a derogatory term and never used it in reference to Iroquois women.

Proud of their traditions, their code of honor, their confederacy, and their ability as warriors, the Iroquois remained foremost among the eastern tribes. They called themselves Ongwe-oweh, "the only true people." The name Iroquois was originally given them by an enemy tribe; it meant "rattlesnakes." Other enemies called them "forest wolves." Still others simply noted that the Iroquois "approach like foxes, fight like angry bears, and disappear like birds."

Within the Great League, the Mohawk, Oneida, Seneca, Cayuga, and Onondaga kept the peace among themselves. But they conducted intermittent and fierce warfare against the Huron and other Algonkian tribes, particularly those north of the Saint Lawrence. This intensified when, early in the seventeenth century, the French established a thriving fur trade along the Saint Lawrence and control of the source of furs became vitally important to Indian tribes.

The first Europeans to explore a portion of what is now New York State met members of the Iroquois group. They were impressed.

This portrait of a geographer, painted in the sixteenth century by an unknown Italian artist, captures the qualities of determination, daring, and scientific curiosity which characterized the European explorers of that age.

1

THE BEGINNING:

THE SEVENTEENTH

CENTURY

The Dutch were the first Europeans to explore and settle in what became the Middle Colonies. For the establishment of their claim to land there, they relied upon an Englishman, Henry Hudson.

After Columbus's voyages, Europeans realized that two continents lay across a western route to the Orient, with its spices and other treasures. In England, France, and Holland especially, attention turned to finding a Northwest passage through North America.

John Cabot, probably born in Genoa and a naturalized citizen of Venice, was the first to try. He was sponsored by King Henry VII of England, who earlier—to his regret—had turned down pleas for support from Bartholomew Columbus, Christopher's brother. Cabot and his crew set out in the small ship *Mathew* late in May, 1497, making first landfall on the northern tip of Newfoundland on June 24. They moved along the eastern coast of the island as far south as Placentia Bay before returning north to the original landfall to head for home. They arrived back in Bristol, England, on August 6.

Henry VII rewarded Cabot with the sum of ten pounds, which he quickly spent "to amuse himself." Later the king granted him an annual pension of twenty pounds, which the able mariner was not long to enjoy.

In 1498 Henry VII dispatched Cabot on a second voyage, this time with five ships. One vessel soon turned back, the others continuing on. The rest is silence. The four ships were

No portrait of John Cabot survives, although this portrait of his son Sebastian is sometimes mislabeled as such. Sebastian (1476–1557) was also a geographer and explorer, sailing at various times under the Venetian, Spanish, and English flags.

never heard from again. Whether they foundered and sank in a mighty storm or were dashed upon rocks and broken, no one knows.

Cabot's significance was threefold. First, he discovered the Grand Banks. These were prime cod and halibut grounds off Newfoundland which the fishermen of Bristol and other English coastal towns would begin to exploit almost at once. Second, he established an English claim in North America which would overlap those of other countries, although nearly a century would pass before England engaged in colonization. And, third, he kept interest in a Northwest Passage alive.

Later, in the 1530's, King Henry IV of France supported westward voyages by Jacques Cartier, the intrepid sailor of Saint-Malo. Cartier found the Gulf of Saint Lawrence, which Cabot missed, and the Saint Lawrence River. He claimed extensive land on both sides of the river for the king of France.

The Dutch Arrive

Dutch interest in a Northwest Passage, and in carving out a portion of North America, surfaced later.

Holland, known also as the Netherlands or Low Countries, consisted of a loose confederation of provinces first united under the French dukes of Burgundy in the fourteenth and fifteenth centuries. In 1506 the area fell under the control of the Hapsburgs, Spain's ruling family. Eleven years later, Martin Luther broke with the Roman Catholic church to mark the beginning of the Reformation. Protestantism spread rapidly throughout the seven northern Dutch provinces. There the Dutch Reformed church was established. Drawing its doctrines from the French theologian John Calvin, this denomination was similar to the Puritan movement that was developing in England.

Protestantism, of course, was anathema to the Catholic Hapsburgs, who soon began a policy of severe religious persecution in Holland. This led to a Dutch revolt, beginning in 1558 and continuing off and on until the two nations signed a truce in 1609. Not until 1648, however, did Spain finally recognize the independence of the Republic of the United Netherlands.

In a modern artist's interpretation of the scene, a group of Indians watch as Jacques Cartier erects a cross to claim the land along the Saint Lawrence River for France. Cartier found the Huron Indians friendly and humorous. They told him of a rich land, filled with precious stones, which lay just beyond the next rapids of the river. Cartier investigated, and when he returned home he carried with him samples of the diamonds he believed he had found. The stones turned out to be quartz crystals, and "Canadian diamonds" became a standard joke in France.

Holland's position on the North Sea and its good ports gave it power as a trading nation all out of proportion to its size. Such trading and manufacturing centers as Amsterdam, Dordrecht, and Deventer flourished. The Dutch East India Company was chartered as a monopoly in 1602. With its ships following the Cape of Good Hope route around the southern tip of Africa, the company quickly became a serious rival to the Portuguese in the Indies trade. Soon a group of merchants in the company, as a private venture, decided to renew the search for a shorter passage to the East—a passage through North America. On January 8, 1609, these merchants contracted with an Englishman, Henry Hudson, for a voyage of exploration.

Little is known about Hudson's background. He apparently lived in London, was married, and had three sons. No one knows how or where he learned his navigation. When the Dutch approached him, Hudson had already made two voyages for England, searching for a passage, one northward along the eastern coast of Greenland. Neither expedition turned up any evidence of a waterway through the North American continent. Hudson's subsequent voyages would fall short of this goal, too, although one, at least, would prove valuable to the Dutch.

In April, 1609, Hudson took command of the small *Half Moon,* a vessel of some eighty tons, sixty-three feet long, with a mixed Dutch and English crew. He sailed out of Amsterdam and the Zuider Zee, westward bound. Reaching Newfoundland, he sailed the North American coast south to Virginia, where Englishmen were in the process of establishing the settlement of Jamestown. After exploring Delaware Bay, Hudson turned north again, eventually finding the mouth of the river which bears his name.

Half Moon, Henry Hudson's ship.

He was not the first there. An Italian navigator, Giovanni de Verrazzano, had seen the river in 1524. In addition, an anonymous English sea captain apparently had sailed into the Hudson's mouth in 1607. On the map he made, he entered the words "Mannahata" on the west of the mouth and "Manahatin" to the east. The words perhaps referred to the Indians living there. Hudson may have had a copy of that map, and Manhattan became the name of the island which is now central to New York City.

For eleven days *Half Moon* cruised up the broad river, past high cliffs and fertile valley land, with low mountains away in the distance. The ship coursed as far north as the present-day city of Albany before encountering shoals and the end to navigation. According to one account, written in 1610:

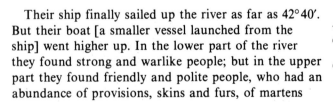

Dutchmen trading for Indian furs.

Their ship finally sailed up the river as far as 42° 40'. But their boat [a smaller vessel launched from the ship] went higher up. In the lower part of the river they found strong and warlike people; but in the upper part they found friendly and polite people, who had an abundance of provisions, skins and furs, of martens

Brown Brothers

and foxes, and many other commodities, even white and red grapes, and they traded amicably with the people. And of all the above-mentioned commodities they brought some home. When they had thus been about fifty leagues up the river [one league is about three English miles], they returned on the 4th of October and went again to sea.[1]

Wrote Hudson himself about the Indians they met:

When I came on shore, the swarthy natives all stood and sang in their fashion. Their clothing consists of foxes and other animals, which they dress and make the garments from skins of various sorts. Their food is Turkish wheat [maize, or corn], which they cook by baking, and it is excellent eating. They soon came on board, one after another, in their canoes, which are made of a single piece of wood. Their weapons are bows and arrows, pointed with sharp stones, which they fasten with hard resin. They had no houses, but slept under the blue heavens, some on mats of bulrushes interwoven, and some on the leaves of trees. They always carry with them all their goods, as well as their food and green tobacco, which is strong and good for use. They appear to be a friendly people, but are much inclined to steal, and are adroit in carrying away whatever they take a fancy to.[2]

Here Hudson put his finger on the nub of underlying Indian-white conflict: wholly opposing values concerning private property. With the possible exception of weapons, Indians did not as a rule honor the idea of private ownership. They held possessions, including land, in common. The ownership of land, in fact, rested in the tribe. Land could not be alienated—that is, its ownership could not be permanently granted to anyone in or out of the tribe. Indians

This drawing of an American Indian owes far more to the imagination of the artist than it does to reality. In fact, just about the only accurate detail is the long cigar—the Indians did make and smoke them.

[1] Emanuel van Meteren, "On Hudson's Voyage," in J. Franklin Jameson, ed., *Narratives of New Netherland, 1609-1664* (New York: Charles Scribner's Sons, 1909), p. 7.

[2] Johan de Laet, "New World," in Jameson, *Narratives of New Netherland,* p. 48.

might permit the use of land for a time—lease it, in effect. But actual title, as far as Indians were concerned, never legally passed from the tribe. Hudson's men had one brief encounter with Indians over theft at the mouth of the river, and one Indian was killed. There was another skirmish over the same issue, and another Indian death, in the upper reaches of the river.

Having claimed all the land he had seen for Holland—as far south as Virginia—Hudson aimed *Half Moon's* bowsprit eastward, arriving at Devonshire, England, on November 7. He had been gone only eleven weeks. And in England he and his crew remained for a time, for King James I had heard of the voyage and ordered that Hudson confine his efforts to his own country. After passing the winter in England, though, Hudson was released to return to Holland to report to his merchant employers.

In 1610 Henry Hudson made one final voyage, this time for English merchants. Searching for the Northwest Passage once more, he discovered Hudson's Strait and Hudson's Bay. Then mutinous crewmen took prisoner the explorer to whom the Dutch owed their claim to a portion of North America. The mutineers cast him adrift in a small boat, and Hudson perished in icy northern seas.

Beginning of Dutch Colonization

The Dutch followed up on Hudson's discoveries. In 1610, merchants sent traders up the Hudson River to open a brisk exchange in furs.

For several years the Dutch interest in America remained purely commercial. The fur trade was steady and, for some, profitable. Dutch traders did especially well with the Iroquois, in whose country they erected Fort Nassau, near present-day Albany. During the first year of Hudson's exploration, the Iroquois had been alienated from the French along the Saint Lawrence. Samuel de Champlain, governor of New France, had joined a war party of Huron Indians and had given the Iroquois their first taste of firepower. Champlain killed two with his musket, scattering the remainder. After that the Iroquois gladly turned to the Dutch as an outlet for their furs. Many of these furs were obtained from Indians west of Lake

Samuel de Champlain, explorer, soldier, and governor of New France, laid the cornerstone of the French empire in North America. In 1608 he founded the great fur-trading center of Quebec.

The Public Archives of Canada

Continental Insurance Co.

A sachem speaks inside the council house of the Iroquois, in a painting by H. E. Smith.

Ontario, and numerous bloody wars were fought over their control. In return, the Iroquois received trinkets, mirrors, cloth, liquor, and eventually guns. Wrote one Hollander who made an extensive tour of Mohawk country:

> The government among them consists of the oldest, the most intelligent, the most eloquent and most warlike men. These commonly resolve, and then the young and warlike men execute. But if the common people do not approve of the resolution, it is left entirely to the judgment of the mob. The chiefs are generally the poorest among them, for instead of their receiving from the common people as among Christians, they are obliged to give to the mob; especially when any one is killed in war, they give great presents to the next of kin of the deceased; and if they take any prisoners they present them to that family of which one has been killed, and the prisoner is then adopted by the family into the place of the

deceased person. There is no punishment here for murder and other villainies, but everyone is his own avenger. The friends of the deceased revenge themselves upon the murderer until peace is made by presents to the next of kin. But although they are so cruel, and live without laws or any punishments for evil doers, yet there are not half so many villainies or murders committed amongst them as amongst Christians; so that I often times think with astonishment upon all the murders committed in the Fatherland, notwithstanding their severe laws and heavy penalties. These Indians, though they live without laws, or fear of punishment, do not (at least, they very seldom) kill people, unless it may be in a great passion, or a hand-to-hand fight. Wherefore we go wholly unconcerned along with the Indians and meet each other an hour's walk off in the woods, without doing any harm to one another.[3]

The Dutch government chartered the Dutch West India Company in 1621, and Holland's New World possession passed to its control. In the spring of 1624 the company sent the ship *New Netherland,* bearing some thirty families. Most were Walloons, French-speaking people of southern Holland. They were led by Cornelis May, who had been appointed governor, or director, of the colony of New Netherland. Some families remained on Manhattan Island, but the majority journeyed upriver to establish Fort Orange, near the then dilapidated Fort Nassau. A few moved to the east bank of the Delaware River, opposite the mouth of the Schuylkill, to begin a settlement also named Fort Nassau.

Ships arrived in New Netherland carrying livestock and food supplies. They returned with furs, tobacco, and maize. More immigrants came. By the end of 1625 the total population stood at about two hundred. The following year the Dutch began a settlement which became New Amsterdam, on the lower tip of Manhattan, with forty cabins initially erected. Willem Verhulst purchased the

[3]Johannes Megapolensis, Jr., "A Short Account of the Mohawk Indians," in Jameson, *Narratives of New Netherland,* pp. 179–80.

Title Guaranty — New York

The purchase of Manhattan Island in 1626, for about twenty-four dollars, has been called "the greatest real-estate bargain in history."

island from the Indians with merchandise worth sixty guilders, or about twenty-four dollars. Later, Governor Peter Minuit bought Staten Island from Indians for an equally small value of "duffels, kettles, axes, hoes, wampum, drilling awls, Jews harps, and diverse other small wares." The demand for labor stimulated the importation of black slaves, beginning in 1626 with the arrival of eleven.

The island of Manhattan, wrote an observer in 1626,

is full of trees, and, in the middle, rocky. On the north side, there is good land in two places, where two farmers, each with four horses, would have enough to do, without much clearing or grubbing [removing tree roots] at first. The grass is good in the forests and valleys; but when made into hay, it is not so nutritious for the cattle as the hay in Holland, in consequence of its wild state; yet it annually improves by cultivation. On the east side there rises a large level field, of about one hundred and sixty acres, through which runs a

The island of Manhattan as it appeared at the time of its purchase in
1626—"full of trees, and, in the middle, rocky."

very fine fresh stream; so that that land can be plowed
without much clearing. It appears to be good. The six
farms, four of which lie along the River Hell-gate,
stretching to the south side of the island, have at least
one hundred and twenty acres ready to be sown with
winter seed, which, at the most, may have been plowed
eight times.[4]

Because the Indians did not value European coins,
preferring the wampum to which they were accustomed, the
Dutch established the manufacture of that medium of
exchange on Long Island. They made white beads out of the
shell of the periwinkle, a marine snail, and black beads out of
part of the inside of the clam shell. Indians valued the black
beads two to one over the white. The Dutch used wampum
mainly in the fur trade. With it they ranged in search of furs
far north along the New England coast, usually meeting with
success. This much annoyed the English Separatist settlers at
Plymouth, in Massachusetts, and later Puritan settlers in
that region. It cut into their own trade with the Indians.

[4]Quoted in John Romeyn Brodhead, *History of the State of New York*
(New York: Harper & Brothers, 1853), vol. 1, pp. 167–68.

New Netherland did not grow rapidly. Past mid-century it held scarcely nine thousand souls. Religious toleration prevailed in Holland. Jobs were not hard to find. And even though wages were relatively low, to most Hollanders life at home seemed preferable to the dangers of a long and stormy ocean voyage and the uncertainties of a new start in an almost unknown land. The colony, and especially the town of New Amsterdam became polyglot as immigrants and traders arrived from other nations. Conversations in French, English, Dutch, German, and Spanish took place daily. One contemporary stated that eighteen Indian languages could be heard there. With respect to religion, the community included Dutch Reformed, Lutherans, Quakers, Jews, Catholics, Puritans, and Antinomians, among others.

In the 1640's the population of New Amsterdam numbered about a thousand people—mostly merchants, craftsmen, government officials, and farmers. Pigs were everywhere, and the stench of pig sties and open privies gravely offended the nostrils of the uninitiated. The Dutch did not keep the fort intended to guard the settlement in good repair. The structure for the Reformed Church went unfinished. On the other hand, the thirty-odd taverns and alehouses appear to have flourished.

Upriver, besides encouraging fur trade, the West India Company made huge grants of land to *patroons*—patrons—who were expected to attract tenants and cultivate their grants. A French Jesuit missionary, Isaac Jogues, left this impression of Rensselaerswyck, an estate which included vast lands on both sides of the Hudson:

> The center of this rude little settlement was Fort
> Orange, a miserable structure of logs. . . . It contained
> several houses and other buildings and behind it
> was a small church, recently erected, and serving
> as the abode of the pastor, Dominie [Reverend]
> Megapolensis. . . . Some twenty-five or thirty houses,
> roughly built of boards and roofed with thatch, were
> scattered at intervals on or near the borders of the
> Hudson, above and below the fort. Their inhabitants,
> about a hundred in number, were for the most part

This sketch of the fort at New Amsterdam and the surrounding buildings was made by a Dutch officer in 1635. The windmill ground grain that was grown on the island's farms or brought by Indians who traveled to the island by canoe.

New York State Library

As an early observer of New Netherland wrote, the settlers "traded, too, with Indians, who profited greatly by the competition among them, receiving guns, knives, axes, kettles, cloth, and beads, at moderate rates. . . ."

rude Dutch farmers, tenants of Van Rensselaer, the patroon, or lord of the manor. They raised wheat, of which they made beer, and oats, with which they fed their numerous horses. They traded, too, with Indians, who profited greatly by the competition among them, receiving guns, knives, axes, kettles, cloth, and beads, at moderate rates, in exchange for their furs.[5]

Government and Indian Wars

At first New Netherland was ruled by the governor, or director, along with a company-appointed council of four or five. There was no popular participation and apparently, during the early years, no demand for it. In towns the principal officials were the *schout* and the *schepens*. The schepens was a combination administrator and magistrate, or judge. The schout was the prosecuting attorney, although at times he might preside over a court as well. All officials were under

[5] Francis Parkman, *The Jesuits in North America in the Seventeenth Century* (Boston: Little, Brown, 1899), vol. 2, pp. 46–47.

the jurisdiction of the West India Company and were ultimately responsible to the laws of the States-General, the government of the Dutch Republic. The huge estates upriver on the Hudson were governed by the patroons, the owners, who possessed legislative, administrative, and judicial powers.

For the most part, council and governor handled everyday matters. Their legislation during 1638, for example, dealt mostly with New Amsterdam—limitations on individual engagement in the fur trade, curfews for sailors and company servants, the sale of arms to Indians, and permits required for leaving Manhattan. The government scolded citizens for idleness and attempted to limit liquor sales. It also provided regulations concerning the quality of tobacco brought to company warehouses for sale and export, at the same time deciding on its value for export duties.

The first warehouse in New Amsterdam.

Between the mid-1620's and thirty years later, the colony of New Netherland passed through the hands of fifteen governors. On the whole they were not impressive, and a few were recalled to Holland on charges of misgovernment. One, Peter Minuit, apparently possessed only loose bonds of loyalty to company and country—he later helped Swedes establish themselves along the Delaware River on land claimed by Holland. Another governor, Wouter Van Twiller, by most accounts drank too much. Willem Kieft, who replaced the too frequently tipsy Van Twiller in 1638, was cited for stupidity in commencing and prosecuting an Indian war. His contemporaries regarded Kieft as "a more discreet and sober" man than Van Twiller, but nonetheless headstrong, autocratic, and "rapacious."

On the whole, relations between the Dutch and the Indians had been friendly since Hudson's time. In the early 1640's, however, things changed.

Indians along the lower river chafed at the strict enforcement of laws against the purchase of guns and brandy, the laws being more carefully applied there than farther north. Indians also resented the frequent failure of the Dutch to restrain their cattle from unfenced Indian cornfields. The Dutch, on their part, complained against Indian dogs that killed and wolfed down poultry and livestock. And they became involved in numerous disputes with Indians over

This tapestry from a New York hotel depicts a scene from New Amsterdam's Cattle Fair, a festival founded by Governor Kieft in 1641 and held on the settlement's bowling green.

land ownership, owing mainly to the Indian policy of leasing rather than selling. Governor Kieft added to the growing tension when he sought to tax Indians along the lower Hudson to pay for the building and maintenance of fortifications. This attempt, Kieft's critics charged, was the final spark that touched off four years of intermittent warfare.

In 1641 Kieft accused Raritan Indians on Staten Island of acts of destruction that were actually committed by whites. The soldiers he sent to the area killed a number of Raritan and mistreated others. The Raritan promptly murdered four whites and laid waste a farm. Then, seeking revenge for the killing of a fellow tribesman several years earlier, a member of a different tribe killed Claes Cornelissen Swits, a wheelwright. Now thoroughly alarmed, Dutch settlers accused Kieft of blundering, of exposing them to attack, and of cowardice for remaining comfortably and securely in the fort on Manhattan.

Seeking support, the governor then established a council of twelve men—the first instance of representative government of any kind in New Netherland—to advise him. The twelve at first refused to agree to an attack on the Indians, but in January, 1642, they finally relented. Eighty men moved out in March that year. But then a truce was made, and an uneasy peace prevailed for the remainder of the year.

Occasional hostile acts on both sides occurred, however, and in February, 1643, war broke out between the Mohawk and Indians along the lower Hudson. At this point Kieft resolved to throw off all restraint and "wipe the mouths of the savages," although his council advised against provoking armed encounters. Kieft's troops made two night attacks. During one they burned an Indian town, killing some eighty warriors, women, and children. In the other raid, on Corlaer's Hook, the Dutch killed forty Indians. One of Kieft's critics recorded:

> As soon as the savages understood that the Swannekens ["people of the salt water," the Dutch] had so treated them, all the men whom they could surprise on the farm lands, they killed; but we have never heard that they have ever permitted women or children to be killed. They burned all the houses, farms, barns, grain, haystacks, and destroyed everything they could get hold of. So there was an open destructive war begun.[6]

Anne Hutchinson and her daughter, as a sculptor imagined they might have looked. No portrait of Anne Hutchinson was made during her lifetime.

Anne Hutchinson, who had been banished from Massachusetts Bay Colony for her religious views, was living in New Netherland. It was during this time of trouble that Indians killed her along with all but one of her children. Another strong woman of colonial times, Lady Deborah Moody, barely escaped harm from Indians.

Born in England in 1600, Deborah Dunch received a good education. At the age of twenty-two she married Henry Moody, whom King James I made a baronet. Henry Moody

(margin, rotated) Library of Congress

---

[6]Quoted in Alexander C. Flick, ed., *History of the State of New York* (New York: Columbia University Press, 1933), vol. 1, p. 289.

died ten years later, leaving his widow with an estate and a five-year-old son. Attracted to dissenting religious groups, Quakers in particular, Lady Deborah got into trouble with the English government. In 1640 she sailed for Boston.

There she found the Puritan religious atmosphere stifling, and after two years she decided to move with her son to New Netherland. The Dutch West India Company granted her land on Long Island—she appears to have been the first woman in America to obtain a land grant—and she established the town of Gravesend, another unusual thing for a woman to do. And Lady Deborah cast a ballot in at least one town election, the first and only time a woman is known to have done so during colonial times.

As the Indian troubles increased, Lady Deborah called and presided over a town meeting in Gravesend. Hers was the deciding vote cast in favor of having the women and children withdraw to New Amsterdam, leaving the men behind. Before their boats were out of sight of the town, Indians attacked and burned Gravesend.

Kieft's continued high-handed conduct of Indian relations increased the number of his enemies. Driven by exasperation, Maryn Adriaensen, a Long Island farmer and a member of the Board of Twelve, tried to assassinate the governor. He failed. Then his servant tried. He too failed and was killed in the attempt. The authorities shipped Adriaensen back to Holland for trial, and he got off with a light sentence.

Since the Board of Twelve offered more advice than he felt necessary, Kieft abolished it, although he later replaced it with a council of eight. This group organized a military company, armed other colonists, and prepared defenses.

In this view of Wall Street on Manhattan Island, the "good, solid fence" built by the Dutch can be seen to the right.

An estimated fifteen hundred Indians outnumbered the Dutch on the lower river. But, fortunately for the Dutch, the Indians failed to act together. They confined themselves to raids by small bands.

In February, 1644, a force of about a hundred and thirty Dutchmen made a night attack on an Indian town near the present Greenwich, Connecticut. The Dutch totally destroyed the town and killed most of its inhabitants, some five hundred to seven hundred Indians. Following this, the Dutch built a "good solid fence" across lower Manhattan for protection. Wall Street, the heart of New York City's financial district, now commemorates that structure.

In June a ship bearing two hundred persons, a third of them soldiers, arrived from Curaçao, a Dutch settlement in northern Brazil which was governed by Peter Stuyvesant. The Dutch force now numbered about four hundred and fifty men, and yet the war dragged on. Finally, in the spring of 1645, the various tribes made peace gestures. In August that year, with seven sachems signing for the Indians and Kieft and the Board of Eight signing for the Dutch, peace was achieved. About two years later, Peter Stuyvesant arrived to take over from Kieft as governor.

Stuyvesant

Judged by historians to have been one of the better of the more than a dozen governors of New Netherland, Stuyvesant was also fated to be the last. He was thirty-seven years old at the time of his appointment. The son of a minister, he had received a classical education and then had entered military service. During an unsuccessful Dutch assault against the Spanish fort on the island of Saint Martin in the Caribbean, a cannonball crushed Stuyvesant's right leg below the knee. That portion was amputated, and thereafter he wore a pegleg over which he draped an embroidered cover fringed with lace. A portrait of about 1660 shows him as a man with piercing eyes, a high forehead, a huge, hooked nose, and a double chin. He wore a benign though aloof expression, as if daring anyone to challenge his authority. Possessing a self-confidence which his enemies considered arrogance, Stuyvesant did not shy from controversy. His rule was often arbitrary and direct. "He proceeds no longer by words or writing," said a contemporary, "but by arrests and stripes [whippings]."

Stuyvesant's term as governor marked a time of conflict between differing interests within New Netherland, and between the New Netherland government and the government of the Dutch Republic at home. At issue were such matters as trade regulation, taxes, land purchases, patroonships, and such problems of public morality as excessive drinking, which the colonial government sought in vain to

Dubbed "Old Silver Nails" because of his silver-studded wooden leg, Peter Stuyvesant was a stern—not to say autocratic—leader. Speaking of one of his critics, he once bellowed, "I will make him a foot shorter, and send the pieces to Holland." On another occasion he announced to his councillors, "We derive our authority from God and the Company, not from a few ignorant subjects."

curb. In 1649 a group of New Amsterdamers petitioned the States-General for popular participation in local government. The States-General directed Stuyvesant to arrange for the election of a schout, two co-mayors, and five schepenses. Stuyvesant did nothing until 1653 when, in his characteristically aristocratic way, he appointed the town officials. No elections were held.

On the whole, however, Peter Stuyvesant appears to have acted in what he believed to be the colony's best interests. He enforced fencing ordinances and made strict fire laws. He applied prohibitions against the sale of liquor to Indians and saw that Indians employed by townspeople were paid promptly for their services. He also enforced laws against smuggling and tried to ensure that everyone attended Sunday services.

A view of New Amsterdam in 1656.

Relations with the Indians did not remain peaceful. An Indian-white quarrel in a peach orchard developed into a wider conflict known as the Peach War. There were massacres and kidnappings. Indians destroyed farms and pillaged small settlements. In all, some fifty colonists and some sixty Indians died before peace was once again restored. Indian access to liquor had much to do with the original outbreak, and Stuyvesant instituted a novel means of dealing with the problem. He kept drunken Indians in jail until they revealed the names of their suppliers; officials then proceeded against the guilty parties with swift punishments. Indian-white relations on Manhattan quieted down.

Peter Stuyvesant also had to contend with foreign encroachment on Dutch territory. On the one hand were the Swedes; on the other, the English.

New Sweden

Seventeenth-century Sweden was a power to be reckoned with, having gained prominence under the great king Gustavus Adolphus, whose interests included both European expansion and New World colonization. Engaged in the Thirty Years' War, however, he was in no position to promote his aims overseas. After the king died in battle in 1632, power in Sweden fell to Count Axel Oxenstierna, who oversaw the government for the girl-queen Christina. Oxenstierna developed plans to stake out a Swedish claim in America and organized a trading company to establish a

Johan Printz, called "Big Tub" by the Indians, was seven feet tall and weighed more than four hundred pounds. Printz served as governor of New Sweden from 1643 until 1653. Then, receiving no supplies or settlers from his government, he resigned and set sail for home.

Swedish Historical Society

colony. Peter Minuit, the former governor of New Netherland, was in Stockholm at the time. He offered to lead the first settlers, and his gesture was accepted. According to an eighteenth-century Swedish historian, the Reverend Israel Acrelius,

> As a good beginning the first colony was sent off, and Peter Minuit was placed over it, as being the best acquainted with those regions. They set sail from Gothenburg in a ship-of-war called the *Key of Calmar,* followed by a smaller vessel, bearing the name of the *Bird Griffin,* both laden with people, provisions, ammunition, and merchandise suitable for traffic and gifts to the Indians. The ships successfully reached their place of destination. The high expectations with which our emigrants had conceived of that new land agreed exactly with the first views which they had of it. They made their first landing on the bay or entrance to the river Poutaxat [the Delaware], which they called the river of New Sweden, and the place where they landed they called Paradise Point.[7]

The Swedish colonists, numbering in all about fifty, purchased land on the west side of the Delaware River from Indians. Acrelius continued:

> The first abode of the newly arrived emigrants was at a place called by the Indians Hopokahacking. There, in the year 1638, Peter Minuit built a fortress, which he named Fort Christina [the present site of Wilmington, Delaware]. This place, situated upon the west side of the river, was probably chosen so as to be out of the way of the Hollanders, who wished to usurp the eastern shore—a measure of prudence, until the arrival of a greater force from Sweden. The fort was built upon an eligible site, not far from the mouth of

[7] Israel Acrelius, "Account of the Swedish Churches in New Sweden," in Albert Cook Myers, ed., *Narratives of Early Pennsylvania, West New Jersey and Delaware, 1630–1707* (New York: Charles Scribner's Sons, 1912), p. 60.

the creek, so as to secure them the navigable water of the Maniquas, which was afterwards called Christina Kihl, or Creek.[8]

So began the short-lived colony of New Sweden.

The possibility of profit in the fur trade initially lured Swedes, and later Finns, to New Sweden, although a number of them soon established farms. But the colony never attracted many settlers. Even though Sweden sent over convicts with the promise of liberty after a few years of service, at its peak the colony numbered no more than four hundred people. And half of those were Finns.

On the strength of Hudson's voyage of 1609, the Dutch claimed the territory that New Sweden encompassed. They resented the Swedish settlement and Swedish activity in the fur trade. But Holland and Sweden, both Protestant nations, were allies in the Thirty Years' War which had begun in 1618 against Spain and other Catholic countries. The New Netherland governor, Willem Kieft, protested the Swedish settlement. Not wishing to endanger their wartime alliance, however, the Dutch government did not press the matter with force. Acrelius noted that "protest was made against the building of Fort Christina, but there also was . . . evidence that the strength of the Hollanders in the river on the first arrival of the Swedes consisted almost entirely in great words."[9]

Earlier the Dutch had settled around Fort Nassau, opposite the mouth of the Schuylkill. The presence of Fort Christina cut them off from contact by water with New Amsterdam. Later the Dutch erected Fort Casimir, south of Fort Christina, which cut off the Swedes.

Peter Stuyvesant inherited the Swedish problem when he took over as governor of New Netherland in 1647. And the following year the Swedish-Dutch alliance lost value as the devastating Thirty Years' War ended.

Stuyvesant, although determined to solve the Swedish situation, did not act in haste. Finally, in 1655, he outfitted a

National Archives

The Swedish colonists along the Delaware River introduced the log-cabin style of architecture to the New World. And, although their own colony was short-lived, the type of building they brought would spread throughout the American frontier.

[8] Ibid., pp. 61–62.
[9] Ibid., p. 63.

fleet and recruited six hundred to seven hundred men, whom he personally led against the Swedes. The appearance of the Dutch on the river off Fort Christina was effective. According to the report of New Sweden's last governor, Johan Clason Rising:

> As soon as the Dutch had nearly completed their works, they brought the guns of all their batteries to bear upon us, and on the 14th instant [of this month], formally summoned Fort Christina, with harsh menaces, by a drummer and a messenger, to capitulate within twenty-four hours. We then assembled a general council of the whole garrison, and it was found to be their unanimous opinion, that inasmuch as we had not sufficient strength for our defence (the Dutch having completed their works against the sconce [a small, protective earthwork], and neither the sconce nor the garrison being able to withstand an assault), and were in want both of powder and other munitions, and had no hope of relief, therefore they were all of opinion, that we should make the best terms that we could obtain with the Dutch; all which may be seen by the documents. So the next day we announced to the enemy, that we would consider their summons within the time prescribed, and being now reduced, by our want of supplies and weak condition, to yield to the violence practised upon us, we concluded a capitulation with Stuyvesant, as may be found by the original among the documents, and surrendered Fort Christina to him on the 15th instant, stipulating that the guns and all the effects belonging to the crown or the Company should be restored by the Dutch, according to the inventory, upon demand, and reserving the restitution of our sovereign's rights in time and manner fitting; providing also, that the Dutch should freely transport to Sweden both us, and as many Swedes as chose to accompany us, for we held it better that the people should be restored to their Fatherland's service than to leave them here in misery, without the necessaries of life, in which case

they would have entered the service of the Dutch or English, and never again advantaged their country.[10]

The English Take Over

The English were another matter. They proved an impossible nut to crack.

By the 1660's New Netherland and its population of about nine thousand people had been far outnumbered by English colonies to the north and south, to which about a hundred thousand immigrants had come. Furthermore, the Dutch claim to the territory of New Netherland was open to dispute. The Dutch, on the strength of Hudson's exploration, claimed all the land between 40° and 54° north latitude. The English king, James I, on the basis of English explorations, had granted English colonists the land between 40° and 48°. The claims overlapped, and the English vowed to drive the Dutch out.

New England colonists spilled over into the Connecticut River Valley, locating at Hartford and then farther west in Greenwich, Stamford, and Milford. These settlements were only a few miles from the Dutch. Eventually, English colonists arrived to settle on eastern and central Long Island. Although the Dutch claimed the land, they were not sufficiently powerful to oust the English. Finally they drew a line which roughly bisected Long Island to separate themselves from English settlements.

In 1660 the English king, Charles II, was restored to the throne following the end of parliamentary rule, which had begun in 1649 with the beheading of his father, Charles I. Charles II made England's fateful move. To his brother James, duke of York, he granted part of Maine, all of Long Island, Martha's Vineyard, Nantucket, "and all the land from the west side of the Connecticutt River to the east side of De La Ware Bay," with "power and Authority of Government and Commaund in or over the Inhabitants of the said

Charles II, restored to the throne in 1660, disliked the Dutch despite their liberal treatment of him during his exile. He gave New Netherland, along with other lands, to his brother, and declared war on Holland.

---

[10] Johan Clason Rising, "Relation of the Surrender of New Sweden," in Myers, *Narratives of Early Pennsylvania*, p. 176.

Territories or Islands." The sweep of the king's pen disregarded not only Dutch claims, but previous charter provisions for the colonies of Massachusetts and Connecticut as well.

Hearing the news and expecting an English fleet, the Stuyvesant government belatedly undertook defense measures. The Dutch had not long to wait, and all preparations proved too little and much too late. Four English ships arrived off New Amsterdam in August, 1664. The commander demanded Dutch surrender.

Peter Stuyvesant fumed. He stumped about on his lace-trimmed peg. He blustered and issued threats. Finally, on September 2, a delegation led by Governor John Winthrop of Connecticut rowed ashore from an anchored man-of-war. Winthrop delivered to Stuyvesant a letter he had written that morning. It said, in part:

> My serious advice therefore to your selfe, & all your
> people, as my loving Neighbours, & friends is this,
> that you would speedily accept his Majesty's gracious
> tender [offer] which I understand hath beene declared,
> & resigne your selves under the obedience of his sacred
> Majesty, that you may avoid the effusion [shedding]
> of blood, & all the good people of your nation, may
> enjoy all the happiness tendered ... otherwise you may
> be assured, that both the Massachusetts Colony, &
> Connecticut, & all the rest are obliged, & ready to
> attend his Majesty's Service.[11]

Winthrop's words were persuasive. Stuyvesant gave up. He accepted the English terms, which allowed the Dutch to remain in the colony, if they wished, under English rule, and to retain their personal possessions, their homes, and their land. Richard Nicolls took over as governor of the colony, now named New York. Nearly ten years later the colony would fall back into Dutch hands for a brief two years. Finally, following an English-Dutch war and the Treaty of Westminster in 1674, it would become permanently English.

[11] Quoted in Flick, *History of the State of New York,* vol. 2, p. 78.

National Archives

After trying in vain to persuade his subjects to resist, Peter Stuyvesant finally surrendered to a contingent of British troops headed by Richard Nicolls.

Summoned back to Holland, Stuyvesant arrived with a letter from his New Netherland officials which stated in part:

> His Honour hath, during eighteen years' administration, conducted and demeaned himself not only as a director-general, as according to the best of our knowledge, he ought to do on all occasions for the best interests of the West India Company, but besides as an honest proprietor and patriot of this province, and as a supporter of the Reformed Religion.[12]

Stuyvesant later returned to the colony, where he died and was buried in 1672. A blunt and colorful man, a stiff taskmaster and an autocrat, he also had been an honest man and a faithful servant to both company and country. He had been a loser, but a gallant and courageous one.

[12]Quoted in Bayard Tuckerman, *Peter Stuyvesant* (New York: Dodd, Mead, 1893), p. 177.

About a hundred years later, Stuyvesant's remains were reburied within the walls of Saint Mark's-in-the-Bowery, a church built in the late 1700's. An inscription on the building honors him but, according to modern scholars, mistakes his age. He was probably sixty-two at the time of his death. The inscription reads:

In this Vault lies buried
PETRUS STUYVESANT,
late Captain-General and Governor-in-Chief of Amsterdam
in New-Netherland now called New-York
and the Dutch West-India Islands, died in A.D.167½
aged 80 years.

The former New Netherland was now a proprietary colony. This arrangement was a holdover from the Middle Ages, when the king owned all the land and could parcel it out as he pleased. With colonial settlement, the theory of feudal ownership was extended to America, although the proprietary idea was not applied everywhere. New York, Georgia, Carolina, Maryland, New Jersey, and Pennsylvania began as proprietary colonies, in which the sovereign granted huge tracts of land to favorites. Not only were the proprietors land owners, but they were also responsible for their colonies' governments. They had the power to appoint deputy governors and to provide for the enactment of laws. The king or his delegated officials, however, retained the right to veto legislation.

The relative toleration of diverse groups—Catholics and Jews usually were the main exceptions—that had been established during Dutch rule was continued in New York under the English. This was the case particularly in the city of New York, formerly New Amsterdam. The decidedly commercial cast that the Dutch had fastened on the colony,

especially on Manhattan, persisted. Dutch place names—
Tappen Zee, Hell Gate, Harlem, and others—prevailed.
And so, as part of the religious landscape, did the Dutch
Reformed church. The Dutch also made architectural con-
tributions, especially the gabled, slate-roofed houses fre-
quently constructed of brick.

These examples of Dutch architecture in New Amsterdam show the gabled, slanted, slate-roofed houses.

For a generation following the Dutch conquest, New
York—city and colony—remained more Dutch than
English. Tributary streams flowing into the Hudson were
still referred to as *kills*. Distances along the river that the eye
could measure remained *reaches*. A farm was still a *bou-
werie* (or "bowery"), and a farm house was a *bouwhyus*. The
terms *cookie, coleslaw, waffle, stoop,* and *baas* (or "boss")
also survived as part of the common speech.

New Jersey Settlements

Much of the huge area that Charles II had lumped under his
grant to his brother James was sheared off within a short
time. Upper Maine, Martha's Vineyard, and Nantucket
were worthless to New York and were given little attention
by that colony. The western half of Connecticut was soon
restored to Connecticut. Ownership of the area along the
western bank of the Delaware River was disputed by Lord
Baltimore and his Maryland colony. And in 1664, James,
duke of York, awarded New Jersey to a proprietary group
which included John, Lord Berkeley and Sir George
Carteret, his kinsmen.

A number of Swedish, Dutch, English, French, and Fin-
nish settlers already lived in New Jersey. Captain Philip
Carteret, Sir George's cousin, immediately brought in thirty
more settlers, mostly Germans. Gradually, such settlements
as Bergen, Newark, Elizabethtown, Middletown, Shrewsbury, and Perth Amboy developed.

Partly to attract colonists and partly because they were of
a liberal cast anyway, Sir George Carteret and Lord
Berkeley granted "concessions." Under these concessions,
new settlers received generous land grants for the payment
of a quit rent—an annual tax, frequently small, which released the settler from traditional feudal services to a lord.
They also received the right to appeal grievances. Freeholders—that is, land owners—gained the right to send

representatives to a general assembly, which could establish courts and provide for taxation. That the proprietors had the power to establish self-government in New Jersey appears to have been questionable. Nevertheless, the first assembly—consisting of a governor, seven councillors, and ten deputies from four or five towns—met on May 29, 1668. There was, and continued to be, considerable strife between the young colonial government and the proprietors over the latters' rights, such as the right to demand an oath of loyalty from the colonists and the right to collect quit rents. At the very least, settlers thought, they should be allowed to pay quit rents in kind (that is, with crops, timber, or other goods) since money was scarce. The proprietors tended to favor the supremacy of the governor, whom they appointed, over the assembly. And on most points they won.

In 1674 Berkeley sold his proprietorship, consisting of land to the west, to a pair of Quakers named Edward Byllinge and John Fenwick. Later, facing bankruptcy, Byllinge and Fenwick sold out to a trio of fellow Quakers—William Penn, Gawen Lawrie, and Nicholas Lucas. As a result, the colony was split into East New Jersey and West New Jersey. The eastern portion remained in Carteret's hands, although in the 1680's it passed to other proprietors following Carteret's death. Because the original Dutch government had paid little attention to New Jersey, and because there were many changes in proprietorship after the English took over, residents were plagued throughout the colonial period by controversies over titles to land. There was also continuous squabbling with New York over New Jersey's right to customs duties at such ports as Perth Amboy, because those duties tended to cut into the income of the port of New York.

The proprietors of West New Jersey laid out the towns of Salem in 1675 and Burlington in 1677. Within a few years they had brought over some five hundred persons. Nearly all of them were Quakers. West New Jerseyites enjoyed freedom of conscience, security from arbitrary arrest, guarantees of individual rights, and trial by jury. They had an elected assembly with broad powers to legislate and to control taxation.

Wrote an unknown contemporary about West New Jersey in 1681:

And there are also many Families, who have settled themselves in this Country; some about Husbandry [farming], others have Erected Mills for Grinding Corn, and several other necessary Tradesmen have There settled Themselves in Towns, and in the Country, fit for their Respective Undertakings.

The Husband-Men have good Increase, as well in large Cattle and Hoggs; as also, in such sorts of Grain which grow in England; and the same are Sold at Easie and Reasonable Rates: The Increase of their Corn [wheat] being considerably Greater than in England; of which they Make good Bread, and Brew good Beer and Ale for their Use. And as for other Provisions, they are Plentiful; as Fish, Fowls, Deer, Pork, Beef, and many Sorts of Fruits; as Grapes, Peaches, Apricocks, Cherryes, and Apples, of which Good Syder is made.

The country also produces Flax and Hemp, which they already Spin and Manufacture into Linnen: They make several Stuffs and Cloath of Wool for Apparrel: They Tan Leather, make Shooes and Hats.

They have also Coopers [barrelmakers], Smiths, Carpenters, Bricklayers, Wheel-Wrights, Plow-Wrights, and Mill-Wrights, Ship-Carpenters, and other Trades, which work upon what the Country produces for Manufacturies.

Colonial women spinning, weaving, and stitching cloth.

For the Soyl it is Good, and capable to produce any thing that England doth: [and] the Yearly Increase is far greater. The Air Temperate and Healthy; Winter not so long as in England: Few Natives in the Country; but those that are, are very Peaceable, Useful, and Serviceable to the English Inhabitants. . . .

Their Houses are some Built of Brick, some of Timber, Plaister'd and Ceil'd as in England: So that they have Materials within the Country, to set Themselves at work, and to make all manner of Conveniency for Human Life: And what they do not

Spend, or have to Spare, they sell to their Neighbours, and Transport the Rest to other American Plantations.[13]

Proprietorship in neither of the Jerseys progressed well. When colonists were not contesting with the proprietors over quit rents, they tended to ignore the owners and their wishes. The proprietors had little control over the governments of their colonies. Finally, in 1702, the owners of both Jerseys turned the governments over to the monarch, retaining only their rights to land. New Jersey, stitched together again, became a crown colony.

Government in New York

As one of his first acts after assuming the governorship of New York in 1664, Richard Nicolls set forth what he called the Duke's Laws, named for the colony's proprietor, James, duke of York. Among other things, these laws provided for religious toleration and established regulations concerning land ownership. But they did not provide for an elected assembly, or for schools or town meetings. Although there was some provision for self-government on the local level, it was vague and confusing. The governor and an appointed council ruled the colony itself. New York City was governed by seven appointed officers—four of whom at first were Dutch—and a mayor.

Colonel Francis Lovelace succeeded Nicolls as governor in 1668. He promoted the establishment of new towns, improved transportation systems by constructing roads and providing ferries, and made laws regulating trade and commerce.

New Yorkers grew restive under what they considered arbitrary government. They increasingly clamored for a representative assembly, although neither Nicolls nor Lovelace nor their successors recommended that the proprietor grant it. But finally, under Thomas Dongan, who became governor in 1683, New Yorkers got their wish.

[13]"The Present State of the Colony of West-Jersey," in Myers, *Narratives of Early Pennsylvania,* pp. 191–92.

Under orders from James, the proprietor, Dongan kept an appointed council of six, but in addition he established a general assembly for the colony. This elected group of seventeen, representing various towns, met for the first time at Fort James, on Manhattan. Among other things, the first assembly produced the Charter of Libertys and Priviledges, which divided the colony into twelve counties. The document also provided that laws enacted would remain in force until vetoed by the duke or repealed. It established individual liberties and the right to vote for freeholders. Further, drawing on the Magna Carta—the great English document of the early thirteenth century which granted certain political rights and human liberties—the charter stated:

Governor Thomas Dongan's house in New York. Dongan, a Roman Catholic Irishman appointed by the duke of York, encouraged the general assembly to pass an act of religious toleration which applied to all Christians in the colony.

> THAT Noe freeman shall be taken and imprisoned or be disseized [deprived] of his Freehold of Libertye or Free Customes or be outlawed or Exiled or any other wayes destroyed nor shall be passed upon adjudged or condemned But by the Lawfull Judgment of his peers and by the Law of this Province.[14]

In addition, the charter placed a mantle of protection over New Yorkers, guarding them from taxation without representation and providing for religious freedom.

This was a good start, but it proved to be short-lived. James, duke of York, the colony's proprietor, became James II, king of England, early in 1685. Soon after, he decided to establish greater centralized control over some of his colonies. New York became a crown colony, and the king voided the charter and the New York assembly. The assembly met for the last time in October, 1685.

In the meantime, New York City had received a new charter. Going into effect in 1684, the document provided for six wards and specified that freeholders from each would elect one alderman and an assistant. This group, along with the appointed mayor and recorder, would be a common council with the power to govern the city.

[14]Quoted in Michael Kammen, *Colonial New York: A History* (New York: Charles Scribner's Sons, 1975), p. 104.

Upriver at Albany, the fur trade remained brisk. There in 1689, for one beaver skin, an Indian could choose from eight pounds of gunpowder, forty pounds of lead from which to make shot, a red or a white blanket, four shirts, or six pairs of stockings. For two beavers, he could obtain a gun. The variety of goods available was a measure of how dependent Indians had become on whites.

The Dominion of New England

Centralized government arrived at last. New Yorkers learned, one day in 1688, that their colony and New Jersey had been lumped together with the New England colonies as the Dominion of New England. Edmund Andros, who had served earlier as governor of New York, was now governor of the Dominion. Francis Nicholson, his deputy, arrived to oversee affairs in New York. And many New Yorkers expressed outrage as public records were placed on a vessel and shipped to Boston, the Dominion's capital.

The Dominion of New England, it turned out, would last but a brief time. The birth of a son to James II brought it down.

James II was Catholic. He accepted the supremacy of the Church of England, but this did not quiet suspicions that if he could have things otherwise, he would. Furthermore, like his father Charles I and his brother Charles II, James II clung to the notion of the divine right of kings. He believed in the absolute power of the monarchy, an idea that was no longer shared by his subjects. In England, by the closing years of the seventeenth century, Parliament had come to dominate.

Still, the possibility that James II might attempt to establish a line of Catholic kings was not too worrisome because he lacked an heir. The English expected that he would be succeeded by his daughter Mary, a Protestant who was married to a Dutch nobleman, William of Orange. But then in 1688, a son—a direct heir to the throne—was born to the king and queen. When James II had him baptized a Catholic, the worst fears of the English were realized. Parliament asserted itself by forcing the king to abdicate in a bloodless

Library of Congress

James II of England. James did not take kindly to being deposed. After a short period of planning in France he sailed for Ireland, where he rallied the Catholic population to armed resistance against English domination. He was successful in the south but could not take the Protestant stronghold of Ulster in the north, and eventually he was defeated by William of Orange's forces at the River Boyne in July, 1690. The uprising was brief but extremely bloody, and James returned to exile in France leaving behind a legacy of bitterness that would linger for centuries. To this day, the Protestants of northern Ireland are known as "Orangemen."

exercise of power known as the Glorious Revolution of 1688. James II fled to France. William and Mary of Orange, at Parliament's invitation, arrived to take over the English throne.

Residents of the New England colonies greeted the parliamentary triumph with joy. Plans were made to demolish the

Dominion of New England, but in Boston there was no waiting for that. Several hundred armed men, led by Wait-Still Winthrop, grandson of the late John Winthrop of Massachusetts Bay Colony, forced Edmund Andros to resign immediately. Andros was imprisoned for a time, then escorted to a ship and sent home. As the Dominion of New England folded, events in New York focused on one Jacob Leisler.

Unrest in New York

The son of a Calvinist clergyman, Jacob Leisler had been born in Frankfurt-am-Main in Germany in 1640. He arrived in New Amsterdam in 1660, a penniless soldier in the employ of the Dutch West India Company. Establishing himself as a merchant, particularly in the wine-importing business, he prospered. Three years after his arrival, he married Altye Tymans, a merchant's widow who was wealthy in her own right. As a man of position, Leisler later became one of six militia captains.

Religious feeling at the time ran high. As a Protestant, Leisler could be expected to be anti-Catholic. He condemned Catholic immigration into New York and expressed fears of Catholic influence on the colony from New France.

His contemporaries characterized Leisler as an energetic man with a talent for business. At the same time, he was regarded as not highly intelligent. He tended to be overconfident, it was said, and suspicious of people. And, depending on how one looked at it, he was either a man of high principle or excessively stubborn. Nothing in his background, however, hinted that he would become the leader of a "rebellion" and would be condemned as a traitor.

Historians have sought in vain to pinpoint a cause for events in New York immediately following the deposition of James II. Numerous factors seem to have been involved, although it appears impossible to weigh accurately the influence of each.

There was plenty of unrest in New York colony, much of it dating back to the English conquest. The current of nationalist feelings ran as strongly as the religious ones. Owing in great part to international rivalry, both the English and the Dutch took dim views of each other. In New York, the

Dutch felt like a conquered people. They resented the loss of power of the Dutch Reformed church there. The fact that ministers no longer were paid from public funds, but frequently had to go door to door to collect contributions toward their salaries, irked the Dutch. Customs duties were more carefully collected under the English, which did not please Dutch merchants. Even the change from the Dutch to the English system of weights and measures helped create ill feeling. English soldiers sometimes mistreated Dutch residents, and the Dutch disliked having their tax money spent to keep the troops.

The Middle Dutch Church in New York.

English residents of such Long Island towns as Oyster Bay, Easthampton, and Jamaica had grievances too. Under the proprietary rule of the duke of York, they were subject to quit rents, which they disliked and which they frequently avoided. They objected to having to channel imports and exports through the port of New York. They protested against the spending of tax money to maintain the fort there. Long Islanders occasionally were given to roughing up tax collectors and to rioting. Most of all, they treasured the nearly independent town governments they had brought with them from New England. They resented the authority of the New York colonial government, in which they had no voice. Constantly they clamored for an elected assembly— and they were not alone in this. When the Dutch returned in 1673, briefly to enjoy control of the colony again, Long Islanders sent no aid to resist the takeover even though requested to do so.

There were sectional quarrels, and contention between farmers and merchants. Albany, the principal settlement up the Hudson, based its economy on the fur trade. When New York City obtained a monopoly on the export trade in 1678, Albany merchants protested vigorously. They finally settled for a monopoly on the fur trade, and the colonial government upheld their efforts to keep non-Albany traders out. In 1682 the city of New York received a monopoly on flour bolting—the final sieving and grading of flour before sale. This aroused farmers against the merchants. Those who supported the monopoly insisted that it was necessary to protect the quality of New York flour. But after much protest, the farmers got the monopoly abolished.

There were constant disputes over land titles, on Long Island and elsewhere. On the one hand, those involved in quarrels deplored the government's failure to solve them. On the other hand, they condemned its occasional efforts, which they considered clumsy, to do so.

Throughout the colony, but especially in New York City, resentment simmered over governors and graft. The record for honesty posted by several administrations left something to be desired. More than one governor freely placed relatives on the public payroll.

The Protestant-Catholic issue continued to course only slightly below the surface. Thomas Dongan, governor during the 1680's, was Catholic, and the Protestant majority suspected him of wishing to promote Catholic interests. The customs collector at the time, Matthew Plowman, was also Catholic, and Dongan brought a number of Jesuit priests with him to New York. There appears to be no evidence that the priests did anything but care for the religious needs of Catholics in the city, but still resentment bubbled.

In the midst of these crosscurrents of grievance and quarreling, King James II was driven from the throne and the Dominion of New England collapsed. New York's deputy governor, Francis Nicholson, failed to act decisively. When he learned of James's fall in March, 1689, he kept the news to himself and removed tax money from the collector's house, storing it in the fort for safekeeping. In April, Nicholson heard of Andros's arrest. He tried to suppress this news too, but it soon was out among Long Islanders, who had New England connections. They greeted the news joyously, and proclaimed their allegiance to the new monarchs, William and Mary. Long Islanders also seized the opportunity to present demands on the colonial government, mainly for the return of tax money. To compound Nicholson's troubles, New York merchants stopped paying customs duties. And because he failed to proclaim allegiance to the new English government immediately, the deputy governor was suspected of remaining loyal to James II.

Jacob Leisler and His Rebellion

On May 31, 1689, the New York militia took over Fort James, soon renamed Fort William. For reasons far from clear, Jacob Leisler was chosen to lead the troops, and on

June 3 he proclaimed William and Mary as Their Majesties. So began what is known as Leisler's Rebellion.

Nicholson sailed for England on June 24. He left the government in the hands of his council.

Sometime later a dispatch from the king, directing Nicholson to control the government and maintain order, arrived in New York. Alternately, the order was addressed "in his absence to such as for the time being take care for Preserving the Peace and administering the Lawes of our said Province in New York in America." Leisler, into whose hands the message fell, took this to mean himself. As head of the militia, the maintenance of law and order seemed up to him. He established a Committee of Safety and sent two men to England to assure the crown of his loyalty and to try to gain the support of the English government.

The War of the League of Augsburg between England and France—known in America as King William's War—broke out in 1689. And the New York frontier soon felt its effect.

Earlier, Albany merchants had agreed to a plan to bring Indians of the far Great Lakes and their furs directly into contact with English traders. The first English expedition westward was successful. This alarmed the French, who were not about to stand by and see their source of furs dry up, especially now that they were officially at war with the English. Early in February, 1690, about two hundred French and Indians moved on Schenectady, a small settlement on the Mohawk River upstream from Albany. It was deep winter, and no Schenectady resident dreamed that hostile forces were out. No watch had been set. The settlement was unguarded. The attack began about midnight, and when it ended a short time later more than sixty English colonists had been killed and twenty-seven taken prisoner. Schenectady was in flames.

Following the Schenectady massacre, Leisler called for the establishment of an elected assembly. One purpose was to provide for defense, although little was actually done about that.

Seeking to provide protection for New England as well as for New York, Leisler proposed an intercolonial conference, the first of its kind in America. Delegates from Massachusetts Bay, Plymouth Colony, and Connecticut met with New Yorkers in New York City in May, 1690. There they discussed not only defense, but an invasion of Canada as well. A small fleet was eventually dispatched against the French, but it had no success.

Meeting in the spring of 1690, the New York assembly passed a tax law. It raised the pay of New York City cartmen, upon whom residents depended for hauling goods. It abolished all monopolies, which pleased farmers. Leisler removed Plowman, the Catholic customs collector, replacing him with a Protestant, Peter Delanoy. Merchants did not mind this, but when customs collections began again their support for Leisler diminished.

Pro and Con Leisler

Jacob Leisler appears to have enjoyed the favor of many artisans and other more or less ordinary people of New York City, and of farmers. Consequently, some historians have labeled him a "man of the people" and a leader of democratic forces against landed aristocracy and merchant oligarchy. The lines, however, were not that clearly drawn.

It is true that a number of well-to-do, prominent men of the colony opposed Leisler. One was Nicholas Bayard, a merchant, a member of the governor's council, and long a city official. Leisler had him—and some others—imprisoned for a time for their unremitting opposition. Another was Stephanus Van Cortlandt, land owner and mayor of New York. Still another was Van Cortlandt's brother-in-law, Frederick Philipse. He was a rich merchant and a large land owner. Albany merchants and civil and military leaders steadfastly opposed Leisler. They labeled him a "restless and ambitious spirit."

On the other hand, Cornelius Pluvier, a well-to-do baker, and Johannes Van Couwenhaven, a wealthy brewer, supported Leisler. So did Gerardus Beeckman and Samuel Staats, prominent physicians. Peter Delanoy, who got the customs job, had been treasurer of the city of New York. The other five militia captains, like Leisler, were prosperous. They stayed with him.

Leisler's chief lieutenant was Jacob Milborne, who became his son-in-law. In England, it was said, Milborne had been convicted of "clipping" coins—shaving minute particles of gold and silver from the edges of coins for one's own profit. For this crime, the story continued, he was transported to America, where he drifted as an indentured servant from master to master. Later, it appears, he became a land owner and a successful trader. He had been with Leisler from the beginning of the "rebellion."

In the meantime, events in England moved slowly. The government there refused to·recognize Leisler's rule as lawful and eventually appointed a new governor, Henry Sloughter. Sloughter, however, did not arrive until a year after his appointment, on March 19, 1691. A contingent of English troops preceded him.

Shortly after his arrival, Sloughter sent orders for Leisler to give up Fort William. Leisler twice refused, on technical grounds. When he finally complied, he and Milborne, along with eight others, were clapped in jail. The council members that Deputy Governor Nicholson had left behind persuaded Sloughter to charge Leisler and the others with treason.

That this was an appropriate charge has been disputed. Treason is a violation of allegiance to one's government or country, or the betrayal of one's country to an enemy. Early in his rule, Leisler had proclaimed allegiance to England's monarchs. It has been argued that sedition would have been a more fitting charge. This involves inciting rebellion against the state's authority—in Leisler's case, against Nicholson's councillors.

In any event, Leisler and the rest stood accused of treason, their trial running from March 31 to April 17, 1691. It ended with two acquitted and the remainder, including Leisler and Jacob Milborne, sentenced to death. Six of those convicted were pardoned, but Leisler and Milborne went to the gallows on May 16. Closing a final speech from the scaffold, Leisler said:

> Gentlemen You will, I hope all Christian like be Charitable to our poor distressed family that are to remain amoung you ... that you will join with us in prayer for the preservation of our immortal Soules in a kingdom of never Dying Glory unto which God of his infinite mercy bring us all Amen, Amen.[15]

[15] Quoted in E. B. O'Callaghan, ed., *The Documentary History of the State of New-York* (Albany: Weed, Parsons, 1849), vol. 2, p. 379.

Jacob Leisler's house in the Strand, New York. When Leisler was executed on May 16, 1691, the crowd carried off locks of his hair and bits of his garments as relics. "These were the days of wrath and utter darkness," said a petition to the New York assembly.

Leisler and Milborne were then hung, drawn, and quartered.

In 1695, friends succeeded in obtaining an act of Parliament clearing Leisler's and Milborne's names. This restored their estates to their heirs. And in 1698, the remains of the two were reburied in a Dutch Reformed church ceremony. Some twelve hundred people attended the funeral.

In filling the power vacuum created by Nicholson's departure, Leisler may have acted in good faith. Or he may have been an opportunist driven by a lust for power, seeking to enhance himself. The issue remains unresolved. Passions at the time ran high; contemporary sources reveal directly contradictory points of view. The Reverend John Miller summed up the problem perhaps as well as anyone when he wrote in 1695: "I do believe that there were some of either side who sought in what they did their own advantage, many who truly did intend his Majesties service & many who blindly followed the leading men."[16]

This much is certain: the rebellion served to deepen the political factionalism which had long characterized New York. For years thereafter, the scene was marked by Leislerians *versus* anti-Leislerians on practically every issue.

Making the Colony English

The government of Holland followed Roman law, and so had the Dutch colonial government. This legal system had continued under the duke of York's proprietorship. In New York, three judges heard cases together, questioning witnesses as well as plaintiff and defendant, and making decisions. There was no trial by jury, and no need for lawyers—a member of the legal profession was a rarity in New York until the 1690's. The English Judiciary Act of 1691 sought to eliminate precedents based on local custom and to bring the colony under the English common law. The act established a supreme court in New York and provided for courts at lower levels. The practice of using lawyers, and trial by jury, habeas corpus, and other characteristics of the English system now began.

[16] Quoted in Jerome R. Reich, *Leisler's Rebellion: A Study of Democracy in New York, 1664–1720* (Chicago: University of Chicago Press, 1953), p. 73.

The Dutch-built Stadt Huys (State House) was located at the corner of Pearl Street and Coentjie Slip. From this drawing of 1679, it is evident that the English made few alterations to the building in the years immediately following their takeover of the colony.

Equally important, New York now legally had and would retain an elected assembly. The group met first in April, 1691, to enact tax laws, deal with land grants, and set up a system of courts. The governor and the king retained veto power over legislation. But until the king was heard from— and months, even years might pass before this occurred— assembly laws remained in effect with the governor's approval.

Procedures for obtaining freemanship—meaning citizenship—were established. The Dutch had controlled admission to citizenship haphazardly. Now one could become a freeman by birth, as a consequence of apprenticeship to a trade, or by paying a small fee. Freemanship was no light matter. Without it, strictly speaking, a person could not vote, practice a trade, carry on any business, or hold public office.

There had been no printing presses in New York. The English government, realizing the advantages such machines bestowed on political opposition, had not encouraged them. But in 1693, Governor Benjamin Fletcher—perhaps to build

A colonial printer setting type.

up his ego—wanted an order printed. Consequently, in April that year William Bradford was brought from Philadelphia to be New York's printer. He found himself overrun with work, turning out some two hundred and fifty titles between 1693 and 1710.

After 1693, the Anglican church gained strength in New York. As the Dutch Reformed church split into bitter factions and membership declined, the Anglican became established, supported in part by public funds.

One thing did not change: New York City's pluralism. Wrote one observer in 1692:

Our chiefest unhappyness here is too great a mixture of nations, and English the least part; the French Protestants have in the late King's reign resorted here in great numbers proportionably to the other nation's inhabitants [following the revocation of the Edict of Nantes, which had granted religious toleration, by French King Louis XIV in 1685]. The Dutch, generally the most frugall and laborious, and consequently the richest; whereas most of the English are the contrary, especially the trading part.[17]

Another, writing in 1695, agreed:

As to their wealth and disposition thereto, the Dutch are rich and sparing; the English neither very rich, nor too great husbands [managers]; the French are poor, and therefore forced to be penurious [stingy]. As to their way of trade and dealing, they are all generally cunning and crafty, but many of them not so just to their words as they should be.[18]

As to religion, Governor Dongan had noted in the 1680's:

New York has first a Chaplain belonging to the Fort of the Church of England; secondly a Dutch Calvinist,

The Dutch Reformed Church at Sleepy Hollow, New York.

[17] Charles Lodwick, "Letter to His Uncle," in *Collections of the New-York Historical Society for the Year 1849,* Second Series (New York: New-York Historical Society, 1849), vol. 2, p. 244.

[18] John Miller, *Description of the Province and City of New York ... in the Year 1695* (London: T. Rodd, 1843), p. 250.

thirdly a French Calvinist, fourthly a Dutch Lutheran—Here bee not many of the Church of England; few Roman Catholicks; abundance of Quakers preachers men and women especially; Singing Quakers; Ranting Quakers; Sabbatarians; AntiSabbatarians; Some Anabaptists; some Independents; some Jews; in short all sorts of opinions there are some....[19]

The First Presbyterian Church in New York City.

A census taken in 1698 showed 18,597 people in the colony. Of these, 5,066 were white men; 4,677 were white women; 6,154 were children; and 2,170 were blacks of both sexes, some but not all of them slaves.

The Founder of Pennsylvania

The area that became known as Pennsylvania was a fertile and forested land. Already a few people had found their way there, and eventually it would have become a colony in any case. But the foundation of Pennsylvania, and the direction it took, undoubtedly would have been different without William Penn. The colony's founder was the most famous convert to the Society of Friends, a group that many people looked down upon as "Quakers" because of their tendency to tremble and quake when, seized by the Spirit, they gave testimony at Friends' meetings. Penn and Quakerism made his colony unique among those in America.

William Penn the younger was born on October 14, 1644. He was the son of Sir William Penn, an English vice-admiral, and later general-at-sea. The Penns were Protestant, the admiral's wife Margaret being a refugee from religious persecution in Europe. She was, from biographers' accounts, a short, plump woman, happy-go-lucky and frolicsome. The admiral was stern, as befitted a naval officer, but he loved his son and was usually indulgent toward him. The family was, at first, rather poor. Naval pay was irregular. And, although the admiral owned land in Ireland, rents from tenants were highly unreliable.

At an early age Penn came down with smallpox. But he suffered no more than the loss of his hair from the disease, and for several years he wore a wig. He received his early

[19]Quoted in Kammen, *Colonial New York,* pp. 118–19.

This contemporary portrait of William Penn as a young man, painted by Francis Place, is considered to be the only authentic likeness of the founder of Pennsylvania.

schooling at Chigwell. There Penn learned Greek and Latin as well as arithmetic and accounting. The Chigwell school day ran ten hours in summer, eight in winter. The Easter and Christmas seasons were vacation times. Penn's education was typical of that given members of the gentleman class, to which he belonged.

By the time Penn was twelve his sister Margaret had been born, and the family had moved to one of the Penns' Irish estates. Although he may have heard of Quakerism before, Penn received a real taste of it when he and his father heard Thomas Loe, an earnest and eloquent member of the Society, speak at Cork. Penn was especially impressed by how deeply Loe's words moved his father.

In 1659, when Penn was fifteen, his father entered him in Christ Church College at Oxford University. College life was boring to Penn. He did not like it. He took to attending meetings of religious dissenters, though not Quakers. For reasons that are not clear he was sent down—expelled—

from Christ Church, and his father awarded him a thrashing. In the summer of 1662, the admiral sent the boy off to Paris.

Penn traveled in France and Italy, and for a time he attended a Huguenot—French Protestant—college at Saumur. He soaked up numerous unorthodox religious ideas. Penn returned to England to study law at Lincoln's Inn. His time there coincided with London's Great Plague, a pestilence which within about a year carried off nearly seventy thousand people out of a population of one-half million. Penn apparently escaped unscathed.

In 1666 Penn went again to Ireland. There he once more listened to Thomas Loe, now gray-haired and bowed but still persuasive. Penn attended several Quaker meetings and finally pledged himself to that faith.

Shocked, the admiral ordered his son home and tried to reason with him. But to no avail. William Penn was a Quaker, and despite stress, turmoil, and hardship, so he would remain. Not until near his death, in 1670, did the disciplined, ramrod admiral begin to understand and accept his son's religious convictions.

Beliefs and Troubles

By the mid-seventeenth century, more than a hundred years after Martin Luther, religious dissent was no stranger to Europe. In the eyes of most people, however, the Quakers went too far.

George Fox, born in Leicestershire, England, in 1624, was stimulated by what he described as a divine call to found the Society of Friends around 1648. The Friends, or Quakers, were individualistic to the extreme. They believed in the "inner light," the "glow of God" each person possessed. They further believed that direct lines of communication between the individual and God were always open. They needed no priest or minister to guide them. Nor were such persons necessary for a Quaker to discover truth. The Holy Spirit within directed each person there. Because there was no need for ministers, the Quakers had none. Moreover, the Quakers considered men and women equal in the eyes of God. Worship together was simplicity itself—sitting in silent thought within the meeting house, each person communing personally with God. When one was inspired to share a religious experience, at that point he or she spoke out.

Friends Historical Library, London

George Fox founded the sect of Protestants which became known as the Friends, or Quakers, around the middle of the seventeenth century. When William Penn was leaving England to join the Quaker colony he had established in Pennsylvania, Fox cautioned him, "Make outward plantations in America and keep your own plantations in your hearts."

Quakers also used their weekly and other meetings as a means of discipline. One might speak out not only as a witness to the Lord. He or she could also raise a voice to criticize

Courtesy Museum of Fine Arts, Boston

This detail from a larger painting shows a Quaker meeting during the seventeenth century.

a neighbor for such un-Quakerlike behavior as using profanity, lying, fighting, or drunkenness. The person would have to offer a defense and, if judged guilty, accept public scolding and promise to reform.

Even though non-believers did not like them much, the Quakers might have escaped official notice if they had been content to pursue their religious individualism. But they did not stop there. They pledged primary allegiance to God, not to a church or a government. And they carried their convictions to the secular realm.

Believing in complete equality, and usually clad plainly in blacks and browns, Quakers would not curtsy or doff the hat in a gesture of respect to social superiors, as was the custom of the time. They addressed each other as "thou" and "thee," words reserved for such lower classes as servants. Further, they addressed all others that way, a practice which did not endear them to non-Quakers. Non-Quakers usually responded with "Thou me, thou my dog!" or "If thou'd thou'st me, I'll thou thy teeth down thy throat." Nor did England's civil authorities take kindly to the Quakers' pacifism, which forbade them to bear arms or support the military. The government also frowned on their refusal to swear oaths in court, which they based on a literal interpretation of Christ's words: "Swear no oaths." The Quakers' steadfast opposition to supporting the established Anglican church with the required tithes—religious taxes—rankled authorities. Quakers also sturdily opposed capital punishment at a time when, in England, conviction for any one of some two hundred crimes called for the death penalty. In addition, Quakers were not above a bit of religious intolerance themselves. Groups of them occasionally invaded and disrupted services in other churches. From the government's point of view, Quakers could hardly be called good citizens.

Parliament legislated against Quakers, and with the same legal blanket sought to smother other religious dissent as well. The Quaker Act of the early 1660's forbade five or more Friends to assemble for worship. Under the Act of Uniformity, all clergymen had to follow the established Prayer Book. No non-conformist preacher could come within five miles of an incorporated town under terms of the Five Mile Act. These last two laws were used against Quakers even though the sect had no ministers.

The Friends were persecuted. Soldiers and government agents stormed into meetings, roughing up Quakers and sometimes dragging them off to jail. The Quaker response was usually passive resistance, which puzzled authorities while making them appear more brutal. It also aroused some public sympathy for the Friends. William Penn himself occasionally suffered.

In and Out of Jail

Late in 1668, Penn was arrested for publishing a religious pamphlet without a license. He was accused of blaspheming the Trinity in its pages. He responded by writing another and wound up in the Tower of London for six months. There he continued to write, smuggling out manuscripts for publication.

On Sunday, August 14, 1670, Penn spoke before three to four hundred Quakers outside the Friends' Meeting House on Gracechurch Street in London. They met in the street because the authorities had recently locked and boarded up the house. The sheriff and some soldiers soon arrived and arrested Penn along with William Mead, a fellow Quaker who stood up for him and protested the seizure. They were accused of preaching sedition and of causing a disturbance. Owing to his rank, Penn was not locked up in the worst part of London's Newgate prison. He went to the more comfortable Black Dog at Newgate Market.

Penn and Mead were brought to trial before a jury, judge, and recorder on September 1. Both were charged with preaching and with attending a meeting and, further, with having caused a great disturbance "against the peace of the said lord the King, his crown and dignity." Denied a copy of the charge, they pleaded not guilty. The trial then adjourned for three days.

When they were returned, a minor court official removed their hats. The judge ordered the hats replaced and then directed the defendants to remove them. They refused, contending that they wore their hats at the court's order. The judge, a short-tempered man anyway, grew angry. He remained angry throughout the entire proceeding which, according to accounts, was extremely loose, irregular, and disorderly to the point of rowdiness. The trial was marked by much shouting, screaming, quibbling, and exhortation on both sides, as well as bullying by the judge. At one point the judge ordered Penn and Mead placed in the bail dock, a partitioned corner of the room where they were shielded from view. From there, with raised voices, the defendants continued to address the court, which the judge had forbidden them to do.

Neither judge nor recorder were learned in the law. On the contrary, they frequently displayed deep ignorance. Penn, on the other hand, had been trained in the law, and his remarks and discourses on the legality of the proceeding reduced his opponents to helpless sputtering and rage. Penn contended that he and Mead had been arrested for worshipping God and that they had broken no law. He pointed out, and rightly so, that neither judge nor recorder would name the law they supposedly had offended. The whole trial, he insisted, was in violation of the Magna Carta, that great cornerstone of English liberties.

At last the exasperated judge sent the jury out. It returned an hour and a half later, hung on an eight-to-four guilty verdict. After haranguing the four hold-outs, and threatening them with prison, the judge sent the jury back to reconsider. The twelve then returned with one guilty verdict— Penn was guilty of speaking on Gracechurch Street. Mead was not guilty of anything.

This was not what the judge had in mind. Once again he addressed the jury, threatening its members for not attending to the charge of unlawful assembly. The foreman stoutly protested that that had not been part of the case. So the judge locked the jury up overnight, denying its members food or even a chamber pot. And the next morning the haggard, hungry, and shivering group returned stubbornly to repeat its verdict. The judge gave up on the jury. He fined Penn and sent him back to Newgate prison until the fine was paid. Penn's father later paid it for him.

William Penn, although a gentle man, was never one to run from a fight. And in this case, with his eloquence, learning, and steadfast stand on principle, he had struck a blow beyond religious liberty. The jurors later brought suit against the court, and eventually won their case. It was decided that a jury had the right to hear evidence and to decide both fact and law. For if the judge alone could do both, and direct a jury's decision, of what possible use were juries? This became an important principle in English law, and later in American law.

Although deeply devoted to his faith, and capable of stubbornly defending it and cheerfully going to prison on its behalf, Penn was not a religious fanatic. His experience with the law, his travels in Europe, his whole upbringing, had made him a sophisticated, cosmopolitan man. Still, although practical in many things, Penn was to prove disastrously impractical and idealistic with respect to his colony, Pennsylvania.

Penn continued to work for the Quakers. He published numerous pamphlets. He visited Germany, and in 1672 he married Guilielma Maria Springett, an attractive Quaker he had met some years earlier. In 1672 Charles II issued his Declaration of Indulgence which freed dissenters, including some four hundred Quakers, from prison. Penn now had

Brown Brothers

Quakers leaving Massachusetts following an order of banishment. Under the laws of the colony, those Quakers who tried to return would be sentenced to death.

more freedom to operate. And among other things, he invested in America, becoming one of the proprietors of West New Jersey.

Quakers in America

For many years, English Quakers had regarded emigration to the American colonies as the only way to avoid persecution. The government, however, did not encourage migration. That merely worked an unimportant geographical change and missed the nub of the Quaker problem.

Brown Brothers

Quakers in America did not avoid harsh treatment entirely. They were welcomed in West New Jersey, and tolerated in Rhode Island. But they were greeted like the plague in Massachusetts and Connecticut. The New England Puritans, like the English, viewed them as a dangerous and disruptive element.

Laws in Massachusetts and Connecticut called for fines, imprisonment, whippings, and banishment for Quakers. Those returning to New Haven, Connecticut, after having been expelled three times were liable to have their tongues pierced with a hot iron. Those coming back to Massachusetts could be put to death. Four Quakers were executed there in the middle of the seventeenth century. One of them

Two members of the Society of Friends being led to the gallows where they would be hanged at the order of a Puritan court for the crime of preaching their religion in Massachusetts.

The artist Howard Pyle painted Mary Dyer as he imagined she must have looked as she walked to her execution, surrounded by militiamen. Her body was buried in an unmarked grave on Boston common.

Friends Historical Library, London

was Mary Dyer. Having left Massachusetts for Rhode Island in 1637 because of religious intolerance, Mary Dyer later returned to England. There she took up with the Society of Friends. Once again in America, she insisted on bearing frequent witness to her faith publicly in Boston. After issuing repeated warnings and banishments, only to have her come back, Boston authorities finally hanged Mary Dyer in 1660.

Sensitive to Quaker hardships, William Penn wished to establish a haven not just for Friends, but for all who suffered persecution. And he finally got his chance to conduct what would be for him a Holy Experiment in love, brotherhood, and tolerance.

At the time Penn's father died, Charles II owed the admiral £16,000 in back pay, loans, and interest. It occurred to Penn that the king might prefer to discharge the obligation with a grant of land in America rather than with cash. Land-rich and money-poor, Charles II was more than happy to do so. He quickly approved a petition for a grant that Penn sent him near the end of 1680.

Under the charter he obtained in March, 1681, Penn received proprietary rights to a huge amount of land. It extended five degrees of longitude west from the Delaware River, and from the forty-third parallel north latitude to the fortieth degree south. This bounded an area larger than Wales and England combined. A year later, James, duke of York, granted Penn rights to Delaware as well. Over Penn's protest—he feared misunderstanding and accusations of un-Quakerlike vanity—the king insisted on naming the new colony Pennsylvania, or Penn's Woods, after the late admiral.

Pennsylvania's northern and southern boundaries later became the subject of dispute between that colony and New York and Maryland. To the north, Penn finally agreed to a boundary at the forty-second parallel. Later in the colonial period, in the 1760's, a pair of English surveyors named Charles Mason and Jeremiah Dixon established a southern boundary fifteen miles south of the fortieth parallel.

In 1681, Penn sent over the first shipload of colonists to an area populated by Indians and a few Swedish, Dutch, and English settlers. His Holy Experiment was launched.

Beginning the Holy Experiment

Charter in hand, William Penn became at once a ruler and a landlord. He could dispose of the land as he wished. He could make laws and appoint officials to enforce them. And he could create courts and select judges to administer the laws. The laws would be subject to veto by English authorities within five years after their enactment, but such vetoes were not likely to occur often. In all cases except treason, the proprietor also possessed the power to pardon.

Penn provided his colony with a Frame of Government. "There is," he said in his preface to it, "hardly one frame of government in the world so ill-designed by its first founders that in good hands would not do well enough, and history tells us the best in ill ones can do nothing that is great and good." Therefore, he went on, "Let men be good and the government cannot be bad; if it be ill they will cure it."

The first Frame of Government called for an assembly to be elected by freemen—in this case meaning land holders or taxpayers—and an elected council. Penn was named governor, with the power to appoint a deputy governor. Because a deputy presided over the Pennsylvania government most of the time, however, the colonists often used the term "governor" to refer to him rather than to Penn.

Anyone believing in God was welcome in Pennsylvania, where there was to be no religious test for holding public office. Prisons would be work houses and places of rehabilitation, not simply institutions for punishment. Prisoners would not be required to pay fees for their own support, as was the custom in England at the time.

In 1683, Penn amended the government structure with his Second Frame. Under this, the assembly would consist of thirty-six members, with more to be added as the population grew. In the beginning, each of the six counties—three in Pennsylvania, three in Delaware—would elect six assemblymen. The council remained, and it was to have the sole power to initiate laws; the assembly could only accept or reject them.

Pennsylvania was also unique with respect to Indian relations. The Dutch and Swedish settlers of the area had laid the foundation for friendly association with the Indians, and Pennsylvania's early colonists took advantage of that. At

Penn's insistence, the right to use land was to be purchased from the Indians and they were to remain unmolested on land they continued to occupy. At a great meeting with Indians—mostly Delaware and Susquehannocks—in the fall of 1682, Penn struck a treaty with them. "The Great Spirit," the document began in Penn's words,

> who made me and you, who rules the heavens and the earth, and knows the innermost thoughts of men, knows that I and my friends have a hearty desire to live in peace and friendship with you, and to serve you to the uttermost of our power. It is not our custom to use hostile weapons against our fellow-creatures, for which reason we have come unarmed. Our object is not to do injury, and thus provoke the Great Spirit, but to do good. We are met on the broad pathway of good faith and good will, so that no advantage is to be taken on either side, but all is to be openness, brotherhood, and love.[20]

And as long as Pennsylvanians kept to straight and fair dealings, relations between Indians and whites in the colony remained peaceful.

Advertising Opportunity

England was not Penn's only source of settlers. He advertised his colony throughout much of Europe with persuasive pamphlets. And because he did not go to Pennsylvania until 1682, he relied for information on reports from his agents there. "The Place lies 600 miles nearer the Sun than England," he said in one advertisement,

> for England begins at the 50th degree and ten minutes of North Latitude, and this Place begins at fourty, which is about the Latitude of Naples in Italy, or Mompellier [Montpellier] in France. I shall say little in its praise, to excite the desires in any, whatever I could

[20]Adapted from a quotation in Thomas Clarkson, *Memoirs of the Private and Public Life of William Penn* (London: Longman, Hurst, Rees, Orme, and Brown, 1813), vol. 1, p. 341.

Library of Congress

An engraving, copied from a famous painting by Benjamin West, of William Penn's meeting with the Indians.

truly write as to the Soil, Air, and Water: This shall satisfie me, that by the Blessing of God, and the honesty and industry of Man, it may be a good and fruitful land.

For Navigation it said to have two conveniencies; the one by lying Ninescore miles upon Delaware River; this is to say, about three-score and ten miles, before we come to the Falls, where a Vessel of Two hundred Tuns may Sail, (and some Creeks and small Harbours in that distance, where Ships may come nearer than the River into the Country) and above the Falls, for Sloops and Boats, as I am informed, to the extent of the Patent [grant]. The other convenience is through Chesapeak-Bay.[21]

[21] William Penn, "Some Account of the Province of Pennsilvania," in Myers, *Narratives of Early Pennsylvania*, p. 207.

Library of Congress

This engraving, "American Friends Going to Meeting in a Settled Frost," conveys the simple, sober life of the Quakers. Those who settled in Pennsylvania came principally from the propertied class in England and were able to bring ample supplies with them to the new colony.

Penn then went on to speak of the resources of the region—timber, game, and furs, the fertile soil, and the crops that could be grown. He spoke of trade with England and with other colonies, and about Pennsylvania's government. Then, with respect to obtaining land:

My Conditions will relate to three sorts of People: 1st. Those that will buy: 2dly. Those that take up Land upon Rent: 3dly. Servants. To the first, the Shares I sell shall be certain as to number of Acres; that is to say, every one shall contain Five thousand Acres, free from any Indian incumbrance, the price a hundred pounds, and for the Quit-rent but one English shilling or the value of it yearly for a hundred Acres; and the said Quit-Rent not to begin to be paid until 1684. To the second sort, that take up Land upon Rent, they shall have liberty so to do, paying yearly one peny per Acre, not exceeding Two hundred Acres. To the third sort to wit, [indentured] Servants that are carried over, Fifty Acres shall be allowed to the Master for every Head, and Fifty Acres to every Servant when their time is expired. And because some engage with me that may not be disposed to go, it were very advisable for every three Adventurers to

send an Overseer with their Servants, which would
well pay the Cost.[22]

He asked for "Industrious Husbandmen" (farmers), day
laborers, and craftsmen of all sorts, discussed "The Journey
and its Appurtenances," and included an abstract of his
charter. Penn closed with some advice:

> To conclude, I desire all my dear Country-Folks,
> who may be inclin'd to go into those Parts, to consider
> seriously the premises, as well as the present
> inconveniences, as future ease and Plenty, that so none
> may move rashly or from a fickle but solid mind,
> having above all things, an Eye to the providence of
> God, in the disposal of themselves. And I would
> further advise all such at least, to have the permission,
> if not the good liking of their near Relations, for that
> is both Natural, and a Duty Incumbent upon all; and
> by this means will natural affection be preserved, and
> friendly and profitable correspondence be maintained
> between them. In all which I beseech Almighty God to
> direct us, that his blessing may attend our honest
> endeavour, and then the Consequence of all our
> undertaking will turn to the Glory of his great Name,
> and the true happiness of us and our Posterity.
> Amen.[23]

Penn's advertising paid off. Pennsylvania rapidly acquired a population as mixed as that of New York. Many
Quakers came, of course, but so did many German Mennonites, whose beliefs were similar, and many other
religious and national groups as well. And right at the beginning, surveyors laid out a community Penn named Philadelphia—"City of Brotherly Love"—between the Delaware
and Schuylkill rivers. Wrote Penn in 1685, describing the colony, its population and resources, and Philadelphia itself:

> We have had about Ninety Sayl of Ships with
> Passengers since the beginning of '82, and not one

[22] Ibid., pp. 208–9.
[23] Ibid., p. 215.

Vessel designed [sent] to the Province, through God's mercy, hitherto miscarried.

The Estimate of the People may thus be made: Eighty to each Ship, which comes to Seven Thousand Two Hundred Persons. At least a Thousand there before, with such as from other places in our neighbourhood are since come to settle among us; and I presume the Births at least equal to the Burials; For, having made our first Settlements high in the Freshes of the Rivers, we do not find ourselves subject to those Seasonings [meaning diseases] that affect some other Countries upon the same Coast.

The People are a Collection of divers Nations in Europe: As, French, Dutch, Germans, Sweeds, Danes, Finns, Scotch, Irish, and English; and the last equal to all the rest: And, which is admirable, not a Reflection on that Account: But as they are of one kind, and in One Place and under One Allegiance, so they live like People of One Country, which Civil Union has had a considerable influence towards the prosperity of that place.

Philadelphia, and our intended Metropolis, as I formerly Writ, is two Miles long, and a Mile broad, and at each end it lies that mile upon a Navigable River. The situation high and dry, yet replenished with running streams. Besides the High Street, that runs in the middle from River to River, and is an hundred foot broad, it has Eight streets more that run the same course, the least of which is fifty foot in breadth. And besides Broad Street, which crosses the Town in the middle, and is also an hundred foot wide, there are twenty streets more, that run the same course, and are also fifty foot broad. The names of those Streets are mostly taken from things that Spontaneously grow in the Country, As Vine Street, Mulberry Street, Chestnut Street, Wallnut Street, Strawberry Street, Cranberry Street, Plumb Street, Hickery Street, Pine Street, Oake Street, Beach Street, Ash Street, Popler Street, Sassafraxs Street, and the like.

I mentioned in my last Account that from my Arrival, in Eighty-Two, to the Date thereof, being ten Moneths, we had got up Fourscore Houses at our Town, and that some Villages were settled about it. From that time to my coming away, which was a Year within a few Weeks, the Town advanced to Three hundred and fifty-seven Houses; divers of them large, well built, with good Cellars, three stories, and some with Balconies.

There is also a fair Key [wharf] of about three hundred foot square, built by Samuel Carpenter, to which a ship of five hundred Tuns may lay her broadside, and others intend to follow his example. We have also a Ropewalk [a place to manufacture rope] and cordage [rope] for shipping already spun at it.

There inhabits most sorts of useful Tradesmen, As Carpenters, Joyners [cabinetmakers], Bricklayers, Masons, Plasterers, Plumers, Smiths, Glasiers [glass fitters], Taylers, Shoemakers, Butchers, Bakers, Brewers, Glovers, Tanners, Felmongers [those who prepare hides for leather], Wheelrights, Millrights, Shiprights, Boatrights, Ropemakers, Saylmakers, Blockmakers [tackle for ships' ropes], Turners [those who work with lathes], etc.[24]

No American colony was begun under more cheerful circumstances, under such a liberal government, and under greater prospects for peace and prosperity.

The Proprietor in the Colony

William Penn did not visit his colony until a year after the first settlers had arrived. On September 1, 1682, he sailed from England on the ship *Welcome* along with about a hundred other passengers, provisions for the colony, and squealing, smelly livestock. After nearly two months at sea, the

[24]William Penn, "A Further Account of the Province of Pennsylvania," in Myers, *Narratives of Early Pennsylvania,* pp. 260–61.

ship reached the settlement of New Castle on the Delaware River late in October.

As governor, Penn presided over a meeting of the legislature, a session which in three days produced some seventy laws. Among other things, the lawmakers provided for trial by jury, guaranteed that no taxes would be collected arbitrarily, and prohibited the use of oaths in court. Another law allowed those accused of crimes to plead their own cases. And whereas English law defined several hundred offenses as capital crimes, the Pennsylvania legislature named only one crime to be punished by death—willful murder.

Religious dissenters of the time deplored the pageantry and ceremony of the Catholic and Anglican churches. They also opposed the luxury, looseness, and extravagance of the courts of the Stuart kings, expecially that of Charles II. Consequently, dissenters tended to be a solemn lot, even stodgy, and Quakers were no exception. Some of the early laws passed in Pennsylvania reflected Quaker plainness and severity. "Offenses against God," the use of profanity, and drunkenness were outlawed. So were stage plays, card playing, and May dances. From a twentieth-century point of view, though,the ban on bull baiting, bear baiting, and cock fighting would seem commendable. Malicious reporting, the spreading of false news, backbiting and defamation were also forbidden. If all of these laws were strictly enforced, as they apparently were not, early Pennsylvania would have seemed a dreary place. The legislature did neglect to provide for a licensing system for drinking houses. Consequently it had no means of controlling their increase in number, or their use.

Penn remained in Pennsylvania for less than two years. One reason for his early return to England was the need to attend to boundary claims made by Lord Baltimore, Maryland's proprietor. Another was a renewed outbreak of religious persecution in England. Penn wished to do what he could for his fellow Quakers, who were now overflowing Newgate prison. He sailed from Philadelphia on August 12, 1684, leaving Thomas Lloyd as president of the council in charge of the colony's affairs.

William Penn successfully settled the boundary dispute. Relying on his friendship with the new king, James II, he

Brown Brothers

The pious, sober Quakers were often objects of ridicule and derision, even in their own colony. A later governor of Pennsylvania, John Blackwell, angry at being driven out of the Philadelphia council chamber by local citizens, vengefully described the Quakers as people who *prayed for* their neighbors on Sunday and *preyed on* them the other six days of the week. Actually, however, most Quakers were scrupulous in their business dealings. They believed, for example, that the usual process of bargaining over prices was immoral and instead offered their goods at fixed prices—the first merchants to do so.

also obtained pardons for more than a thousand imprisoned Quakers. He was, however, criticized on this account. James II tended to hold himself above the law. And, even though Penn's actions were humane, he appeared to support arbitrary rule by encouraging the king to act independently of Parliament and the judicial system. Remaining in England until 1699, Penn sent David Lloyd, who had been trained as a lawyer, to represent his interests in Pennsylvania.

Factionalism and Dissent

Lloyd, a Welshman who was to become important in Pennsylvania's political history, was a relative of Thomas Lloyd, president of the council. At the time David Lloyd was not a Quaker, although some of his relatives were and had suffered persecution. Arriving in the colony on July 15, 1686, he met with the council in August that year. He brought most unwelcome news.

William Penn had been paying much of the cost of colonial government—legislators' allowances, for example—out of his own pocket. He had gone deeply into debt. The colony's merchants had not paid him custom duties as agreed upon. Moreover, the collection of quit rents was well in arrears. Consequently, Penn suggested that the colonists be taxed to support their government. This did not sit well with the council, nor with the assembly, which had tended to assume powers that Penn's Frame of Government of 1683 had not granted it. David Lloyd himself proved lukewarm in his defense of Penn's proprietary rights. He carried out few of his employer's instructions. Lloyd soon identified himself with local interests and turned to land speculation, which eventually brought him wealth. Penn finally dismissed the man in 1699.

Occupied with Quaker affairs and with his estates in Ireland, Penn kept delaying his return to the colony. In 1688 he sent over John Blackwell, a non-Quaker, as deputy governor. The Quaker majority resented the appointment of an outsider, and the two Lloyds in particular opposed Blackwell. Owing to strong opposition, Blackwell was unable to keep the assembly within the boundaries of power Penn had granted in 1683. That body continued to debate, amend, and alter bills, and, finally, to begin legislation itself. Furthermore, contrary to Penn's instructions, Blackwell failed to gain control of the courts.

Much squabbling appeared within the assembly itself. Members from the Lower Counties—Delaware—were frequently at odds with those representing Pennsylvania counties. One issue in dispute was defense measures during King William's War, which began in 1689. Lower County representatives favored contributing to colonial defense against the French in Canada. Pacifist Quakers, in control of the government, refused to budge from principle. Besides, they pointed out, the French were far away. Furthermore, Pennsylvania Indians remained friendly and tribes within the League of the Iroquois were pro-English. They saw no danger. The defense issue would remain a thorny one in colonial Pennsylvania politics. It eventually had severe implications for Quaker rule.

Factionalism developed among Quakers themselves. A man named George Keith, a Scotsman, led a minority of Quakers in an effort to wrest control of the government from the orthodox group. The orthodox Quakers managed to place Keith on trial for sedition, slander, and malicious criticism. Convicted, he got off lightly with a small fine and no right of appeal. But the whole affair had spread much ill feeling. All in all, the Holy Experiment was not working.

George Keith.

Penn's problems continued to grow. His closeness to James II, who was driven from the throne in 1688, landed him in trouble with the new monarchs, William and Mary. He was charged, falsely, with plotting to restore James II as king. And in 1692, King William removed Pennsylvania from Penn's hands. He made it a royal colony and sent Colonel Benjamin Fletcher over as governor.

Fletcher trimmed the assembly's power somewhat, and he made other changes in the colonial government. But the assembly, led by David Lloyd, hamstrung him over money, tax, and defense bills. In 1694, less than two years after it began, Pennsylvania's experience as a royal colony ended when King William restored Penn's proprietorship. Pennsylvania would remain in the hands of the Penn family throughout the remainder of the colonial period.

The Experiment Fails

At last, on November 30, 1699, William Penn arrived back in the colony he founded. With him was twenty-six-year-old James Logan, then Penn's secretary and a man destined to place his stamp on eighteenth-century Pennsylvania. Upon landing, Penn almost immediately called a meeting of the legislature. By law, however, it could not assemble until January, so Penn used the period between to tour the colony. He spent some time on his eight-thousand-acre estate, Pennsbury, still being cleared, where an elegant house fit for a proprietor had been erected.

William III.

Pennsylvania colonists had many complaints. They detested quit rents. The judicial system was uncertain, partly because the division of authority among the various courts had not been clearly defined. Many land titles were in dispute. The 1690's had been a time of economic depression, with prices low and trade slack. There was little hard money—gold or silver—to be had. Factionalism between the Lower Counties and the others continued. And so did strife between the orthodox Quakers and the pro-Keith forces. In addition, there was growing tension between Anglicans and Quakers in the colony. Colonists and political leaders demanded change, although there was little agreement as to what direction it should take—except, apparently, that it should involve a reduction of the proprietor's rights and privileges.

Legislative meetings, with Penn presiding, were disastrous. King William's War had ended in 1697, but now renewed conflict with the French was brewing. Following instructions from the crown, Penn asked the lawmakers to raise three hundred and fifty pounds to aid New York's defense against New France, which was just across the Saint Lawrence. They refused. So Penn was prevented from keeping a promise made to King William when the king returned the colony to him in 1694. Although the proprietor had paid many colonial costs out of his own pocket, and remained in debt, the legislators refused to contribute a penny to his expenses. There was haggling over land sales and how they should be administered. Much was said about quit rents. The legislators wanted a new frame of government, but they could not agree on its form. Penn grew especially concerned when he learned that once again a strong movement to abolish proprietorships was afoot in England. He had to return to defend his interests. With this on his mind, Penn's stand against the legislators' onslaught was weak.

The colonial legislature finally agreed to a new government structure in 1701. Hereafter the governor would appoint the council, which would have few but advisory powers. The assembly would continue to be elected, and it would be the lawmaking group. Pennsylvania thus acquired a unicameral (one-body) legislature, which it would keep until 1790. The proprietor would continue to appoint a deputy governor. And the Lower Counties were now free to form their own legislature, although they would continue under the Pennsylvania governor. Preparing to depart, Penn appointed Colonel Andrew Hamilton to be his deputy, and left James Logan in charge of his affairs in the colony.

A sad and embittered William Penn sailed from Pennsylvania late in 1701. "God forgive those wretched people who have misused me so," he wrote to Logan. The Holy Experiment was in shambles.

To William Penn, religious liberty and toleration were the bedrock of government. Were liberty to prevail, then harmony and good government would naturally follow. Events in Pennsylvania proved him wrong. Political factionalism and economic self-interest buried religious considerations. Penn had not reckoned on that.

In England the danger to proprietorship passed, temporarily. Penn retained his colony, but it profited him and his family as little as it had in the past. He never returned to Pennsylvania.

Penn spent many of the declining years of his life in controversy with the government over his proprietary rights. He was also involved in litigation with Philip Ford, a Quaker merchant whom Penn had earlier placed in charge of his Irish estates. Ford and his wife swindled Penn out of thousands of pounds, made a bramble patch of his affairs, and tried to wrest his proprietorship from him. Unfortunately, Penn had frequently been a poor judge of the characters of those in whom he entrusted responsibility and the management of his wealth. And at one point he went to prison for a brief time because he was unable to pay his debts. To add to his troubles, the riotous living of his first and wastrel son William, in Philadelphia, was a constant embarrassment. Arrested in a tavern brawl, the younger William renounced Quakerism and finally returned to England.

On October 4, 1712, while writing a letter to James Logan, William Penn suffered a stroke. He lived another six years, however, dying on July 30, 1718. He was just short of seventy-four years of age.

Penn had ventured much and, even though he had not achieved his goals, he had been outstanding as a colonial leader and as a testament to the Quaker faith. And he left a colony to his widow and children.

SUGGESTED READINGS

Andrews, Charles M. *Our Earliest Colonial Settlements: Their Diversities of Origin and Later Characteristics.* Cornell University Press.

Irving, Washington. *Knickerbocker's History of New York.* Edited by Anne C. Moore. Frederick Ungar.

Irving, Washington. *"Rip Van Winkle," "The Legend of Sleepy Hollow," and Other Tales.* Grosset & Dunlap.

Kammen, Michael. *Colonial New York: A History.* Charles Scribner's Sons.

Morison, Samuel Eliot. *The European Discovery of America: The Northern Voyages.* Oxford University Press.

Reich, Jerome R. *Leisler's Rebellion: A Study of Democracy in New York, 1664–1720.* University of Chicago Press.

Wildes, Harry E. *William Penn.* Macmillan.

Wilson, Edmund. *Apologies to the Iroquois.* Random House, Vintage Books.

A Currier and Ives print depicts Benjamin Franklin's experiment with electricity, an event which could be seen as symbolic of the coming of age of the Middle Colonies of North America. The experiment took place in a field in Philadelphia, with Franklin's son as his only assistant.

2

COMING OF AGE

Leisler's Rebellion, which lasted from 1689 to 1691, left New York scarred and bitter. During the administrations of Governor Henry Sloughter and his successor Benjamin Fletcher, from 1691 to 1698, anti-Leislerians controlled the assembly. And they were preoccupied with revenge.

In a resolution, the assembly condemned the Leisler movement and passed a bill broadly defining treason. New codes concerning workers, especially New York City cartmen, were drafted. Leislerians who had fled the colony after Leisler's arrest were offered pardons if they returned, even though they had never been formally accused of crimes. Lawsuits charging Leisler's followers with false imprisonment and property damage were begun. In 1695, Governor Fletcher threatened to shoot anyone who voted for Peter Delanoy, the former customs collector and Leisler supporter, who was running for a seat in the assembly. Fletcher conferred freeman's status on English soldiers and sailors so that they could vote. He also appears to have threatened impressment—enforced enlistment—into the army or navy for those who voted "incorrectly." Later, however, he denied all threats and anti-Leislerian acts.

Leislerians, in turn, accused the governor of permitting piracy, associating with pirates, and receiving pirated goods. There apparently was truth to these charges, for the English Board of Trade scolded Fletcher for leniency to pirates. Nicholas Bayard and other anti-Leislerian merchants were also accused of aiding piracy and profiting from it. Fletcher

81

defended himself by pointing out that pirates brought hard money into New York—estimates ran as high as one hundred thousand pounds a year—and that this gold and silver money was badly needed. This indeed was the case. In New York as in other colonies throughout the colonial period, hard money was scarce and paper currency was uncertain in value. Charges and countercharges over the issue elevated feelings to a high level.

Among the leaders of the Leislerian faction were Gerardus Beeckman, Peter Delanoy, Samuel Staats, and Abraham Gouverneur. Their prospects brightened after Richard Coote, earl of Bellomont, arrived in New York to replace Fletcher as governor in 1698. At first Bellomont attempted to be impartial, but eventually he seemed to swing toward the Leislerian side. He nullified some of Fletcher's land grants, enforced customs regulations, and appointed some Leislerians to public office. All of this earned him abuse from anti-Leislerians.

Leislerians gained control of the assembly in 1699, and the political uproar continued. It was now their turn for vengeance. They tried to get opponents disqualified from holding seats in the assembly. They succeeded in having a number of large land grants nullified. The assembly voted money to Leisler's son, Jacob, Jr., for expenses his father had incurred. That body also granted the colony's coopers a lucrative monopoly by forbidding the importation of casks, or barrels. After William Bradford printed an anti-Leislerian pamphlet, the assembly dismissed him as public printer. And the assembly instigated the arrest and imprisonment of some anti-Leislerians accused of working with the notorious Captain William Kidd, who was later hanged in London on charges of piracy. Leislerians remained in control of the assembly after the election of 1701, which their opponents accused them of stealing.

Edward Hyde, Viscount Cornbury, arrived as governor in 1702, following Bellomont's death. Then the political seesaw tipped the other way. It appears that Cornbury's major purpose was to increase his wealth, and he decided that his best interests lay with anti-Leislerian merchants and large land owners. But Cornbury did not realize his ambitions. Recalled by the English government in 1708, he fled New York to escape his many creditors, to whom he owed several thousand pounds.

By the time Robert Hunter arrived to take over as governor in 1710, the intensity of the old quarrel was diminishing. Many of those personally involved in the events of 1689–1691 were dead. Their successors, although equally capable of factionalism, did not inherit the bitterness that had marked the 1690's and early 1700's. In addition, Hunter made it clear that he would govern impartially and that he wanted an end to squabbling. Addressing the assembly, he said that "if any go about to Disturb your Peace by reviving buryed parties & piques or creating new ones they shall meet with no Countenance or Encouragement from me & I am sure they deserve as little from you."[1]

Other Controversies

Hunter did not have his way entirely. As tattered animosities were laid aside, new controversies appeared. Two such controversies stood out during Hunter's administration and the one that followed it. First, there was a struggle for control between the governor and the assembly, a common eighteenth-century American colonial experience. Second, merchants opposed land owners in contesting for political control, which each group wished to use for its own economic advantage.

The assembly insisted that the council could not amend money bills. It wished to nominate a colonial treasurer responsible only to itself. It wanted the power to approve any courts the governor might create. And the assembly used the power of the purse—its right to enact tax bills and appropriate money—as a weapon against governor and council.

The colony of New York, like the other English colonies in North America, relied mainly on two sources of public income. One was taxes on trade. There were duties on furs exported from the colony, and on rum, wines, and certain

Lord Cornbury, a first cousin of Queen Anne, was appointed governor of New York and New Jersey in 1702. According to one description, he proved to be "a drunkard, a spendthrift, a grafter, an embezzler, a religious bigot, and a vain fool, especially when he appeared in public dressed as a woman." The latter charge, at least, seems to have been well founded—in his official portrait, Cornbury is indeed dressed as a woman, and a vain one at that.

[1] Quoted in Jerome R. Reich, *Leisler's Rebellion: A Study of Democracy in New York, 1664–1720* (Chicago: University of Chicago Press, 1953), p. 167.

The Royal Exchange in New York during the eighteenth century. The building was supported by a series of arches, leaving the ground floor open for merchants and tradesmen to meet and transact their business.

other goods imported into the colony. In addition, a "tonnage duty" on ships using the colony's ports was sometimes levied. The second source of income was a property tax, although this was used only when the assembly considered it necessary. And herein lay the basis for conflict between land owners and merchants. Each group favored shifting the burden of taxation to the other.

Members of the landed group argued that merchants simply added import duties to the prices of the goods they sold. Land owners, if subjected to property taxes, would really be doubly taxed. Because of import duties, they would also be paying higher prices for the goods they had to buy.

Governor Hunter tended to side with the landed faction, perhaps because it possessed so much strength in the assembly. This did not help him, however, for he failed to develop sufficient influence in the assembly to obtain passage of the money bills he desired. Hunter dissolved the assembly more than once, only to have the same members return to stage the same performance. The governor had to rely on money from England—which usually was not enough—and watch the public debt grow.

This situation persisted until 1713, when the governor and the assembly struck a bargain. The governor agreed to a treasurer appointed by the assembly. He also agreed to clear up the citizenship status of certain wealthy merchants of French Protestant and Dutch background. Under the English Navigation Act of 1660, aliens could not engage in colonial trade. This was not strictly enforced, but it left some merchants under a cloud. Hunter approved a bill granting citizenship to New Yorkers of foreign birth. In return, the assembly voted to issue twenty-seven thousand pounds in bills of credit—paper money. This would relieve the hardship caused by the flow of hard money to England to pay for goods imported from there. The issue of paper money would be paid off from duties on imported liquors, slaves, and European goods. The merchant group vigorously opposed the tax bill, but without success. Furthermore, in 1715 the assembly provided for a five-year term of financial support for the governor.

In 1717 the assembly authorized another public issue

amounting to thousands of pounds, again to be backed by customs duties. Merchants protested the tax, and they opposed the issue itself. It would, they said, be inflationary, cheapening the money supply. Again they lost.

Governor Hunter returned to England in 1719 believing that he had brought some stability to the colony. William Burnet arrived the following year to replace him.

Land owners remained politically strong because Burnet refused to call new elections, although this was customary upon the arrival of a new governor. He preferred to leave the assembly as it was. And he further offended the merchant group.

During times of French-English peace (and sometimes even in wartime), Albany merchants dealt with French fur traders as well as with Indians. The French obtained most of their pelts from the far Great Lakes region. The earlier plan to make direct contact with fur-gathering Indians of that area, which had led to the Schenectady massacre in 1690, was revived. Burnet wished to cut out French middlemen. With his support, the assembly passed a bill prohibiting trade with the French. While Albany merchants welcomed direct contact with fur sources, they bitterly deplored the loss of the French contacts. The French, despite the presence of English traders in the west, would continue to draw furs from that region.

Finally bowing to the merchants' clamor, Burnet called for elections in 1726. The merchant class gained strength in the assembly. In addition, after receiving many complaints from New York merchants, the English government that year vetoed the prohibition on trade with the French.

Although the merchant group won some points, it was becoming less of a solid front. New York City and Long Island merchants increasingly resented the cost of frontier defense, which aided Albany merchants. What had been a New York–Albany alliance was weakened further as Albany merchants gradually obtained more and more of their goods directly from England through their own agents on the coast. They purchased less from seaboard merchants. In Albany itself the economy had broadened. The fur trade grew less important. Population increased in the upper

This 1797 drawing by John Joseph Holland details a section of Broad and Wall Streets in New York. Dutch architecture prevails in the gabled, tiled roofs.

Hudson and the Mohawk valleys, and such food products as meats and grains became increasingly prominent as regional exports.

A Stormy Time for Cosby

The basis of political struggles was gradually shifting from economic to sectional—it was now more or less a matter of backcountry versus seaboard. And in New York City itself, factionalism centered more on the drive for political power than on the pursuit of economic advantage. This was particularly apparent during the administration of Governor William Cosby, which began in 1732.

Born in Ireland, William Cosby was a man with important connections. He was a close friend of the duke of Newcastle, who controlled the Board of Trade, which oversaw numerous colonial matters. His wife was a sister to the earl of Halifax. Cosby had been governor of the island of Minorca, then an English possession, off the coast of Spain. There he had illegally seized a Spanish ship and sold its cargo at auction. Then he changed the records to try to hide his deed. The English government ordered Cosby to pay back the ship's owner. But, despite this, Cosby found no trouble in obtaining the New York appointment. Writing about it later, one of his opponents remarked:

How such a man, after such a flagrant instance of tyranny and robbery, came to be intrusted with the government of an English colony and to be made Chancellor and keeper of the King's conscience in that colony, is not easy for a common understanding to conceive.[2]

Like his predecessor Cornbury, Cosby seems to have considered the governorship mainly as a means of increasing his fortune. He hoped to do well in land speculation. He also offered appointments to public office at a price. He angered the people of Albany by nullifying a deed under which Indians had conveyed 1,200 acres of land in trust.

Yet, from all reports, the man had considerable charm. He played host at glittering parties. He got on well with the assembly, at least at first. On the whole, he enjoyed good will and popularity early in his administration. But then he crossed Lewis Morris, a wealthy land owner, member of a long-respected family, and chief justice of the colonial supreme court. Morris was a political powerhouse who never shied from a fight or missed an opportunity for vengeance when he felt wronged. The quarrel began with Rip Van Dam who, as president of the council, had been acting governor until Cosby's arrival.

According to a custom which derived from a verbal order made by King William in 1698 but which was not always observed, the acting governor could be asked to split his salary evenly with the new arrival. But when Cosby requested that Van Dam do so, Van Dam balked. He noted that Cosby had drawn certain income as governor while still in England. The sum may have been as much as £6,500. Van Dam's salary had come to slightly less than £2,000. He suggested that each split his income and give half to the other. Cosby did not see things that way. He sued to collect.

This was a suit at equity—concerning a right or a claim. Under English common law such cases were usually heard by a judge and jury. But Cosby sensed that a jury made up of

Rip Van Dam.

---

[2]Cadwallader Colden, "History of William Cosby's Administration as Governor of the Province of New York . . . through 1737," in *Collections of the New-York Historical Society for the Year 1935* (New York: New-York Historical Society, 1937), p. 286.

New Yorkers would probably find for a fellow colonist, not the governor, no matter how popular he might be. Technically the supreme court could hear equity cases. The supreme court then became what was called a court of exchequer, dealing with money matters. Such a court, however, sat without a jury. The judges sometimes dealt with cases not precisely covered by law, and the possibility of arbitrary rulings was great. For that reason, American colonists took a dim view of exchequer courts. Moreover, no exchequer court had convened in New York for many years. Still, such an arrangement seemed well suited to Cosby, and he took his case to the supreme court.

Lewis Morris, the chief justice, may have foreseen a possible problem. New Jersey was then under the governor of New York. Before Cosby arrived, Morris had served as acting governor of New Jersey. Cosby might possibly demand half of his salary too, although there appears to be no evidence that Cosby had that in mind. In any event, Morris accepted the arguments of Van Dam's lawyers, who suggested that it was improper, even illegal, for the supreme court to hear the case. James De Lancey and Frederick Philipse, the associate judges, were friends of Cosby. They disagreed. Morris overrode them.

The Fight Heats Up

Cosby promptly removed Morris from the court, making De Lancey chief justice. The governor had pulled a tiger's tail. Counterattack was not long in coming as Morris set out to drive Cosby from New York.

Morris and his son ran for the assembly in the fall of 1733. Despite Cosby's efforts to rig the results, they won by healthy majorities. Lewis Morris now had a forum in which to attack Cosby, and he used it. Before long, he had whipped up considerable opposition to the governor, both in the assembly and among the public.

Among other things, the governor was denounced for accepting a possibly illegal gift of a thousand pounds from the assembly, the gift representing compensation to Cosby for expressing opposition to certain English legislation affecting the colonies. His opponents also faulted him for allowing a French ship to take on provisions in New York harbor. They criticized him for sitting with the council when it was considering legislative matters, a practice that was illegal. They scolded him for not notifying council members who opposed him of the dates and times of council meetings. Cosby had, his enemies declared, appointed incompetents as sheriffs. The battle eventually shifted to paper.

The only newspaper in the colony was William Bradford's *New-York Gazette,* established in 1693. Because he was official printer, Bradford could publish no criticism of the government. He could, however, publish Cosby's praise. Francis Harison, a friend of the governor's, began planting pro-Cosby items in the *Gazette* and occasionally pieces lampooning the opposition. He characterized Cosby as "the mild, the happy, good and great." The opposition, on the other hand, was "loquacious, loud, and turbulent of tongue" and "scandal busy."

Fearing that this propaganda might sway opinion against them, Cosby's enemies established their own paper, the *New-York Weekly Journal.* John Peter Zenger became its printer.

Zenger had been born in the Palatinate, a German province, in 1697. In 1710, when he was thirteen, he came with his family to the colonies. Soon after, he began an eight-year apprenticeship as a printer under William Bradford in New York. Completing his time, Zenger looked about for a place to set up shop on his own. He settled in Maryland, where he became official printer. He also married Mary White of Philadelphia, who bore him a son, John. Following his wife's death, Zenger returned to New York in 1725, joining Bradford in partnership. This did not last long, though. Zenger soon went into business for himself in New York City. He also married again. His second wife was Anne Catherine Maulin, a native of Holland.

New York's second printer did well enough to make a living. But he did not do so well that he could afford to turn down new business from the anti-Cosby faction. And for this he spent nearly a year in jail.

Zenger's participation in the Cosby affair seems to have been limited to his role as printer. He composed ads and put together foreign news in the paper, but he appears to have written no articles about the governor. James Alexander, an able lawyer and friend of Morris, edited the articles. He probably wrote some of them too. Other contributors published anonymously or under assumed names. With the *Journal* now in action, and the *Gazette* continuing, New Yorkers could expect new digs and accusations, increasingly nasty, each and every week.

Cosby was labeled a "Nero," after the oppressive Roman emperor. His friend Francis Harison was characterized in this way:

> A large spaniel of about five foot five inches high has lately strayed from his kennel with his mouth full of fulsome [sickening] panegyrics [praises], and in his ramble dropped them in the *New-York Gazette*. When a puppy he was marked thus (FH), and a cross in the middle of his forehead; but the mark being worn out, he has taken upon him in a heathenish manner to abuse mankind by imposing a great many gross falsehoods on them. Whoever will strip the said panegyrics of their fulsomeness, and send the beast back to his kennel, shall have the thanks of all honest men, and all reasonable charges.[3]

All previous accusations concerning Cosby's conduct in office were rehashed.

The *Gazette* responded in kind, labeling the opposition "seditious rogues" and "disaffected instigators of arson and riot." It equated Zenger's name with "liar." It nicknamed Rip Van Dam "the Amsterdam Crane," referred to Lewis Morris and his son Lewis, Jr., as "Philip Baboon, senior and junior," and called James Alexander "the Scythian Unicorn." Zenger became "Wild Peter from the Banks of the Rhine."

Both sides had a case for libel. Cosby finally instituted one.

Copies of Zenger's *Journal* are burned on Wall Street, November 6, 1734.

Printer on Trial

At first Cosby tried to get a grand jury investigation to determine who had written the *Journal* articles. The grand jury refused to consider the matter. Then Cosby had four copies of

[3] *New-York Weekly Journal,* 26 November 1733.

the *Journal* burned in public. Finally, on November 17, 1734, he had Zenger arrested and held for trial on a charge of seditious libel. Bail was set at four hundred pounds, an impossible sum for Zenger to raise.

In the meantime, in an attempt to get Cosby removed from office, Lewis Morris went to England to lay charges against the governor before officials there. Morris spent eighteen months in England. He met with no success. And, although he tried hard, he never won back the chief justiceship.

Zenger remained in jail for nine months awaiting trial. He steadfastedly refused to name the authors of the anti-Cosby articles he had printed. It is altogether possible that he did not know them. In the meantime, the *Journal* missed only one issue. Zenger's wife, Catherine, got the paper out each week.

James Alexander and William Smith, Zenger's lawyers, sought first to discredit De Lancey and Philipse, the judges who would hear the case. The justices disbarred Alexander and Smith for their pains. The anti-Cosby group now cast about for another lawyer. They found Andrew Hamilton of Philadelphia.

Hamilton's birthdate is uncertain. It was said that he was eighty years old when he journeyed from Philadelphia to New York to defend John Peter Zenger. He may have been fifteen years younger. In any case, he was an immigrant from Scotland and enjoyed a reputation as the best lawyer in the colonies. He had handled cases for the Penn family. He had also been a member of the Pennsylvania assembly, serving for a time as its speaker. Hamilton had been the object of attacks by William Bradford when Bradford ran his printing shop in Philadelphia, before coming to New York. And Hamilton had helped to prosecute Bradford on a charge of seditious libel brought by the Pennsylvania assembly. Now he was on the other side.

When Zenger's trial opened on August 4, 1735, the prosecution rested its case on one leg. Under English law and practice, only the *fact* of libel had to be proved. Libel was defined as the publication of a statement damaging to a person's reputation. Seditious libel, with which Zenger was charged, was the publication of a statement that tended to undermine governmental authority by damaging the reputation of a person

The front page of the *New-York Weekly Journal* for November 25, 1734, contains a column written by John Peter Zenger reporting his own arrest for libel.

Andrew Hamilton helped to establish the tradition of a free press in America with his defense in the Zenger case. Among other accomplishments in his busy and productive life, he helped to design Independence Hall in Philadelphia.

The trial of John Peter Zenger. This nineteenth-century engraving shows Andrew Hamilton, Zenger's attorney, defending his client. Hamilton declared, "It is not the bare printing and publishing of a paper that makes it a libel: The words themselves must be libelous, that is, false."

in public office. The *truth* of the statement was not considered. All the jury had to decide was whether or not the libel had in fact occurred—that is, whether or not Zenger had published the statement in question. If they agreed on the fact of publication—and they could hardly do otherwise, since Zenger did not dispute it—the judge would interpret the law by deciding whether or not the statement constituted seditious libel and would then pass sentence.

Realizing that he had little chance to win under the law, Hamilton presented a political argument. He spoke of self-government and freedom of the press, and he described Zenger's motivations in terms that the jury could identify with.

In his remarks, Hamilton noted the English law on libel. But he contended that what was good for England, where ruler and ruled were widely separated, might not be good for an American colony, where governor and governed were much closer. Freedom of the press, Hamilton argued, helped hold governments accountable, forcing them to attend to the people's needs and wishes. The people must have the power to check governors and governments in order to protect their liberties. They must see that governments function for the public good. Because governors could control assemblies and courts, the only sure way to call governments to account was through a free press.

Finally, Hamilton offered the jurors a choice. They could choose to follow the English precedent. Then they would simply decide that Zenger printed the material, which everyone knew. He would be guilty of libel and the judge would dispose of the case. Or they could choose to move beyond the English law. Hamilton insisted that a jury had the right to decide both fact and law in libel cases. Furthermore, he argued, truth was a defense against a libel charge. That is, the jurors could decide who was responsible for the anti-Cosby articles, and John Peter Zenger was willing to accept responsibility there. That was the finding of fact. Then they could interpret the law by deciding whether or not the printed statements were libelous. If they agreed that the statements contained truth, they could rule that libel had not been committed and that Zenger therefore was not guilty of the charge.

Hamilton's was a bold, new argument. And the jury bought it. Its members found Zenger not guilty as courtroom spectators cheered.

What had begun as essentially a personal quarrel had blossomed into something larger. But what the Zenger case meant has undergone revision over the years. It was long hailed as the first step toward the establishment of freedom of the press in America, and as a beginning of change in libel laws. It was also considered the first important instance in which a newspaperman—in the case of Zenger, perhaps the term is used loosely—had refused to reveal the source of his information.

It remains possible that Zenger did not know who wrote the articles. If this were so, he had nothing to reveal. As to freedom of the press, the case does not seem to have set a precedent. Even after the First Amendment to the Constitution guaranteed freedom of the press, governments in America stifled it from time to time. Important changes in libel laws were still more than a century away. Nonetheless, the Zenger case did bolster those who believed that public opinion should be brought to bear on government, and that government should be held accountable.

John Peter Zenger is carried in triumph from the courtroom following his acquittal on charges of libel.

One of those in the case, Andrew Hamilton, is also remembered as the designer of what became Independence Hall in Philadelphia. John Peter Zenger, a year after the trial, was made public printer. He died in 1746, and his wife and son continued the paper until it folded in 1751. The trial broke Governor William Cosby. He died after a brief illness in 1736. Cosby never collected from Rip Van Dam, but shortly before he died, he had the satisfaction of removing Van Dam from the governor's council. Cosby made sure that Van Dam would not be acting governor again.

Power and James De Lancey

Two men dominated New York politics during the 1740's and into the 1750's—Governor George Clinton and James De Lancey, the same man Governor William Cosby had elevated to the chief justiceship to replace Lewis Morris.

The DeLancey Mansion.

Young De Lancey was of French Huguenot stock, his father Stephen having come to New York in 1686. The elder De Lancey did extremely well as a merchant, amassing a fortune. He married into money when he wed Anne Van Cortlandt, daughter of Stephanus Van Cortlandt, member of a powerful merchant family. Educated at Cambridge at Corpus Christi College, beginning in 1721, James De Lancey later read law at Lincoln's Inn, in London. He began his law practice in New York City with a gift of three thousand pounds from his father. In 1728 he married Anne Heathcote. As the daughter of Caleb Heathcote, a Westchester County squire, she came from landed wealth. In a sense, the marriage symbolized a union of land holding and commercial interests. At age twenty-six, De Lancey became a member of the governor's council. In 1731 he was made a supreme court justice and then, during the Cosby conflict, chief justice.

De Lancey enjoyed outstanding political connections, both in the colony and in England. His father was an assemblyman. Three brothers later were active in New York City and colonial politics. De Lancey's wife's first cousin, Sir John Heathcote, was a member of Parliament. His sister Susannah married Commodore Peter Warren of the British navy. Warren became a hero in actions against the French during the War of the Austrian Succession—known as King George's War in America—which England fought from

1744 to 1748. De Lancey's position on the supreme court itself overflowed with political influence. The court was a center of attention not only because it met four times annually in New York City, but also because the justices acted as circuit judges throughout the colony during other times of the year.

Clinton became governor of New York in 1743. De Lancey became his chief adviser. He used his influence in the assembly to obtain a salary grant of £1,560 for Clinton. In return, the governor appointed De Lancey's friends to four of the five council seats.

Governor and adviser eventually fell out. Partly, perhaps, their differences hinged on De Lancey's ambitions for the lieutenant governorship. More important, though, were Clinton's plans for defense during King George's War.

Upper New York merchants still profited from the fur trade with the French. Moreover, they recalled past disasters, especially the Schenectady massacre during King William's War, which had resulted from breaking the informal alliance with French interests. Consequently they wanted nothing to do with Clinton's plan, in 1746, to send an expedition up the Hudson Valley to attack Quebec, in Canada. For that matter, few New Yorkers anywhere in the colony wanted to participate in the war. As far as they could see, it was a European affair that could hardly further their interests. And James De Lancey, who did not mistake the political winds, sided with the majority.

As it turned out, Clinton's discussion of invasion plans with the Iroquois and with representatives from Albany dragged on until winter came. By then it was too late to undertake the expedition. The presence of English troops quartered during the winter at Albany annoyed residents there. Commissioners responsible for provisioning the soldiers refused to do so. The troops then broke into warehouses and supplied themselves. This might seem justifiable, but it did not improve the soldiers' relations with Albany's people.

Events in Albany during the winter of 1746–1747 helped solidify opposition to Clinton. He had to cancel plans for attack again in 1747. The war ended the following year. De Lancey's opposition served to enhance his political fortunes. Clinton's influence diminished.

Governor George Clinton.

Library of Congress

The assembly now had a firm clutch on the public purse through its power to tax and appropriate money. A governor was financially helpless without the good will of the assembly. Governors previously had exerted influence with respect to land grants, but much of this authority had gradually slipped into the hands of the supreme court. Formerly, by doling out jobs and favors, governors had kept a firm grip on the powers of patronage. They decided where military supplies would be distributed and made appointments in the colonial militia as well as to lower courts. But by Clinton's time, the practice of having local favorites pass on civil and military appointments had seriously eroded the governor's patronage power. And during Clinton's administration, much of what had been lost—influence over the assembly, land matters, and patronage—moved into James De Lancey's hands. His power proved roughly equal to, if not greater than, the governor's. With the end of King George's War, George Clinton set out to alter the situation. This touched off four years of bitter political warfare.

By firing and appointing, Clinton could gain and maintain control of the council, which he did. The assembly, however, with its power over the purse, was another matter. Clinton had to develop a grassroots organization to get out the vote for his supporters, a weapon James De Lancey and his followers already possessed. Clinton tried.

In September, 1748, Clinton dismissed the assembly after it refused to grant him five-year financial support. He then set out to build a local political power base and to reassert his authority over appointments to local civil and judicial offices. About two years later, the governor concluded that he might risk a showdown. He called for elections to a new assembly.

For Clinton, the 1750 election was a disaster. Even with the aid of bribery, Clinton's candidate Lewis Morris, Jr., son of the old Cosby adversary, could not defeat Peter De Lancey, the chief justice's brother. Bribes and "threatenings" used "barefacedly," Clinton glumly reported afterward, "did prevail by about 8 or 10 votes."

Clinton and De Lancey forces then declared a truce. The governor accepted a one-year appropriation from the assembly. But the war was on again in the fall of 1751 when Clinton dissolved the assembly and called for new elections. Again he lost, even more heavily than before.

In the spring of 1753, Clinton was recalled to England. Ironically, from Clinton's point of view, James De Lancey was made lieutenant governor. Then came further irony. The new governor, Sir Danvers Osborne, grieving over his wife's death and doubtful of his ability to govern, hanged himself soon after arriving in New York. That left James De Lancey as acting governor.

James De Lancey now had to defend much of what he had been attacking—the governor's powers and prerogatives.

Astute politician that he was, he did well, steering clear of the shoals of confrontation. He reconciled those who had supported Clinton. He accepted without murmur annual appropriations for salaries and other items. He defended the assembly in communications with the English Board of Trade. At the same time, he saw to it that New York City's commercial interests benefitted at the expense of those in Albany. The assembly passed a law requiring colonial authorities to inspect such upper New York products as meats, fish, and leather which passed through New York's port, and the governor approved it. In addition, Sir William Johnson, long an Indian agent, was made commissioner for Indian affairs. This removed Indian policy completely from the hands of Albany officials, who had conducted Indian relations for nearly a century.

De Lancey continued as acting governor until 1760. That year he died of a heart attack, at the age of fifty-seven.

Personal politics as well as the politics of assembly *versus* governor had marked the Clinton period. For the colonial future, the latter element had been especially important. By the mid-eighteenth century, in New York as in other colonies, the assembly had attained considerable power. And this power would be jealously guarded as relations with Britain became increasingly strained after 1763. The colonials' defense of it would be an important ingredient in revolution.

Across the Hudson

New Jersey had become a crown colony in 1702 after the original proprietors had surrendered their powers of government while keeping their rights to land. From then until 1738 the colony shared its governor with New York. And the first governor under the new regime in 1702 was Edward Hyde, Lord Cornbury, the center of a stormy administration.

During Cornbury's time there was controversy over proprietary land titles. The governor squabbled with the assembly over the amount of his salary and over the number of years of financial support which that body could vote at one time. There were battles over property taxes, which proprietary groups usually opposed. As a matter of conscience, Quakers continued to refuse to support appropriations for the military. Nor would they serve in the militia. Frustrated, Cornbury dissolved the assembly several times, but this did not solve his problems.

Only nine laws were enacted in New Jersey during Cornbury's administration, bleak witness to the conflict between governor and assembly. Evidence also indicates that Cornbury accepted bribes. He made life miserable for Quakers. He stole land from proprietors. Cornbury ran up debts in New Jersey as well as in New York, and the relief of his departure was no less great in New Jersey than in the neighboring colony.

New Jersey experienced three governorships between the recall of Cornbury in 1708 and the appointment of Robert Hunter in 1710. Hunter labored as even-handedly and as firmly in New Jersey as in New York, but his administration was not free from problems.

The New Jersey assembly, like that in New York, had by now assumed a tight grasp of the purse strings. It could, and did, use its power to tax and to appropriate money as a weapon against governors. Hunter advised English officials that Parliament should pay governor's salaries, to take them out from under assembly control. Nothing came of this, however.

There was also controversy over the matter of court and legal fees. The governor and council had the power to set these fees, but the trend in the assembly was to take over this authority. As a rule, the New Jersey assembly favored lower fees than the governor and council. Lower fees would ease legal burdens on ordinary citizens, who elected assemblymen. After failing under previous governors, the assembly got its foot in the fee-setting door during Hunter's administration, much to his dissatisfaction.

At the same time, the assembly made other gains. Some of them seemed of small importance, but they all added up to greater authority. As one example, Hunter permitted the assembly to pay its sergeant-at-arms, its clerk, and its doorkeeper on the say-so of the speaker. Previously no payments could be made except on the basis of a warrant signed by the governor.

As in other colonies, the question of paper money arose in New Jersey. And twice, early in Hunter's administration, the assembly issued bills of credit—in essence, paper currency.

These bills continued in circulation, although their buying power gradually decreased.

The early 1720's proved a time of economic hardship in New Jersey, and groups pressed for additional paper money to be issued. Consequently in 1723 the assembly set up a loan office and a land bank. It issued forty thousand pounds' worth of legal tender paper. People could obtain a share of this as loans, within limits of not less than twelve pounds, six shillings, or more than one hundred pounds. Borrowers had to pledge a mortgage on land or a house, pay five percent interest, and retire the loans in at least twelve years. How to treat interest from these loans became a matter of contention between assembly and governors. The assembly wished to use the money for general purposes. This, as one effect, would keep taxes low. Governors, on the other hand, preferred to keep the interest money separate and use it for certain specified purposes, including the payment of official salaries. The assembly usually carried the point here.

Lewis Morris of New Jersey

Lewis Morris.

Lewis Morris had long advocated separate governorships for New Jersey and New York. And when New Jersey came under its own governor in 1738, Morris got the job. He had served briefly as acting governor in 1719 and again from 1730 to 1732 while New York and New Jersey awaited the arrival of William Cosby. And this man, who had fiercely contested the governor's rights and privileges in New York, now found himself defending them. Morris' eight years in office were filled with controversy.

Governor Morris did remove himself from council meetings having to do with lawmaking. This gave the council greater freedom to debate and decide. He also appointed his son, Robert H. Morris, to fill the vacant chief justiceship of the New Jersey supreme court. At the time, helping a son in this way was not noteworthy. The important thing was that Morris made the appointment "during good behavior." This shielded the office from the kind of arbitrary action Morris had experienced under Governor Cosby in New York.

But Morris, like other governors, disputed with the assembly over his salary. He was thoroughly dissatisfied with the initial one thousand pounds appropriated and the sixty pounds for house rent. He thought that he should get

New Jersey Historical Society

additional reward for his efforts to obtain a separate governorship for the colony. The assembly figured that his getting
the office was reward enough in itself, and that the thousand
pounds was sufficiently generous. Morris tried to persuade
the Board of Trade to set governors' salaries, without success. He continued the fight over what to do with loan-office
interest money. He vetoed a bill calling for a meeting of the
assembly at least every three years, for this would remove
from his hands the authority to call meetings. Morris also
quarreled with the assembly over whether or not the governor had the power to change—instead of just veto—
money bills. The Board of Trade insisted that he had. The
assembly said no. In 1740, the governor failed to stir up
much enthusiasm with his request for troops and money to
aid an English expedition against the Spanish in the West
Indies during the War of Jenkins' Ear, which began in 1739.
(One cause of the war was the action of Spanish coast guards
based in Havana, who had cut off the ear of Robert Jenkins,
a British merchant seaman, after boarding and looting his
ship as it lay in Cuban waters.) Morris had only slightly more
success in persuading the assembly to support military operations against the French during King George's War, which
began in 1744. He did, however, stir up a hornet's nest when
he vetoed a paper money bill.

The English government opposed the issuance of paper
money because it tended to be inflationary and because it
placed too much financial power in the colonies. In 1744,
plans were laid in Parliament to forbid bills of credit entirely.
Upon hearing of this, the New Jersey assembly passed a resolution. It insisted that such a move would be an "encroachment upon the fundamental constitution of this colony" and
"destructive of the liberties and properties of his Majesty's
subjects." Twenty years later, similar declarations would be
hurled against bills and laws considered oppressive. Colonial agents in London lobbied furiously against the idea of a
law prohibiting paper money, and nothing came of it at the
time.

Quarrels over Land

During the Morris administration, much time was spent on
struggling over land titles. The battle boiled down to proprietary *versus* other interests.

Sailors on a British warship patrolling the Caribbean.

As an example, proprietors held title to half a million acres of land around Elizabethtown. Incoming settlers, however, were unwilling to pay the proprietors' relatively high prices. Since the acreage was unused, settlers took up land on the outskirts of the proprietors' claims. They either "squatted"—paid nothing—or made purchases directly from Indians. This displeased the proprietors, and the dispute finally evolved into a conflict between the East Jersey Council of Proprietors, in which Lewis Morris and his son Robert were involved, and the Elizabeth-Town Association. In drawn-out lawsuits, neither group gained a clear-cut victory at first.

A similar, although not quite as intense, situation existed in West Jersey, where Morris had interests also. There, proprietors estimated that some thirteen thousand acres of land belonging to them had been taken up illegally. The alleged wrongdoers were not impressed. They simply drove off the proprietors' agents who, from their point of view, were annoying them.

In East Jersey, by 1745, the tide was running in favor of the proprietors. They had won some lawsuits and had managed to eject numerous land holders they considered to be without valid titles. What the proprietors regarded as the most important lawsuit began early in 1745. When the Elizabeth-Town Association proved unready to proceed at the appointed time, ejections commenced. Then one of the Association members, Samuel Baldwin, was arrested for cutting timber illegally. He was jailed in Newark. A mob overran the lockup and rescued him. Later, four men were jailed for taking part in the ruckus. Even though the militia surrounded the jail, those armed men proved no match for a mob of three hundred which soon descended. After some fist fights and wrestling, the four were released.

The assembly refused to take action against the rioters, nor did the English government do anything. Following Governor Morris's death in 1746, the controversy continued. Rioters even took to driving those holding titles issued by proprietors from their homes. Summing up the rioters' spirit, some opponents of the proprietors declared in 1747:

When the King shall have Notice that such a
Multitude of his Subjects in the Jerseys are turned
Mob, and act as they do, He will say, Or think, what's
the Matter with my Subjects? Surely they are wronged
or oppressed, or else they would never rebell against
my Laws, sure some previous Oppression had caused
them to act thus, or else they would never have done
it, and so he will order us to have our Land.[4]

In July that year came another jail rescue, this time in Perth Amboy. John Bainbridge, Jr., had been arrested for participating in a jail outbreak in Somerset County. According to the sheriff at Perth Amboy:

About Eleven a Clock the Justices the City
Magistrates & I attended by my Deputies and the
constables went to the Market House & Walked there
till between Twelve and one when a mob of about One
hundred & fifty, Armed with Great Clubs Came into
the Town on horse back, Rode by my door, then
alight, Tyed their Horses to Mr. Johnson's fence &
Came on foot up the Street with Edmond Bainbridge,

[4]Quoted in W.A. Whitehead et al., eds., *Documents Relating to the Colonial History of the State of New Jersey* (Newark: *Daily Journal,* 1880–1886), vol. 3, p. 423.

Simon Wyckoff & one Amos Roberts at their head
and two Fiddles playing. We meet them at the Corner
of the Court house I asked their Business,
Commanded them to Disperse, Read the
Proclamation, which they Suffered me to do but when
I began to read the Writt by which I had taken
Bainbridge I was knocked down & have a Grievous
Wound in my head they also Struck the Mayor, broke
one of the Constables' head beat several of the others
and then violently with a Sledge and Iron Barr & a
Hatchet broke open the Outward & Inward Doors of
the Gaol [jail] took out the Prisoner and Carried him
off Huzzaing.[5]

Rioting over land in New Jersey continued off and on into
the 1750's.

The New Jersey land controversy was similar to that in
other proprietary colonies where a small group of men had
been granted huge tracts. In New Jersey, however, matters
went to greater lengths than elsewhere. Land monopolies,
with quit rents and relatively high prices, infuriated many
colonials. Immigrants had come to America for greater freedom and for opportunities to better themselves economically. Acreage was abundant, and many would not tolerate
restrictions imposed by a small group. Unsupported by
either the assembly or the English government, and with a
strong popular tide running against them, New Jersey proprietors by and large lost their case.

The Proprietor's Man

For nearly half a century after William Penn's second, and
final, visit to Pennsylvania, James Logan, the representative
he had left behind, remained influential in colonial affairs.
Logan had been born into a Scottish family in October,
1674. His family had been transplanted to Ireland and were
living in a little town near Belfast. Logan's father was a tight-
fisted schoolmaster, with a master of arts degree from
Edinburgh University, and a convert to Quakerism. For
Scottish as well as English Quakers, life was hard. Stern

[5]Quoted in ibid., vol. 4, pp. 469–70.

James Logan.

Presbyterians—the majority—held little sympathy for the strange Quaker ways. And so Patrick Logan moved his family to County Armagh. The Logans found life in Ireland scarcely better than in Scotland, but with care and diligence Patrick was able to survive as a teacher.

Matters grew worse in 1688 when armies of the deposed king, James II, retreated westward into northern Ireland. James's men wreaked havoc on Protestants, and lay seige to Londonderry. Patrick Logan fled with his family back to Scotland, and later to Bristol, on the west coast of England. There James received an education in Greek and Latin from his father. And, like his father, he became a teacher. He also tried, with little success, to become a merchant. Then in 1699 he met William Penn and accepted Penn's invitation to cross the ocean to Pennsylvania as his secretary.

James Logan immediately set himself to disentangling Penn's affairs, a mighty task. Rent rolls were practically nonexistent. Many land surveys had been made improperly. And the matter of quit rents remained a sore point. If paid at all, the rents were usually offered in kind—in goods or commodities such as wheat. And, during the time of economic depression early in the eighteenth century, grain fetched little at the market place. Only with difficulty did Penn persuade Logan not to chuck it all and return to England.

Upon leaving Pennsylvania, Penn placed Logan in full charge of his affairs there. He also made him clerk of the council and secretary of the colony. Logan's main task was to oversee his employer's interests, which mostly meant generating income from the land. This was not easy. In 1702, for example, Logan reported that he had managed to collect barely twelve pounds in quit rents and only about forty-eight pounds from land sales. Hoping to supplement his own and his employer's income, he invested in trade. While this proved hardly more profitable, it did afford relief from the carping criticism he received from those owing rent.

Penn's man later became involved in the fur trade as a merchant furnishing goods to traders for the Indians. This eventually proved financially beneficial, as did some of the land deals he made. In 1714 James Logan married Sarah Reed, a wealthy merchant's daughter. This helped him both economically and socially. And almost from the beginning Logan was involved in Pennsylvania politics.

Logan leaned toward the aristocracy. He found the Pennsylvania government defective because there was no real upper house of wise and able men of property to serve as a check on the possible impulsiveness of the popularly elected assembly. Throughout much of his life in Pennsylvania, in fact, he insisted that the council had legislative powers. And gradually there gathered around him a proprietary party composed of large land holders and conservative, well-to-do merchants. David Lloyd, who for many years had been speaker of the assembly, led the opposition. Most of those opposing Logan were artisans and shopkeepers from Philadelphia, and a considerable number of Quakers from both town and country. Throughout Pennsylvania's colonial history, many Quakers opposed the proprietors' rights and privileges. Quit rents were always a sensitive issue. So were matters of defense and service in the militia. And so was the Penn family's insistence that they pay no taxes on land they owned, which amounted to hundreds of thousands of acres.

David Lloyd was a formidable opponent. He had been anti-proprietor since Penn dismissed him from office in 1699. Upholding assembly privilege and rights, and doing much to strengthen that body's power, Lloyd sometimes opposed the crown itself. His attitude toward authoritarianism attracted Quakers with keen memories of persecution. Most assembly bills bore Lloyd's stamp. And in 1719 he became chief justice of the Pennsylvania supreme court. He could now interpret laws he had helped to pass.

Both Lloyd and Logan had risen in the world largely through their own efforts. Both were arrogant, jealous of power, and vindictive. They clashed frequently. Between 1706 and 1708, the assembly did little more than listen to Lloyd denounce Logan, accusing him of violating the Frame of Government of 1701 and of mismanaging land policies. Lloyd tried, and failed, to get Logan removed from office. Ill feeling between the two persisted until Lloyd's death in 1731.

The Oath Controversy

In addition to personal controversies in Pennsylvania, there were struggles pitting Quakers against non-Quakers. One had to do with oaths.

During the early eighteenth century, Quakers made up about two-thirds of Pennsylvania's population. They dominated the assembly. And while they might disagree among themselves on some issues, on those that touched their faith they tended to unite. They enforced their convictions on the remainder of the colony's population. The oath was a case in point.

Quakers opposed the swearing of oaths in court. Yet in England no person's unsworn testimony was allowed. Therefore, owing to their position on oaths, Quakers could not give evidence in criminal cases, sit on juries, or hold any civil office.

The oath issue arose from time to time in Pennsylvania. In 1711 the Quaker-dominated assembly legalized affirmations as a substitute for oaths. The governor at the time, Charles Gookin, signed the legislation. The act began:

> That when any person who for conscience's sake cannot take an oath shall be called before any

Quakers on trial in England. Because Quakers opposed the swearing of oaths, under English law they could not give evidence in criminal cases, sit on juries, or hold civil office.

magistrate or proper officer to give evidence in any matter or case whatever, such magistrate or officer shall administer the affirmation as hereinafter directed to such person or persons in these words, "A.B., thou art called here to give thy evidence; dost thou protest solemnly and declare that the evidence thou shalt give be the truth, the whole truth, and nothing but the truth?"[6]

Queen Anne nullified the law in 1714. The assembly promptly passed it again, and again Gookin signed it.

In 1715 two men were arrested for the murder of Jonathon Hayes, a wealthy farmer of Chester County. Noting the absence of an oath, Gookin ruled that they could not be legally tried. The men were released on bail.

Two years later a new governor, William Keith, saw matters differently. He ordered that the accused be tried under Pennsylvania law. Eight Quakers were on the jury, and they were affirmed. The men were found guilty. And after Keith and the council concluded that there were no grounds for appeal, the two were executed. The incident created a storm of protest in England, where opinion held that it was monstrous to execute persons following the decision of an unsworn jury, an illegal body.

In 1718 the assembly passed another law which asserted that an affirmation enjoyed equality with an oath. The English government allowed this legislation, apparently because it was part of a trade-off. Long under pressure from England to do so, the assembly at the same time broadened the list of capital offenses—which had been limited to murder—to include many other crimes, such as burglary, maiming, and highway robbery. This brought Pennsylvania more in line with the English criminal code.

The affirmation law proved double-edged. Quaker beliefs were upheld. But at the same time the law cut conscientious Friends out of judicial office. If they could not take an oath, neither could they administer one to a person demanding it.

[6]Quoted in Isaac Sharpless, *Two Centuries of Pennsylvania History* (Philadelphia: J.B. Lippincott, 1900), p. 110.

The victory was not worth much. And it contributed to the eventual decline of Quaker influence in Pennsylvania.

Logan versus Keith

During the eighteenth century, in Pennsylvania as in other colonies, there was considerable dueling between the governor and the assembly. The assembly's right to adjourn itself, and money matters such as the governor's salary were among the points at issue. However, the administration of Governor William Keith, which began in 1717, proved a period of relative calm. The focus of controversy shifted to governor *versus* council.

Keith and the assembly got along well. They kept government expenses relatively low, and agreed on property taxes and import duties to raise money. And in 1723 the assembly provided for a paper money issue amounting to fifteen thousand pounds in one-shilling to twenty-shilling notes. Pennsylvanians could acquire these by pledging gold or real estate and paying five percent interest over a period of one year for gold and eight years for real estate. The limits per person were twelve pounds minimum and a hundred pounds maximum. In 1724, the assembly authorized an additional issue of thirty thousand pounds.

James Logan and other conservatives both within and outside the council opposed the issues of paper money as inflationary, but they were powerless to prevent them. To Governor Keith, Logan continued to make a nuisance of himself with his insistence that the council had legislative power. Keith sided with David Lloyd and other members of the assembly, contending that the Frame of Government of 1701 did not provide for that. Relations between Keith and Logan became so poor that in the spring of 1723 the governor dismissed Logan as council secretary. He accused Logan of altering certain council minutes. The power of dismissal, however, lay with the proprietor. Logan left for England to confer with Hannah Penn, whom Penn had married in 1696, two years after the death of his first wife.

The late proprietor's widow upheld Logan. In a communication to Keith, she reminded him that he was accountable to the Penn family. He must not interfere with those responsible for the proprietor's business, especially in matters concerning land and rents. He must seek and attend to the council's advice. And the governor must agree to issue no more paper money, which displeased many merchants. Finally, she told Keith to restore Logan to his position on the council.

Logan later learned that Keith, in a letter to Hannah Penn, had brought up the matter of falsifying council minutes. He then accused Keith of defamation. David Lloyd and the governor struck back with pamphlets against Logan, featuring themselves as defenders of the Frame of Government and, incidentally, of the people. The "paper war" produced charge and countercharge for many months, and in the end Keith lost. The Penn family dismissed him, replacing him with Patrick Gordon, an army officer well along in years.

Although Logan won his battle with Governor Keith, neither the Penns, the Board of Trade, nor Parliament could stem the issue of paper money. The Pennsylvania assembly authorized thirty thousand pounds more in 1729, another forty thousand pounds two years later, and still another eighty thousand pounds in 1739. And in England, Pennsylvania representatives lobbied hard against legislation that would forbid paper money. It would appear, though, that in Pennsylvania paper money issues were well managed. When Parliament finally forbade them in the colonies, it exempted Pennsylvania.

In January, 1728, James Logan suffered a bad fall on the ice. The accident permanently injured his left hip, forcing him to use crutches. Despite his handicap, Logan continued to care for the proprietor's business. Then in 1731 his old enemy, David Lloyd, died and the position of chief justice of the Pennsylvania supreme court fell open. Logan accepted the office. In 1735, when Governor Gordon died, he became president of the council and, in effect, acting governor. He remained so until the arrival of Governor George Thomas from the West Indies. At about this time two related issues—defense and Indian relations—boiled to the surface more strongly than ever before.

The Indian Matter

Indian-white relations had, with some exceptions, been peaceful since William Penn's meeting with tribal leaders in 1682. But over the years the situation grew increasingly complex. One reason was the constant influx of new settlers. As more and more land was taken up, pressure on the Indians increased. Relations between one group in particular—the Scotch-Irish—and the Indians were rough from the start.

The Scotch-Irish had their origin during the reign of England's King James I, which began in 1625. Following rebellions in northern Ireland, English authorities invited Scots to settle in Ulster. They came in large numbers, bringing their Presbyterian religion with them. As Protestants, they did not get along well with Irish Catholics. Nor were their relations with the established Church of England always good. All this reinforced Scotch-Irish clannishness and tended to develop in them such character traits as self-sufficiency and toughness. To those who did not care for them, though, the Scotch-Irish were simply quarrelsome, cantankerous people.

Many Scotch-Irish supported themselves and their families by weaving woolen cloth. Their product was good, and it was cheaper than English woolens, offering keen competition to English weavers. To protect the English weavers, Parliament in 1699 passed the Woolen Act, forbidding the export of cloth from Ulster to any foreign country. This severe blow was followed five years later by another—the Test Act for Ireland. Under this, no one who failed to follow the doctrine of the Anglican church doctrine would have the right to vote.

Droves of Scotch-Irish soon began arriving in America. Puritan New England did not appeal to them. Nor did the southern colonies, where they would have to compete with slave labor. Later many Scotch-Irish did, however, drift southward along the mountains into the backcountry of those colonies, beyond the fall line. Most came to the Middle Colonies at first, particularly to Pennsylvania. And finding the coastal region relatively crowded, and land prices high, the Scotch-Irish tended to move west, into the wilderness.

With respect to land, some ignored legal niceties. Choosing a spot, these people simply squatted. They built their cabins, cleared the land, and began to farm. Possession equaled ownership.

Like numerous other frontiersmen, many Scotch-Irish possessed none of the Quaker regard for the Indians' rights with respect to land or any other item. The Indians, like the forest and underbrush, were simply obstacles to settlement. They were to be cleared away. This did not make for good relations, and there were ever more frequent white-Indian clashes on the frontier.

The French were another factor. During the French-English wars, Indians friendly to the French were a constant menace. Even in peacetime the French were not above encouraging Indian attacks on English settlers, especially as the French expanded their fur trade into the Ohio Valley, where they met competition from English traders.

In eastern Pennsylvania, the Walking Purchase of 1737 became yet another ingredient damaging to Indian-white relations. Thomas Penn, a son of the late proprietor who came to the colony in 1732, figured in this. And so did James Logan.

The land in question lay in an area known as the Forks, in the upper part of Bucks County, north of Philadelphia. Here two branches of the Delaware River came together to form the larger stream. Settlers wished to move into the region, but they were hampered by Delaware Indians who claimed it as their own. Logan had an interest in an ironworks there, and he foresaw a need for more timber land to provide charcoal for his ovens. Furthermore, both he and Penn wanted the land open to settlement to gain income for the Penn family. Logan insisted that the land was part of that which the ancestors of the Delaware had given over to William Penn many years before. The Delaware denied this.

Logan as last produced a deed dated 1686. According to this document, the Indians had granted Penn a tract of land west of the river "back into the woods as far as a man can go in a day and a half." Although the deed may have been false, the Delaware accepted it. They contended, however, that it referred to land south of the Forks.

With Thomas Penn's cooperation, Logan hatched a plan. He sent men into the area to discover how much ground they could cover in a day and a half of hard traveling. What he found satisfied him. And in September, 1737, ignoring Delaware claims, he and Penn began the Walking Purchase as three stout young men set out for the west from the banks of the Delaware River north of Philadelphia. A path had been cleared, horses loaded with provisions, and boats provided to ferry the walkers across streams. And, as Indian observers quickly discovered, the three men did not linger. They moved at a rapid trot, somewhat faster than a walk. The Indians' bitter protest had no effect.

By the end of the day, one "walker" had collapsed from exhaustion. Another went down the following morning. The third continued until noon, halting twenty miles west of the Kittatinny Mountains, fifty-eight miles from the starting point. Logan, however, drew the line of purchase at the mountains, leaving the land beyond to the Indians. The purchase netted twelve hundred square miles, and the land was opened to settlement. Ten square miles were reserved as hunting grounds for the Delaware.

Nutimus, the Delaware chief, furiously defied the whites to move his people. This, Logan concluded, was easy enough. He had only to speak to the Iroquois.

The powerful Iroquois had long before established themselves as overlords to the Delaware and numerous other Pennsylvania tribes. The Iroquois were "uncles" to them. Since the Iroquois were allies of the English, this in itself contributed to keeping Pennsylvania Indians friendly to whites. When a delegation of Onondaga showed up to collect payment on some land along the Susquehanna River which they had sold to Pennsylvania authorities, Logan showed how powerful the Iroquois were.

He spent twenty pounds of his own money lavishly entertaining the Onondaga with food and drink. He and Thomas Penn assured the delegation of undying English friendship, and they in return made their own friendly declarations. Then, when Logan and Penn asked Canasetego, the Onondaga leader, for help with the Delaware situation, things turned out as they expected.

Canasetego concluded that by refusing to accept the terms of the 1686 deed, and by refusing to move, the Delaware endangered Iroquois relations with the English. Besides, when they supposedly had sold the land long ago, the Delaware had not cut the Iroquois in on the payment they received for it. Holding out a belt of wampum and turning to the Delaware attending the conference, Canasetego said:

> Let this belt of wampum serve to chastise you. You ought to be taken by the hair of the head and shaked severely, till you recover your senses and become sober. You don't know what ground you stand on, nor what you are doing. Our brother's cause is very just and plain, and his intentions to preserve friendship. On the other hand, your cause is bad; your heart far from being upright; and you are maliciously bent to break the chain of friendship with our brother and his people. We have seen with our eyes a deed signed by nine of your ancestors above fifty years ago for this very land, and a release signed, not many years since, by some of yourselves and chiefs now living, to the number of fifteen or upwards.
>
> But how came you to take upon you to sell land at all; we conquered you; we made women of you; you know you are women, and can no more sell land than women; nor is it fit you should have the power of selling lands, since you would abuse it. The land that you claim is gone through your guts; you have been furnished with clothes, meat, and drink, by the goods paid you for it, and now you want it again, like children as you are.
>
> But what makes you sell land in the dark? Did you ever tell us that you had sold this land? Did we ever receive any part, even the value of a pipe-shank, from you for it? . . .
>
> And for all these reasons we charge you to remove instantly; we don't give you the liberty to think about it. You are women. Take the advice of a wise man, and remove immediately. You may return to the other side of the Delaware where you came from. But we do

not know whether, considering how you have demeaned yourselves, you will be permitted to live there; or whether you have not swallowed that land down your throats as well as the land on this side. We therefore assign you two places to go, either to Wyoming [north along the Susquehanna] or Shamokin [to the northwest]. You may go to either of these places, and then we.shall have you more under our eye, and shall see how you behave. Don't deliberate; but remove away, and take this belt of Wampum.[7]

Although embittered, the Delaware had no choice but to comply. When an Iroquois ordered, one obeyed. Logan and Penn awarded the Onondaga with three hundred pounds' worth of additional goods.

The Walking Purchase was among James Logan's last public acts in Pennsylvania. He gave increasing attention to his ironworks and to the book collection housed on his estate, Stenton, along Wingohucking Creek, which flowed into the Delaware. He had received a sound education, and through his library he hoped to pass one on to his sons, William and James. The collection included volumes of such ancient Greek and Roman writers as Homer, Aeschylus, Sophocles, Horace, and Virgil. It also held such more recent books as Sir Isaac Newton's *Principia Mathematica.*

In February, 1740, a stroke felled Logan, who was already partially crippled. He lived on, unable to walk or to speak, until 1751. He died near the end of October, leaving his heirs his estate and a total of 18,000 acres of land, his library, and £8,500 in cash and bonds.

The Defense Problem

In matters of defense, James Logan opposed the majority of his Quaker faith. Yet he had no influence on the Quaker majority in the assembly, and even in wartime the defense

---

[7]Quoted in John Fanning Watson, *Annals of Philadelphia, and Pennsylvania in the Olden Time: Being a Collection of Memoirs, Anecdotes, and Incidents ...* (Philadelphia: E.S. Stuart, 1898), vol. 2, p. 171.

A Quaker meeting in Philadelphia. Twice a week, Friends would meet for public worship and would sit together in quiet contemplation until one of them was moved to share his or her spiritual experience with the others.

question was complicated by Quaker pacifism. As a matter of conscience, most Quakers opposed appropriating money for arms, fortifications, or troops.

Queen Anne's War—known in Europe as the War of the Spanish Succession—began in 1702 and lasted until 1713. England and France were on opposite sides, and the English government asked for colonial help against the French in Canada. The Pennsylvania assembly refused to act.

That an assembly would not act on behalf of intercolonial defense was not uncommon. Each colony was an authority unto itself, and each jealously guarded its independence. Frequently a colony did not see its own best interests in terms of another's. A European visitor to the colonies in the mid-eighteenth century had this to say:

> From [each colony's independence] it happens, that in time of war, things go on very slowly and irregularly here: for not only the sense of one province is

sometimes directly opposite to that of another, but frequently the views of the governor, and those of the assembly, of the same province, are quite different: so that it is easy to see that while the people are quarrelling about the best and the cheapest manner of carrying on the war, an enemy has it in his power to take one place after another. It has commonly happened that while some provinces have been suffering from their enemies, the neighboring ones were quiet and inactive, and as if it did not in the least concern them. They have frequently taken up to two or three years in considering whether they should give assistance to an oppressed sister colony, and sometimes they have expressly declared themselves against it. There are instances of provinces who were not only neutral in these circumstances, but who even carried on a great trade with the power which at that very time was attacking and laying waste to other provinces.[8]

So the Pennsylvania assembly's attitude was not unique, although that colony's situation, where Quakers opposed even internal defense measures, certainly was.

Early in Queen Anne's War, the young and impulsive governor, John Evans, who had arrived in 1704, concluded that the assembly might be scared into action. In the spring of 1706, he faked a letter from the governor of Maryland which said that a French fleet had been sighted off the coast. The threat of invasion drove Philadelphians to panic, although it had no effect on Quakers. In their weekly meeting on the day the letter was made public, they paid no attention to the din and clatter. James Logan exposed the letter as a hoax, and the incident did nothing to make the assembly more willing to meet requests for help against the French.

[8] Peter Kalm, "Travels into North America," in John Pinkerton, ed., *A General Collection of the Best and Most Interesting Voyages and Travels in All Parts of the World* (London: Longman, Hurst, Rees, Orme, and Brown, 1812), vol. 13, pp. 460–61.

In the Lower Counties—Delaware—the residents of such riverside settlements as New Castle were especially open to attack from the sea. Non-Quakers controlled the assembly in the Lower Counties, and they decided to take matters into their own hands. The assembly voted to build a fort at New Castle and found an unusual way to pay for it. To provide for construction and maintenance costs, the law imposed a fee on ships using the Delaware River. This could hardly have pleased Philadelphia merchants, whose goods reached them by way of the Delaware.

Governor Evans had been in New Castle when the assembly discussed the bill, and he had done nothing to prevent its passage. So James Logan went into action. After hearing him, the Delaware assembly voted to exempt Philadelphia's ships from the law. It required only that such vessels stop at New Castle so that their captains could prove that they were owned by Philadelphians.

The fort was built. And in the spring of 1707, Richard Hill guided his new sloop, named after the city, out of port and down the Delaware. He was bound for the island of Barbados in the West Indies with a cargo of lumber. Hill declared that he would not, under any circumstances, heave to at the fort. Nor did he. On the spot, Governor Evans ordered the ship fired upon. Two cannons were touched off. Both balls missed, and Evans pursued *Philadelphia* in a small boat as Hill made for Salem on the Jersey side. There Lord Cornbury, governor of New York and New Jersey, was in residence. Cornbury prevented Hill's arrest and scolded Evans for trying to arrest a person in New Jersey.

A comic incident indeed, but it demonstrated the conflict between Quakers and non-Quakers over the defense issue. And as it turned out, Quakers proved willing to bend a little on the matter.

The English government later requested that Pennsylvania furnish one hundred and fifty men to join an expedition to invade Canada. Governor Charles Gookin, who followed Evans, thought the assembly might appropriate money to pay and supply the men if he promised to raise the force without violating the Quaker conscience. Here is what happened, according to a communication from the governor to English authorities:

The Queen having pressed me with her command that this province should furnish 150 men for its expedition against Canada, I called an assembly and demanded £400. They being all Quakers after much delay resolved that it was contrary to their religious principles to hire men to kill one another. I told some of them [that] the Queen did not hire men to kill one another but to destroy her enemies. One of them answered [that] the assembly understood English. After I had tried all ways to bring them to reason they again resolved that they could not directly or indirectly raise money for an expedition to Canada but they voted the Queen £500 as a token of their respect &c. and that the money should be put into safe hands till they were satisfied from England it should not be employed for the use of war.[9]

The next assembly went a little further. It decided that it would not "be inconsistent with our principles to give the Queen money notwithstanding any use she might put it to, *that* not being our part [our business] but her's." The assembly message said, in part:

That the majority of the people of this province being of the people called Quakers religiously persuaded against war and therefore cannot be active therein; yet are as fully persuaded and believe it to be their bounden duty to pay tribute, and yield due obedience to the powers God has set over them in all things, as far as their religious persuasions can admit; and therefore we take this occasion to express our duty loyalty and faithful obedience to our rightful and gracious Queen Anne and accordingly have voted the sum of £2,000 to be raised by the inhabitants of this province for the Queen's use which we hope will be taken in good part and accepted as a token of our duty.[10]

[9]Quoted in Sharpless, *Two Centuries of Pennsylvania History,* vol. 2, pp. 105–6.
[10]Quoted in ibid., p. 106.

A Changing Tide

In 1739, the War of Jenkins' Ear broke out between England and Spain over an incident in the West Indies. The assembly refused Governor George Thomas's request for money to raise troops. So he put together a company on his own, made up largely of indentured servants—persons having agreed to serve a four- to seven-year term of labor for an employer who paid their fare to America. This displeased both the assembly and those who depended on indentures. In 1740 the assembly voted £2,500 to compensate the employers.

The War of Jenkins' Ear lasted but a short time, and then in 1744 King George's War began between England and France. And again the age-old defense controversy arose. This time the non-Quakers had a new and most forceful champion—Benjamin Franklin, who had arrived in the colony in 1723 and who would become, in the words of those who knew him, "the greatest American of them all."

Benjamin Franklin was born in Boston in 1706, the fifteenth child and youngest boy in a family of seventeen children. He received only two years of formal schooling. Later he taught himself foreign languages, mathematics, sciences, grammar and logic, and how to write lean, clear prose. At the age of twelve Franklin became an apprentice to his brother James, a printer, who published the *New England Courant* in Boston. He soon mastered the craft.

Impatient under his brother's control, Franklin broke his apprenticeship when he was seventeen and left for New York. Finding no printer's jobs available there, he continued on to Philadelphia. He arrived after a stormy thirty-hour voyage, hungry, tired, and low on money. Purchasing a bun, he munched it as he made his way from the waterfront into the main part of town.

An excellent printer despite his extreme youth, Franklin easily found work in Philadelphia. Then in 1730, when he was twenty-four, he opened his own shop and began publishing the *Pennsylvania Gazette,* which he continued to publish until 1748. Also in 1730, he took as a common-law wife Deborah Reed, in whose father's house he had found lodging when he first arrived in the city. A devoted couple, they produced four children. One of them, William, later became governor of New Jersey.

"It is now forty years (1785) since I worked, like you, at this press, a journeyman printer."

BENJAMIN FRANKLIN.

Benjamin Franklin's life as a printer and publisher is traced in this nineteenth-century engraving.

A page from *Poor Richard's Almanac*, which Franklin published under the name Richard Saunders. Included among the weather predictions, times of the tides, medical remedies, and other useful information were such Franklinisms as "Three may keep a secret if two of them are dead" and "Some are weather-wise, some are otherwise."

In 1732 Franklin for the first time issued his annual and famous *Poor Richard's Almanac.* This was outstanding among almanacs of its time and is best remembered today for the proverbs Franklin placed in the mouth of the fictional Richard Saunders. He gathered such sayings as "An empty Bag cannot stand upright" and "The sleeping Fox catches no Poultry. Up! Up!" from various sources. They delighted *Poor Richard's* many readers.

Three years after beginning his almanac, Franklin was made clerk of the Pennsylvania assembly. In 1737 he became Philadelphia's postmaster, later becoming deputy postmaster general for all the colonies. His civic contributions were remarkable. Franklin established a public library, organized Philadelphia's first fire department, and persuaded the city council to undertake a program of street lighting and paving. He also helped establish a city hospital for the insane, the academy which became the University of Pennsylvania, and the American Philosophical Society. His scientific interests were boundless. Franklin experimented with electricity, invented an efficient stove and bifocal eye glasses, studied Gulf Stream currents, and conducted experiments with plants. The Royal Society of London elected him to membership, a signal honor for anyone, let alone a colonial.

In his *Gazette,* Franklin spoke frequently and strongly in favor of defense measures against the French and their Indian allies. He warned that the economic interests in America made further French-English clashes inevitable. In 1745, during King George's War, some other colonies supported an expedition against Louisbourg, a fortress near the mouth of the Saint Lawrence River. Pennsylvania did not, and in the *Gazette* Franklin criticized both Governor Thomas and the assembly. He asked Quakers what better reason they might need for legal warfare than "the Defense of Country, and the Protection of the Helpless and Innocent." In 1747 Franklin published *Plain Truth,* an essay on the danger of a French invasion following French naval raids along the Pennsylvania coast. "Prepare, and thus avoid bloodshed," he wrote, "for 'tis a wise and true saying, that *One Sword often keeps another in the Scabbard.*"

Using his imagination, Franklin found a way around the assembly's lack of action. He produced a plan for an association of military volunteers, and within a few days five hundred citizens had joined up. Eventually the ranks swelled to one thousand. Franklin also published a manual of arms, and he suggested ideas for fortifying Philadelphia. The city council—though not the assembly—supported Franklin's efforts. In February, 1748, the council made him an honorary member.

King George's War ended in 1748. Pennsylvania had escaped practically unscathed. But thanks in part to Franklin's efforts, the anti-defense policy was beginning to change. The final war for empire between England and France was not far off. That war would commence in Pennsylvania and it would spell the beginning of the end of Quaker rule.

Buildup to Final Conflict

Intermittent warfare between European powers marked much of the eighteenth century. Mainly, the nations struggled over the domination of Europe. But with respect to England and France in particular, the conflict also spilled overseas. And although such powers as Austria, Prussia, Spain, and Russia occasionally shifted alliances, England and France were always on opposite sides. Abroad, their scenes of contention were North America, the West Indies, and later India.

French possessions in North America ran along the Saint Lawrence Valley, the Great Lakes, and the Mississippi Valley to New Orleans. English fur traders controlled the Hudson's Bay region. South of the Saint Lawrence, thirteen English colonies were firmly entrenched. The final point of conflict lay in the Ohio Valley, a land rich in fertile soil and furs. Which nation would control that area?

Both sides made moves to secure the Ohio Valley at about the same time. A group of speculators, mostly Virginians, formed the Ohio Company in 1749. They received a grant of half a million acres of land in the Ohio country. The fur trade there was profitable, but the company also looked forward to opening the area to settlement. In their turn, the French erected forts in their attempt to control the Ohio region.

Young George Washington practices the surveyor's skill in this drawing. Washington gained much experience as a surveyor while establishing the boundaries of the estate of his employer, William Fairfax, for whom he worked at the age of twenty-one.

Governor Robert Dinwiddie.

With much at stake, in 1753 Virginia's Governor Robert Dinwiddie decided to warn the French out. Besides his concern for the Ohio Company, Dinwiddie had two other reasons for action. Virginia claimed land in western Pennsylvania. Furthermore, the Pennsylvania assembly was doing nothing about western defense. Governor Dinwiddie chose as his messenger to the French one George Washington, a rising young member of a planting family, then twenty-one years old.

Washington had learned surveying at age fifteen. And he had become acquainted with the frontier on surveying trips, particularly on behalf of Lord Fairfax who, with five million acres, was the largest land owner in Virginia. In February, 1753, Washington became a major in the Virginia militia and in November of that year he set off with six others on his mission to the French.

The party reached Fort Le Boeuf, just south of Lake Erie, about a month later. Not surprisingly, the French commander there rejected Dinwiddie's demand that the French

In this painting, George Washington is selecting the site of Fort Pitt at the strategic junction of the Ohio, Allegheny, and Monongahela rivers.

depart the area. And he made it clear that they were in the Ohio country to stay. After much hardship, Washington and his men arrived back in Williamsburg, Virginia's capital, in the middle of January, 1754. Reporting to Dinwiddie, Washington recommended that the governor have a fort built at the spot where the Allegheny and Monongahela rivers flow together to form the Ohio.

In the meantime, anticipating renewed warfare with France, the English Board of Trade in 1753 called for a colonial convention, to meet at Albany the following year. The delegates were to discuss defense. Addressing themselves particularly to relations with the Iroquois, they were to try to remove any chance that those tribes might go over to the French. The Mohawk especially had become unhappy about white encroachments on their land, contrary to treaties and agreements.

New York, New Hampshire, Massachusetts, Connecticut, Pennsylvania, Maryland, and Rhode Island sent delegates to the Albany Congress in 1754. Benjamin Franklin was the outstanding member there. He proposed a plan of union and an overall colonial council that would have the power to raise money and look after defense and Indian matters.

Colonial governments, however, proved cool to the idea. They could see no necessity for cooperation and clung

JOIN, or DIE.

Ben Franklin's famous "Join or Die" cartoon underlined his plea for colonial unity. Tories, on seeing the cartoon, chanted: "Ye sons of sedition, how comes it to pass that America's typed by a snake—in the grass?"

General Edward Braddock. Before his assignment to America, Braddock had been a parade-ground soldier who had seen no real combat in forty-five years.

jealously to their individual rights and powers. Nothing came of Franklin's plan. Only a few Iroquois, mostly Mohawk, attended the Albany meeting. They made no alliance with the colonies, but they did depart the town richer by thirty wagonloads of trade goods.

Benjamin Franklin returned to Philadelphia to publish his famous segmented-snake cartoon, each piece representing a colony, with the caption, "Join or Die." Franklin's plan of union was ahead of its time.

Back in Virginia, Dinwiddie followed Washington's advice. He had the fort built, and in April, 1754, Washington set out with 160 men to garrison it. On the way he learned that the French had captured the fort and named it Duquesne. Washington was determined to retake it.

About sixty miles south of Fort Duquesne, Washington's men constructed Fort Necessity. Additional militia were sent to reinforce the garrison there. Washington and his troops were not to hold Necessity long.

The French and their Indian allies attacked in July, 1754. A third of Washington's force of four hundred men were sick, and food supplies were low. A violent rainstorm during the battle dampened the fort's gunpowder. The garrison suffered about a hundred casualties, with thirty killed. By midnight on the day of battle, Washington realized that the situation was hopeless. He surrendered, and the French allowed him to march his men back to Virginia.

French forces at Duquesne were not allowed to rest, however. In 1754 Major General Edward Braddock became commander of English forces in America, and the following year he landed with 1,200 troops at Alexandria, Virginia. Braddock made the reclaiming of Fort Duquesne his first order of business. He assembled his army at Fort Cumberland, in Maryland, about ninety miles from the French stronghold.

With his force strung out for a mile, dragging artillery, Braddock's progress toward Duquesne was slow. His men made scarcely three miles a day. Washington finally persuaded the general to ditch his artillery, and the column now moved at a faster pace, although Indians still picked off stragglers here and there. Then the expedition bogged down for lack of supplies and Benjamin Franklin had to hurry out from Philadelphia to round up food, horses, and wagons.

State Historical Society of Wisconsin

Braddock's defeat is recreated in this painting by E. W. Deming. Of 1,459 British troops, 977 were casualties. Braddock was killed, and his aide-de-camp, George Washington, had two horses shot from under him.

Washington-Custis Lee Collection, Washington and Lee University

A force made up mostly of Indians had been sent out from Fort Duquesne. At a ford of the Monongahela River, about seven miles south of the fort, it met the English-colonial army. The red-coated troops moved forward to the attack, but the Indians refused to meet them head on. The red coats made bright targets as the Indians, firing from behind trees, logs, and rocks, decimated the opposing ranks while the English fired blindly at unseen targets. Braddock himself received a death wound, and Washington had two horses shot out from under him. The regulars were soon fleeing in retreat, and it fell to Washington to organize the withdrawal. Fort Duquesne remained in French hands as the French and Indian War—known in Europe as the Seven Years' War— began in earnest.

George Washington at the time of the French and Indian War.

The End of Quaker Power

Settlers on the frontier from Pennsylvania to North Carolina bore the most immediate effect of Braddock's defeat. Impressed with their own success and that of the French in fighting the English, Indians scrambled to the warpath.

An additional factor was the Ohio Indians, who had become dependent on the French for guns and other goods. They felt that they had little choice but to join the French against the English. Some two dozen German settlers at Penn's Creek were killed, and another forty-seven were killed or captured at Great and Little Coves. This was only the beginning. Between Braddock's defeat in July, 1755, and March, 1756, more than seven hundred whites were killed or taken captive along the Pennsylvania, Virginia, and Carolina frontiers.

Frontier warfare was far from romantic. Indians killed and scalped, they burned, they pillaged, and they sometimes tortured. Whites also committed their share of atrocities.

The need for defense measures in Pennsylvania was obvious, but this troubled Quakers in the assembly. There, in 1756, they held a majority of twenty-six out of thirty-six seats. Quaker footdragging on military matters had long irked non-Quakers. Now that frontier settlements were burning, the situation appeared desperate. Non-Quakers were anxious that something be done.

The assembly finally voted £55,000 for defense, to be raised by a property tax. Most of the money was to be used to build a line of forts along the Kittatinny Mountains to the Maryland border. Quakers in the assembly managed to live with this, although they would have preferred to spend the money trying to reconcile the Indians instead of warring on them. Merchants, many of them Quakers, supported peace measures because war was harmful to profits in the Indian trade.

A related issue had to do with taxing proprietary lands as part of the general property levy for defense. The Penns opposed this as part of their proprietary rights. Anti-proprietary Quakers in the assembly favored taxing Penn lands as well as any other. The bill passed without taxing the Penns, but Thomas Penn made a personal gift of £5,000 toward defense.

The governor and the council laid the final straw on the camel's back in the spring of 1756 when they declared Pennsylvania at war with the Shawnee and the Delaware Indians. A bounty was to be offered for both female and male Indian scalps. To be part of a government openly at war was too much for many Quakers. Six resigned from the assembly immediately. Several refused to stand for re-election in the fall of 1756, and four others resigned after the balloting. Only twelve Quakers now remained in the assembly. And this marked the end of the strong Quaker influence in the Pennsylvania government.

Forming a "Friendly Association," Quakers did, however, serve as go-betweens for Pennsylvania authorities and the Indians in an attempt to make peace with the Shawnee and the Delaware. The Association sent Christian Frederick Post, a member of the Moravian church, to parley with Ohio Indians almost under the shadow of Fort Duquesne. Post's mission was successful. The Pennsylvania frontier gradually quieted down.

The Course of Conflict

Most of the fighting in the colonies during the French and Indian War took place in New York. In Pennsylvania there continued to be scattered Indian raids off and on. And at first, English-colonial forces met with little success.

In the spring of 1756, the French destroyed Fort Bull on the Mohawk River and the garrison at Oswego on Lake Ontario. Early the next year the French, led by the outstanding general Louis Montcalm, took Fort William Henry on Lake George, from which Indians pursued the English in retreat to Fort Edward. The French destroyed Fort William Henry. French and Indian raids along the Mohawk River caused great loss of life and property damage. By the end of 1756, most New York frontier settlements lay deserted. Then came disaster at Fort Ticonderoga on Lake George.

The English general, James Abercromby, pitted 15,000 English and colonial troops against 3,500 French and Indians defending Ticonderoga. Montcalm outgeneraled Abercromby, who threw wave after wave of men against the fort only to see them mercilessly cut down. The attacking force suffered 1,600 casualties before Abercromby finally broke off.

Under a new English government led by William Pitt, who was determined to pursue the war in America with the fullest of English resources, the tide turned in 1759. In July of that year English-colonial forces took Fort Niagara on Lake

William Pitt, popularly known as "The Great Commoner," was admired so much by the common people of England that on occasion they kissed his horses. Pitt, as head of the British government, was instrumental in planning and executing the successful campaign against the French in Canada, an achievement which won him another title, "Organizer of Victory."

Ontario. Fort Duquesne fell that summer too, as the French abandoned it. It was renamed Fort Pitt. General Jeffrey Amherst led troops to retake Ticonderoga. The French evacuated Crown Point and scuttled their fleet on Lake Champlain. Then, in a daring night move, General James Wolfe sent a detachment to scale the cliffs that guarded Quebec, on the Saint Lawrence. There, in the climactic battle of the war, the English defeated Montcalm and the French on the Plains of Abraham. Both commanders died from wounds. The following year Amherst took Montreal. Soon thereafter the French sued for peace, and a treaty was signed in 1763.

The Treaty of Paris made the British empire the greatest in the world. Save for a few West Indian islands, and two tiny ones at the mouth of the Saint Lawrence, the French lost all their American possessions. They lost nearly all they had gained in India, too.

More Indian War

The Americans' center of attention now shifted to the West, to the country on the other side of the mountains.

The French presence in the Ohio and Mississippi valleys had been removed. The entire West lay open to settlement, and already there had been pioneers across the Allegheny Mountains. Yet Indians remained, and they had grievances—the Walking Purchase of 1737 was only one example of questionable white dealing. Some Indians realized that, if they were to survive, the white advance must be stopped at the mountains and, if possible, pushed back. One of these Indians was Pontiac.

An Ottawa Indian, Pontiac lived in northern Ohio. He was a gifted orator and organizer. In 1762 he held a great council of Indian tribes. He urged them to have no more to do with whites, to return to their traditional ways, and to prepare for war and white extermination. He sent messengers bearing blood-stained tomahawks and wampum war belts throughout the Ohio and Mississippi valleys, and he gained many recruits. In June, 1763, Pontiac's followers struck.

Pontiac, chief of the Ottawas.

Ohio Historical Society

One after another, Indian forces took Fort Venango, Fort Le Boeuf, and Fort Presque Isle, all in western Pennsylvania. They lay siege to Fort Pitt and to Detroit. The

General Wolfe lies mortally wounded in this painting by Benjamin West.

whole Pennsylvania frontier was aflame again. Settlers fled eastward for safety. It was estimated that during the summer of 1763 Indians killed or carried off some two thousand persons. Several thousand, it was reported, were driven from their homes.

A five-hundred-man force under Colonel Henry Bouquet marched to relieve Fort Pitt. Twenty-six miles from the fort, Indians attacked the detachment. After two days of heavy fighting the Indians withdrew, which marked the engagement a white victory, and the siege of Fort Pitt ended. Following a few additional skirmishes, the so-called Pontiac conspiracy petered out, but it left much bitterness behind, especially in Pennsylvania.

A group of some twenty Conestoga Indians—six men, the remainder women and children—lived in Lancaster County. Far removed from their old way of life, they eked out a living making and peddling brooms and baskets. Although apparently innocent of any hostile activity, one had been accused of murder and the group was suspected of harboring hostiles. The tiny band of Conestoga would pay dearly for the western uprising.

On December 14, 1763, more than fifty settlers, most of them from the community of Paxton, rode on the Conestoga settlement. They found six Indians there, and killed them. And so began what was known as the Paxton Rebellion, a short-lived but—for the Conestoga—bloody affair.

The Paxton Boys, as they were called, resented Indians and the frontier's lack of protection. They also resented the fact that the frontier was underrepresented in the Pennsylvania assembly. This was one reason, they believed, why frontier defense had been so long neglected. But the killings horrified most Pennsylvanians, and warrants were issued for the arrest of the Paxton Boys.

For safety, authorities placed the remaining Conestoga in a workhouse—really a jail—in Lancaster. John Hay, the sheriff of Lancaster County, wrote a letter to Governor John Penn telling what happened next:

> Since writing the above, the poor Indians whom we imagined were placed in safety are destroyed. A number of Persons to the amount (by their appearance), of fifty or Sixty, armed with Rifles, Tomahawks, &c, suddenly, about Two o'clock, rushed into the Town & immediately repaired to the Work House where the Indians were confined, & notwithstanding all opposition of myself and the Coroner, with many others, broke open the Work House, and have killed all the Indians there, being the fourteen mentioned in the List to have survived the former Affair at their Town. After which they in a Body left the Town without offering any insults to the Inhabitants, and without putting it in the power of any one to take or molest any of them without Danger of Life to the Person attempting it; of which both myself and the Coroner by our opposition were in great danger.[11]

The Paxton Boys kept Pennsylvania in an uproar for several weeks, although no more Indians were killed. At

[11] Quoted in John R. Dunbar, ed., *The Paxton Papers* (The Hague: Martinus Nijhoof, 1957), p. 28.

The attack of the Paxton Boys upon the Conestoga Indians depicted in a contemporary drawing by an unidentified Quaker artist.

last, in February, 1764, the group presented a petition to Governor Penn listing numerous grievances, one of which was the removal of bounties on Indian scalps. The Pennsylvania government agreed to only one demand—it restored the bounty. There the Paxton matter rested.

SUGGESTED READINGS

Bonomi, Patricia. *Fractious People: Politics and Society in Colonial New York*. Columbia University Press.

Franklin, Benjamin. *Autobiography and Other Writings*. Edited by Russel B. Nye. Houghton Mifflin, Riverside Editions.

Franklin, Benjamin. *Poor Richard's Almanac*. David McKay.

Frost, William J. *The Quaker Family in Colonial America*. St. Martin's Press.

Latham, Frank B. *The Trial of John Peter Zenger, August 1735: An Early Fight for America's Freedom of the Press*. Franklin Watts, Focus Books.

Parkman, Francis. *Montcalm and Wolfe*. Macmillan, Collier Books.

Peckham, Howard H. *Colonial Wars, 1689–1762*. University of Chicago Press.

Pomfret, John E. *Colonial New Jersey: A History*. Charles Scribner's Sons.

Seamen, merchants, and others carrying out their business on the riverfront of New York in 1680.

3

PEOPLE, CLASSES,

AND INSTITUTIONS

Aside from Quakers, no group made a deeper impression on Pennsylvania than the Pennsylvania Dutch. These people were not Hollanders. They were Germans, with some German-speaking Swiss mixed in. Their name in America derived from "Deitsch" or "Deutsch," words meaning "German" which they used in referring to themselves. At the height of the colonial period they made up fully one-third of Pennsylvania's population.

Church and Plain People

Some Pennsylvania Dutch were Quakers. The others fell into three broad groups, divided along religious lines. There were the "plain people," the "church people," and, in between those two groups, the Moravians. The Quakers, of course, could be considered plain people too, but usually the term was used in reference to the Mennonites, the Amish, the Brethren (or "Dunkards"), and the Schwenkfelders. They were "plain" because they lived, worshipped, and dressed with little or no ornament. Amish men, for example, wore severe dark clothing and broad-brimmed hats, and they shaved only the upper lip. Amish women, though, were not averse to some colorful clothing, and the men liked to display colored shirts.

The Mennonites traced their beginning to Menno Simons, a German Protestant reformer who lived between 1496 and 1561. Like the Quakers, Mennonites opposed oaths in court and military service. The Amish were an offshoot of the Mennonites. Jacob Amman, a Swiss, founded the sect in the late seventeenth century. The Brethren were a German Baptist group. The nickname "Dunkard" came from the Pennsylvania Dutch word "dunk," referring to the Brethren's ceremony of baptism which involved total immersion in a stream. The Brethren dunked candidates for baptism not once but three times, and the only difference between a winter and a summer ceremony was that in the winter they had to break the ice several times. The Brethren too were pacifists and opposed to oath-taking. The Schwenkfelders were a small group, first organized by Kaspar Schwenkfeld von Ossig, a German nobleman and Protestant mystic who was born in 1489. Schwenkfelders, like Quakers, believed not only in the words of the Bible but also in revelation through the "inner light." The second main group of Pennsylvania Dutch, the "church people," were made up of Lutherans, German Reformed, United Brethren, and Evangelicals. The third group, the Moravians, were named after the province of Moravia, now part of Czechoslovakia. They traced their religious origins to John Hus, a Protestant reformer born probably in 1369, who was accused of heresy and burned at the stake by Catholic authorities in 1415.

Religious persecution drove most of the Swiss and the Moravians to America. Intermittent warfare in Germany, and particularly in the Palatinate region, was responsible for the migration of many of the Germans. Late in the seventeenth century, a group of Germans learned of William Penn's colony in the New World—a colony which accepted all comers. The group selected Francis Daniel Pastorius as their agent and sent him on ahead. Pastorius arrived in Philadelphia on August 20, 1683. He chose a site for settlement which became Germantown. And, after thirteen families arrived aboard the ship *Concord* on October 6 of that year, clearing and building commenced.

Germantown prospered from the start, a reflection of the settlers' willingness to work. A year after settlement began, William Streypers could write: "I have been busy and made a brave dwelling-house, and under it a cellar fit to live in; and I have so much grain, such as Indian corn and buck-

John Hus.

Library of Congress

wheat, that this winter I shall be better off than I was last year."[1] Another Germantown settler, Cornelius Bom, wrote in 1684:

> I have here a shop of many kinds of goods and edibles. Sometimes I ride out with merchandise, and sometimes bring something back, mostly from the Indians, and deal with them in many ways ... I have no rent or tax or excise to pay. I have a cow which gives plenty of milk, a horse to ride around; my pigs increase rapidly, so that in the summer I had seventeen, where at first I had only two. I have many chickens and geese, and a garden, and shall next year have an orchard, if I remain well, so that my wife and I are in good spirits.[2]

It has been estimated that by 1727 around twenty thousand Pennsylvania Dutch occupied land in the colony. Some of them had been among the Palatines from Germany who had first settled in New York during Queen Anne's War, 1702–1713. Making their way overland from New York to the Susquehanna River, a number of families had then floated downstream on rafts to establish the community of Tulpehocken. Records indicate that between 1727 and 1775 a total of 68,872 Germans and Swiss, mostly the former, arrived in Pennsylvania. There may have been even more. What with the natural increase in the colony, the number of Pennsylvania Dutch on the eve of the War for Independence was probably over a hundred thousand. Settlements flourished in Montgomery, Lancaster, Berks, York, Cumberland, and other counties.

Most of the newcomers were poor. But, like those who settled Germantown, they were industrious. Most plunged into forested land, cleared trees (taking care to grub out the stumps immediately, unlike some other settlers), and

---

[1] Quoted in Oscar Kuhns, *The German and Swiss Settlements of Colonial Pennsylvania: A Study of the So-Called Pennsylvania Dutch* (New York: Henry Holt, 1901), p. 41.

[2] Quoted in ibid., pp. 41–42.

established farms. Given their enthusiasm for hard labor and their frugality, and given Pennsylvania's fertile soil, they did not remain poor for long. One Andrew Ferree of Lancaster County may not have been typical, but he serves as an example of what could be done. Ferree died in 1735, leaving an estate, aside from land and buildings, valued at one hundred fifty-six pounds, eight shillings, and sixpence. It included farm produce and implements, carpenter's tools, four working horses, a mare and two colts, six cows and ten head of yearlings, and eleven sheep. In the context of his time, Ferree had been well-to-do.

Thomas Pownall, an English official who later served as governor of Massachusetts, visited Lancaster in 1754. He found it "a pretty considerable town, encreasing fast and growing rich." He continued:

> I saw some of the finest farms one can conceive, and
> in the highest state of culture, particularly one
> that was the estate of a Switzer [Swiss]. Here it was
> I first saw the method of watering a whole range of
> pastures and meadows on a hillside, by little troughs
> cut in the side of the hill, along which the water
> from springs was conducted, so as that when the
> outlets of these troughs were stopped at the end the
> water ran over the sides and watered all the ground
> between that and the other trough next below it.[3]

Equipment and Methods

The tools and equipment used by the Pennsylvania Dutch farmers, like those employed by other colonial farmers, were primitive and inefficient. Many farmers, especially in early colonial days, made their own. A typical inventory of farming implements was that listed as essential by Thomas Budd in 1695:

> A Share [plow] and Coulter [cutter for the plow], a
> Plow chain, 2 Schythes, 4 Sickles, a Horse Collar,
> some Cordage [rope] for Harness, 2 Stock Locks, 2
> weeding Hoes, 2 grubbing Hoes [for digging out

[3]Quoted in ibid., p. 90.

roots and stumps], 1 cross-cut Saw, 2 Iron Axes,
1 broad Axe, 1 Spade, 1 Hatchet, 1 Fro [chisel] to
cleave Clapboards, Shingle and Cooper's Timber.[4]

Plowing the soil.

Until the mid-eighteenth century, iron was scarce and
expensive. Even plows were made almost entirely of wood,
and they were heavy and clumsy. The colonial plow
consisted of a wooden shaft, one or more wooden coulters to
cut the soil, and a wooden moldboard to turn the soil over.
Usually the only metal on it was a thin sheet of tin or
iron attached to the cutting edge. The coulter was perhaps
three or more feet long, but it was shallow and a farmer
could cut only a few inches deep into the soil. Some farmers
mounted their plows on wheels, which reduced friction and
made it easier for horses or oxen to pull them. But even with
wheeled equipment, plowing was heavy, back-breaking
work that no one looked forward to in spring and fall. Not
infrequently, two or three men had to work together to
perform the task.

Sowing the seed.

After plowing, farmers used the broadcast method of
sowing grain. Walking slowly up and down a field, they
scattered seeds by the handful. To cover the seeds, they
often used a harrow. This implement was constructed by
joining two or three eight-to-ten-foot logs together with
crosspieces; rows of large wooden pegs or nails were then
attached to the underside of the logs, the points projecting
downward. Oxen or horses dragged the harrow up and down
the field, spreading the loose soil over the seeds. As the
crops grew, most weeding was accomplished with a hoe.

Harrowing.

Reaping.

Farmers harvested such grains as wheat with sickles or
scythes, tools dating back to ancient times. With these a
man could reap only about an acre a day, and consequently
harvesting was a cooperative project. Gangs of up to fifty
or seventy-five men moved from farm to farm at harvest
time. According to one account of harvesting in Fayette
County, Pennsylvania,

Binding the grain
into sheaves.

[4]Quoted in Stevenson Whitcomb Fletcher, *Pennsylvania Agriculture
and Country Life, 1640–1840* (Harrisburg: Pennsylvania Historical and
Museum Commission, 1950), p. 90.

Flailing the sheaves.

Flailing the stalks.

Taking the wheat to the mill.

It was a beautiful sight to look upon a gang of twenty or more reapers. . . . The best reaper was selected as a leader and the rest had to follow not far behind. At the end of a "through," which extended across the field, one half of the reapers took up all the sickles and carried them back half way to the starting point where, on the arrival of the other half, the sickles were taken up; thus the cut grain was bound into sheaves by the time the gang reached the beginning. The two reapers on each hand always put their grain in one grit [pile] to facilitate binding. Generally before another round was made cold water from an adjoining spring and whiskey from the green glass bottle were handed around and each partook freely to brace up the physical nature.[5]

As a field was cleared, wagons pulled by horses or oxen hauled the sheaves to the threshing floor, usually in the barn. Flailing was the most common method of threshing, or separating the kernels of grain from the chaff (the husks that cover the kernels). The flail consisted of a flat piece of wood which was attached to a round handle by a strip of rawhide so that it swung freely. The thresher first flailed the grain while it was still bound, striking the sheaves over and over again. Then he untied the sheaves and flailed the stalks. Finally, the whole mass was winnowed, or thrown repeatedly into the air. The loosened chaff blew away, while the heavier kernels fell back to the floor where they were gathered for storage. Most of the kernels would later be ground into flour, but a portion would be saved as seeds for the next season's planting.

Those Towering Barns

Most Pennsylvania Dutch farm houses were snug and firm, many being built of stone. But the farmers gave even greater attention to their barns, placing themselves second after their livestock and produce. As Dr. Benjamin Rush observed, "They always provide large and suitable accommodations for their cattle before they lay out much money

[5] Quoted in ibid., p. 120.

in building a house for themselves." Rush cited one good reason for this: "They keep their horses and cattle as warm as possible in winter, by which means they save a great deal of their hay and grain; for these animals when cold eat much more than when they are in a more comfortable situation."[6] Huge barns came to dominate the eastern Pennsylvania countryside. According to another source:

> They are two stories high, with pitched roof,
> sufficiently large and strong to enable heavy farm-
> teams to drive into the upper story, to load or unload
> grain. During the first period they were built mostly
> of logs, afterwards of stone, frame, or brick, from
> 60 to 120 feet long, and from 50 to 60 feet wide, the
> lower story, containing the stables, with feeding-
> passages opening on the front. The upper story was
> made to project 8 or 10 feet over the lower in front,
> or with a forebay attached, to shelter the entries to
> the stables and passageways. It contained the
> threshing-floors, mows [bins], and lofts for the storing
> of hay and grain.[7]

Conestoga wagons were the farmers' main means of transportation. These stoutly built vehicles, with their white linen coverings, were frequently painted red and blue and fitted with chiming bells. They were pulled by four or six horses, or sometimes by oxen. Wrote Benjamin Rush,

> In this wagon, drawn by four or five horses of a
> peculiar breed, they convey to market, over the
> roughest roads, 2,000 and 3,000 pounds of weight of
> the produce of their farms. In the months of
> September and October it is no uncommon thing on
> the Lancaster and Reading roads to meet in one day
> fifty or one hundred of these wagons on their way
> to Philadelphia, most of which belong to German
> farmers.[8]

[6] Quoted in ibid., p. 82.
[7] Quoted in Kuhns, *The German and Swiss Settlements of Colonial Pennsylvania,* pp. 94–95.
[8] Quoted in ibid., pp. 98–99.

The Pennsylvania Dutch guided their farming and their lives with frequent references to signs and omens. As one historian has noted:

Things planted when the moon was in the sign of the Twins [Gemini] would be abundant. When the horns of the moon were down onions must be planted; beans, and early potatoes, however, when the horns were up. Apples should be picked in the dark of the moon, else they would rot. Hogs should be slaughtered during the waxing of the moon, otherwise the meat would shrink and be poor. Even the thatching of houses should be done when the horns of the moon were down, or the shingles would curl; and when fences were built, the first or lower rail should be laid when the horns were up, while the stakes should be put in and the fence finished when the horns were down. Such are a few of the affairs of life which were supposed to be done literally "by the book."

Omens were frequent. It was a sign of death if a bird entered the room, if a horse neighed or dog barked at night, or if a looking-glass were broken; the same thing was supposed to be true of dreaming of having teeth pulled, or of seeing someone dressed in black.

As water was one of the most important things for every house, it is not surprising that supernatural means were employed to discover it. The following device of "smelling" for water was common: "Hold a forked willow or peach limb with the prongs down, and move over the spot where water is desired. If water is present, the stick will turn down in spite of all you can do; it has been known to twist off the bark. The depth of water may be known by the number and strength of the dips made. Ore can be found in the same way."

Also curious in their way were the weather signs. If the ears of corn burst, a mild winter will follow; but it will be cold if they are plump. If the spleen of a hog be short and thick, the winter will be

"Hex signs," like this one, were thought to be used by the Pennsylvania Dutch to prevent the devil from entering their barns to give the cows milk fever. Always of the same basic design, a star within a circle, these signs probably were meant only as decoration—"chust for nice," as the farmer himself would say.

Walt Shelly

short, and *vice versa*. If on February 2d the ground-
hog comes out and sees his shadow, he will retire
to his hole and six more weeks of cold weather will
follow. So, when the snow is on the ground, if
turkeys go to the field or the guinea-hens halloo,
there will be a thaw. If cocks crow at 10 P.M., it
will rain before morning.[9]

It was not uncommon for a Pennsylvania Dutch family
to inscribe a stone placed over the front door of their
house. This was a typical inscription:

Got segne dieses Haus.
& Ales was da geh ein & aus.
Got alein die Ehr
& sonst keinen antern mer.
Adam & Cathrina Orts
17   I.M.S.   62

Translated, the inscription means:

God bless this house.
& all who there go in and out.
To God alone the glory
& to no one else besides.
Adam and Catharine Orth
17   I.M.S.   62[10]

For the most part, the Pennsylvania Dutch kept to themselves during the colonial period. Their communities became
islands within the colony's British culture. They jealously
guarded their customs and their ways of life, and they main-
tained their dialect, a form of what is known as Low
German. They were not long on literature and learning;
intellectual matters concerned them hardly at all. They were,
in a word, industrious. And most were better off in America
than they had been in their homeland.

[9] Quoted in ibid., pp. 103–5.
[10] Fredric Klees, *The Pennsylvania Dutch* (New York: Macmillan, 1950),
p. 387.

American Jewish Archives

Jews of the Sheareth Israel congregation in New Amsterdam, forced to worship in their homes under Peter Stuyvesant's rule, were finally allowed to construct this small synagogue on Mill Street in 1730, after the English took over the colony.

Jews in the Middle Colonies

The Jews, too, were industrious immigrants. Many of the earliest arrivals were Sephardic Jews—Jews who had lived for hundreds of years in Spain and Portugal, often achieving great wealth and influence, until the systematic program of religious persecution known as the Inquisition began driving them out in the late fifteenth century. A number fled to Holland, where they soon became prominent in the life of that nation and its colonies.

Several Jewish merchants appear to have been active in the early days of New Netherland. The first sizeable group, however, arrived in September, 1654, landing from the French frigate *Saint Charles* at New Amsterdam. The party included four men, six women, and thirteen children. They had come from Recife, Brazil, after the Portuguese had retaken that settlement from the Dutch. They were not universally welcomed. Peter Stuyvesant, who had no use for any religion but his own, wrote to the Dutch West India Company: "Giving them liberty, we cannot refuse the Lutherans and the Papists [Catholics]." But Jews were among the investors in the West India Company, and the refugees were allowed to remain. They were joined, in the years that followed, by more Jewish immigrants from Holland and from the Dutch island of Curaçao.

Stuyvesant's anti-Semitism continued to be a problem for the early immigrants. In his usual high-handed way, he announced laws denying citizenship to Jews and prohibiting them from owning real estate or engaging in various forms of trade and employment. A series of petitions detailing the governor's discriminatory policies was drawn up and sent to the Dutch West India Company by the leaders of the Jewish community, notably Salvador Dandrada, Jacob Henriques (the family name later became Hendricks), Abraham de Lucena, and Joseph d'Acosta. As a result, Stuyvesant received a rebuke from his employers, company officials noting with particular "displeasure" his policy of excluding Jews from the fur trade. Jews were granted the status of burghers, or citizens. However, the company did uphold Stuyvesant's ban on public worship, requiring members of the city's Jewish congregation, Shearith Israel ("Remnant of Israel"), to conduct services in their own homes. The congregation was allowed to establish a cemetery in 1656, but it was not until 1730—well after the English takeover of the colony—that construction of a synagogue was permitted. It was located on Mill Street in Manhattan.

The offices of the Dutch West India Company in Holland. To the company, New Netherland was a disappointment—it cost money to administer, and it never returned the profits that were expected of it.

Like other immigrants to the Middle Colonies, the Jews pursued a variety of occupations. They were, however, notable for their enterprise. The Hendricks family, for instance, founded the first copper mill in America, using ore mined around Newark, New Jersey, and they were among America's first millionaires as a result of its success.

Often the same person followed several professions at the same time. An early example was Asser Levy, one of the original twenty-three to arrive. Levy began as a butcher, and by 1678 he had become prosperous enough to build a slaughterhouse at the east end of what is now Wall Street. Then, nearby, he opened a tavern that soon became popular as a gathering place for the city's businessmen. He was also a merchant, specializing goods for the Indian trade. An active member of the Jewish community, Levy was instrumental in winning rights for Jews from the Stuyvesant government—one being the right to stand guard duty in the town. But he is also worth remembering for his ecumenical spirit. In 1671 he loaned money to the city's Lutherans (who had also suffered from Stuyvesant's prejudice), thus enabling them to build their first church. When he died in 1682, Asser Levy left his family well established. His estate consisted of £53 in cash, a comfortable house, several business properties, substantial land holdings, and a large stock of trade goods.

Daniel Gomez was another New York merchant. Born in 1695, at the age of fourteen he joined his father and brothers in the West Indies trade, dealing mostly in wheat. Before long he extended his operations to include trade with England and Ireland and with the Indians in New York. By about 1713, Gomez had purchased 2,500 acres of wilderness in the vicinity of Newburgh, north of New York City. There he built a large, fortlike house of stone in which he could spend the winter months—the most active season in the fur trade—without sacrificing any of the luxuries he enjoyed in the city. Joined eventually by his sons, Gomez operated his trading post profitably for many years. (One of the firm's employees was a young German immigrant named John Jacob Astor, who learned the fur-trading business from the Gomezes so well that he went on to make a fortune in his own right.) After the British took over New York during the War for Independence, Daniel Gomez grew to dislike the Loyalist character the city acquired. He moved to Philadelphia, where he died in 1780.

By then a number of Jews had been active in Philadelphia's commercial and cultural life for a long time. Among them were Moses Franks (originally Franco), head of a large mercantile firm, and Haym Salomon, a financier who raised substantial sums of money for the Revolution by selling bonds for the struggling Continental government. Two were brothers, Barnard and Michael Gratz.

The records of the Gratz family in America appear to date from 1754. They refer to Barnard, who came to Philadelphia that year from Europe, where the original family name was Gracia or Garcia. In 1759 Barnard was joined by his brother Michael. Both had been trained as merchants under a cousin, Solomon Henry, in London. The Gratz

Haym Salomon used his financial genius and his considerable assets to aid the cause of the Revolution. He was twice arrested by the British as a spy, but on both occasions he managed to escape.

American Jewish Archives

brothers engaged in trade in the West Indies, in Nova Scotia, along the Atlantic coast, and in London. The Indian trade was also an important part of their business. A ledger entry of December, 1760, showed beaver pelts valued at nearly £190, a large sum at the time. It appears that the Gratz brothers did business with George Croghan, an Indian trader and land speculator, supplying him with goods for barter in his dealings with the western Indians. The two certainly appear to have been interested in Croghan's scheme to establish a new colony in the Ohio Valley—his Vandalia project. And, although nothing came of Croghan's plans, the Gratzes' business prospered as the West began to fill with settlers, especially after the War for Independence. Like many of their fellow merchants, the brothers left well-endowed descendants who continued to distinguish the family name. Worthy of note is Michael's daughter Rebecca Gratz, a celebrated beauty who encouraged such literary figures of her time as Washington Irving, James Fenimore Cooper, and William Cullen Bryant, and who was said to be the model for the character named Rebecca in Sir Walter Scott's novel *Ivanhoe*.

The Working Class

Merchants and farmers were not the only groups in colonial society. Most of the remainder of the population was made up of the working and servant classes.

English and European society was stratified, or organized into layers of differing status. Everyone had a place, and a person's position depended more on birth and occupation than on wealth. A member of the nobility or gentry, even though broke and in debt, could still expect to enjoy certain rights and privileges. Merchants ranked higher on the social scale than craftsmen, even though some of the latter might be fairly well-to-do. The working class itself was subdivided into master craftsmen, journeymen, apprentices, common laborers, and agricultural workers. Workingmen's associations, known as guilds, reinforced those classifications.

Although colonial society was stratified to some extent—in the Middle Colonies merchants and large land owners were on top—it was not nearly so rigid as in Europe. With

Brown Brothers

Clothing styles of the eighteenth century included, for the men, a scarflike neckcloth, a waistcoat worn under a knee-length coat, knee breeches, a sword, and heeled, buckled shoes. The large curled wigs they wore were called "periwigs." The women favored gowns with bell-shaped skirts and three-quarter-length sleeves, and often a "fontange," a high headdress fastened to the front of a cap, as worn by the woman on the right. Muffs and long gloves usually completed their outfits.

a small stake, hard work, and sometimes luck, one could jump class barriers. This happened, although the evidence indicates that most people in America, as in England and Europe, remained from birth to death in the same class.

Not all categories of labor survived the Atlantic passage. No distinction between masters and journeymen prevailed in the colonies. People referred to both groups as artificers, handicraftsmen, or mechanics. The strict system of apprenticeship, or training, that was enforced by guilds did not take hold in America. Guilds themselves did not. It is true enough that apprenticeship was common—Benjamin Franklin served part of a term under his brother James—but it was not absolutely necessary to go the apprentice route to enter a trade. In many cases a person's competence

Shelburne Collection

This reproduction of a colonial kitchen shows the many handmade utensils the colonists produced. The kitchen features a large open fireplace used both for cooking and for heating, pewter tableware, and many iron pots of various sizes. Hanging between the large fireplace and the oven is a warming pan, which was filled with embers at bedtime and used to warm sheets and blankets in the cold rooms.

was judged not by whether he had spent a certain number of years in apprenticeship, but whether he displayed sufficient skill to satisfy his customers. The market place applied the test. And demand usually determined wages. A carpenter in New York City, for example, might earn five to eight shillings a day, depending on the amount of building going on at any one time.

The fact that farmers in the normal course of their work engaged in skilled labor further blurred distinctions. Most farmers had to be jacks of all trades. A craftsman might ply a particular trade and farm on the side, or a farmer might engage in a certain trade on the side. Some craftsmen resented farmers' intrusion in trades. Wrote one to the *New-York Post-Boy* in 1753:

It should not be permitted for one man to carry on
the Business of Tanning, Currying and Shoemaking;
much less ought a Farmer to do one, or all those
Occupations within himself ... A Farmer also ought
to employ himself in his proper occupation without
meddling with Smiths, Masons, Carpenters, Coopers,
or any other mechanical Arts, except making and
mending his Plow, Harrow, or any other Utensil for
Farming.[11]

Nor did everyone care for the casual way in which a person
could enter a craft. A New Jerseyite wrote in 1753:

The first Grievance that calls for Remedy is; that
Tradesmen (if I may call them so) are permitted to
follow their Occupations, after having served a
Master-Workman not above two or three Years, and
sometimes not above a few months; such as
Carpenters, Masons, Shoemakers, Tanners, Smiths,
Taylors and many other Trades; who are rather
Jobbers and Coblers than Workmen; by which the
country is imposed on, having their work done by
the Halves: It is almost incredible to think what a
Number of such Insects infest this Country.[12]

What counted most among skilled workers in urban areas
was freedom of the city. This, in effect, was citizenship and
a license to practice a trade. It could be purchased or
obtained by birthright—that is, a craftsman's son, having
learned a trade, would automatically be eligible. The
freedom-of-the-city idea began in New York under the
Dutch, and the English continued it. The practice was a
means of regulating the labor supply and its quality, and
of controlling competition. Without such a license, strictly
speaking, a person could not earn a living as a craftsman
in a city. In the 1690's in New York, it cost an artisan one
pound, four shillings to obtain freedom of the city. Working

---

[11] Quoted in Samuel McKee, Jr., *Labor in Colonial New York, 1664–1776* (New York: Columbia University Press, 1935), p. 24.
[12] Quoted in ibid., p. 27.

without the license laid one open to a fine of five pounds.
Later the license fee was reduced to six shillings.

Having paid his fee, a person took an oath as a freeman.
In New York during Queen Anne's reign, the oath was
lengthy:

> Ye shall Swear, That ye shall be good & true to
> our Soveraign Lady Queen Anne, and to the Heirs
> of our said Soveraign Lady the Queen. Obeysont and
> Obedient shall ye be to the Mayor and Ministers
> of this City, the Franchises and Customs thereof.
> Ye shall..maintain, and this City Keep harmless, in
> that which is in you is. Ye shall be contributing to
> all manner of Charges within this City, as Summons,
> Watches, Contributions, Taxes, Tallages [occasional
> taxes], Lot and Scott [city taxes according to ability
> to pay], and all other Charges, bearing your part as
> a Free-man ought to do. Ye shall know no Forreigner
> to buy or sell any Merchandise with any other
> Forreigners within this City or Franchize thereof, but
> ye shall warn the Mayor thereof. Ye shall implead
> or sue no Free-man out of this City, whilst ye may
> have Right and Law within the same. Ye shall take
> no Apprentice, but if he be free-born, (that is to say)
> no Bond-man's [indentured servant's] Son, nor the
> Son of an Alien, and for no less term than for four
> years, without fraud or deceit; and within the first
> year ye shall cause him to be enrolled, or else pay such
> Fine as shall be reasonably imposed upon you for
> omitting the same; and after his term ends, within
> convenient time, being required, ye shall make him
> free of this City, if he have well and truly served you.
> Ye shall also Keep the Queens Peace in your own
> Person. Ye shall Know of no Gatherings, Conventicles
> [meetings] or Conspiracies made against the Queens
> Peace, but you shall warn the Mayor thereof, or let it
> to your Power. All these Points and Articles ye shall
> well and truly Keep, according to the Laws and
> Customs of this City. *So help you God.*[13]

[13] Quoted in ibid., p. 36.

A person then received a freeman's certificate, of which the following is an example:

> Isaac De Riemer Esq'r Mayor and the Alderman
> of the Citty of New Yorke. To all to whom these
> presents shall Come *Send* Greetings Whereas Thomas
> Evans Bricklayer hath made application to be made
> a Freeman and Cittizen of the said Citty. These
> are therefore to Certifie and Declare that the said
> Thomas Evans is hereby Admitted Received and
> allowed a Freeman and Cittizen of the same City to
> Have, Hold, Enjoy and Partake of all the Benefits,
> Liberties, Privileges, Freedoms & Immunities
> Whatsoever Granted or belonging to the same. In
> Testimony whereof the said Mayor hath hereunto
> Subscribed his Name and Caused the seale of the
> said City to be affixed the first day of October,
> Anno. Dom 1701. *Annoq. Rog. Regs. Will, tertii.*
> *Nunc. An &c Decimo Tertio.*
>
> I.D. Riemer, Mayor
>
> Will Sharpas Clk.[14]

Craftsmen tended to guard the right to work in a community jealously. In 1675, the coopers—barrelmakers—of Hampton on Long Island complained of "foreigners" plying that trade in their midst. They spoke of Boston coopers in particular. Coopers of Hampton, they pointed out, were forbidden to work in Boston. In 1737, New York City carpenters petitioned Governor George Clinton to exclude members of their trade who came over from New Jersey to work by the day. These workers paid no taxes, the petitioners argued, and consequently they could work for lower wages, which they took back to New Jersey to spend. Furthermore, the Jerseyites brought their own materials with them, thus avoiding any expenditure of money in New York. Clinton referred the matter to a committee. That group suggested that the New York carpenters follow the usual procedure and report such offenders who, upon conviction, would be liable for a five-pound fine.

[14] Quoted in ibid., p. 37.

A view of the southern tip of Manhattan Island in 1704.

New York City's regulation of cartmen—independent haulers of goods—seems to have been more extensive than that of any other group. Cartmen in 1667 petitioned for a monopoly, which the city granted provided that they agreed also to help put out fires. Over the years more duties were added. Cartmen had to clean and repair streets, and in addition they were required to labor for the city one or two days a week without wages. Cartmen also had to obtain a license and pay annual fees. The city government set their wages.

The list of crafts in Philadelphia was as long as that in New York, and regulations concerning them were much the same. Shipbuilding was the Quaker City's largest industry—William Penn had brought a shipbuilder on his first visit there—and it employed more artisans than any other business. "Here is a great employ of ship-work, it increases and will increase," Jonathan Dickinson, a Philadelphia merchant, wrote in 1718. And during the 1720's as many as twenty ships at one time could be seen under construction on the ways in Philadelphia. Philadelphians owned about half the total tonnage of ships trading in the city, and ships were also constructed there for merchants in other colonies and in England.

Apprenticeship

Until 1766, when a second law was passed, a section of the Duke's Laws of 1665 generally regulated apprenticeship in New York. Parents and masters were urged to "bring up their children and Apprentices in some honest Lawfull

Historical Society of Pennsylvania

The city of Philadelphia, seen in the background across the busy Delaware River. Shipbuilding was the largest industry in the city during colonial times.

Calling Labor or Employment." The 1766 law provided for contracts in writing "to bind any Infant [minor] or other Person for a Term of Years." Furthermore, the act declared that each person should "be liable to such Correction as any apprentices are liable to in England, and may be relieved and discharged for Misusage, Refusal of Necessaries [food, clothing, and shelter, all of which the master was supposed to provide], Cruelty or Ill treatment in the manner Apprentices are relievable in England for any of the Causes aforesaid."[15] This legislation simply turned common practice into law.

Apprenticeship meant a contract between a craftsman and a young person with the consent of the parents. For a certain term of years an apprentice agreed to work for the master, sometimes at household tasks as well as other labor. The craftsman was to teach the apprentice his trade. Apprenticeship was a source of cheap labor, but it was also an important educational institution. Agreements were lengthy and restrictive, as this example shows:

[15] Quoted in ibid., p. 64.

Recorded for Nathaniel Marston, ye 24th day of
August, 1697. This Indenture Witnesseth that
Nathaniel Lynus by and with the Consent of his
Parents hath put himselfe and by these Presents
doth Voluntarily and of his own free will and Accord
put himselfe Apprentice to Nathaniel Marston of
New Yorke Barber to learn his Art, Trade or Mystery
and after the manner of An Apprentice to Serve from
ye Date hereof till the full Terme of Seaven Years be
Compleat and Ended. During all which Terme the
said Apprentice his Said Master Nathaniel Marston
and Mistress Margarett Marston faithfully Shall Serve,
his Secretts keep, his Lawfull Commands Gladly
Everywhere obey. He Shall do no Damage to his
Said Master Nor See it to be done by others without
letting or Giving Notice thereof to his Said Master.
He Shall not waste his Said Masters goods nor lend
them Unlawfully to Any. He Shall not Committ
Fornication Nor Contract Matrimony within the Said
Terme. Att Cards, Dice or any other unlawful Game
he shall not play whereby his Said Master may have
Damage with his own goods Nor the Goods of others.
During the Said Terme without Lycense from his Said
Master he Shall Neither buy nor Sell. He Shall not
absent himselfe Day or Night from his Masters
Service without his Leave, Nor haunt Ale houses,
Taverns or Playhouses. But in all things as a
faithfull Apprentice he shall behave himselfe toward
his Said Master and all During the Said Terme. And
the said Master in the Same Act which he Useth by
the best means that he Can Shall teach [his apprentice]
or Cause [him] to be taught and Instructed, finding
onto him meate, Drinke, Apparell, Lodging and
washing fitting for an Apprentice During the Said
Terme. And for the true Performance of all and
Every of the Said Covenants and Agreements Either
of the Said Parties Binde themselves unto the other.

In Wittness whereof they have Interchangeably put
their hands and Seals this Nineteenth day of
August in the Ninth Year of the Reign of our
Sovereign Lord William the third by the Grace of

In this photograph, taken in Williamsburg, Virginia, a silversmith recreates articles of colonial design using eighteenth-century methods to hammer out bowls and plates from silver bars.

God King of England, Scotland, France and Ireland &c: Annoq. Dom. 1697.[16]

Fewer occupations were open to girls than to boys. Girls who accepted apprenticeships usually entered the trades of seamstress, milliner (hat maker), or servant. They entered into agreements similar to the one above. One such agreement was made between Aulkey Hubertse, who was to be a servant, and John Delemont, her master in Albany. After listing the ordinary mutual obligations, the document stated:

> It is further agreed between the said parties that the Master shall before the expiration of the said Term teach [the apprentice] or cause [her] to be taught to read.[17]

Numerous laws dealt with apprentices' conduct. Many of the laws covered stealing and the use of alcoholic beverages. Others had to do with disobedience and laziness, and permitted a master to go so far as to whip an apprentice for such conduct. Running away—and a number of apprentices, like Benjamin Franklin, did—could be punished by adding double the time of absence, beyond twenty-four hours, to an apprentice's term of service.

A Large Industry

Probably the largest single employer of skilled labor in the colonies was Peter Hasenclever. And his was a most unusual case.

Hasenclever, a Prussian, became an English citizen in 1763. A real entrepreneur, he envisioned great possibilities in the iron and potash business in America. He proposed to establish a huge iron and potash works and to grow hemp, flax, and madder (a dye plant) on the side. The British government approved his scheme, and Hasenclever formed a company capitalized at £21,000, of which he put up £8,000. He then sent agents to Germany to round up workers

[16]Quoted in ibid., p. 69.
[17]Quoted in ibid., p. 71.

Colonial Williamsburg

and transport them to America. Altogether, he paid the fare of 535 workers and their families. Among them were miners, carpenters, masons, and blacksmiths.

Arriving in New York in April, 1764, Hasenclever purchased five thousand acres of land in that colony and in New Jersey. He also bought more than three hundred horses and oxen. The building of furnaces, forges, blacksmiths' shops, storehouses, sawmills, stamping mills, and so on was completed late in 1766, in settlements located at Ringwood and Charlottenburg, New Jersey, and at Long Pond, Cortland, and New Petersburg, New York. Hasenclever incurred debts of £54,600, several thousand pounds more than he and his partners possessed.

Hasenclever expected to produce what was known as bar iron for £14.5s.7d. a ton. The London price was £17.10s. This would yield Hasenclever and his associates a good profit, but unfortunately labor troubles and mismanagement doomed the scheme. His workers demanded higher wages and performed badly until he gave in. Many took sick, others deserted. In an advertisement listing the names of workers who had left his employ in violation of their contracts, Hasenclever said,

Hand-operated printing presses like this one produced the first newspapers in the colonies. Even the paper was entirely made by hand.

> They are all Germans, and talk very little English, had on when they went away, soldiers jackets, and carried with them their miner's clothes, black turn'd up with red, likewise guns and hammers. As these men are still engaged by contract for 3 years and 4 months and have been brought into this country from Europe at a very great expense, all gentlemen, well-wishers to their country, are respectfully desired not to engage these people in their service, but to . get them secured in any of his majesty's gaols [jails]. Five pounds reward is offered for anyone so secured, and if sent back to the works, all charges besides.[18]

In November, 1766, Hasenclever departed New York for London. There he found that one of his partners who had pledged £8,000 was bankrupt. Hasenclever scrambled

[18] Quoted in ibid., p. 58.

successfully for credit and returned to America the following year. He found his company a mess. One iron works in the Mohawk Valley lay abandoned. Additional debts had piled up because costs had exceeded income. The project collapsed, and Hasenclever declared personal bankruptcy in England in 1770. Lawsuits seeking to settle the company's accounts and affairs cluttered the courts for years.

Colonial Classifieds

People seeking the services of skilled craftsmen frequently advertised for them. The newspapers also carried many "help wanted: servant" ads. The following example appeared in the *New-York Mercury* in 1764:

> Wanted, A Decent middle-aged Woman, who has been used to the Care of Children; She must be able to teach young Ladies to read, and the Use of the Needle; Such an one, (if well recommended) may hear of a Place, by enquiring of the Printer.[19]

Another ran:

> Wanted, Two White Servant Maids, to serve in a small Family; the one for a Nurse-maid, to take Care of a Child or two; the other to Cook and do the other necessary Work about the House; They must be well recommended and engage to stay a Twelve-month at least in the Family. Enquire of the Printer.[20]

Unemployed servants also placed "situation-wanted" ads. Here is one example:

> Wants a Place A Woman that is capable of taking Care of Children and serving, or doing occasional Work in a Gentleman's Family; She could undertake to Keep House for a Tradesman, and cook and do House Work. For Particulars apply to Hugh Gaine [the printer].[21]

[19] Quoted in ibid., p. 47.
[20] Quoted in ibid.
[21] Quoted in ibid., p. 49.

Forty Shillings Reward.

RAN away this morning from the fubfcriber, an Apprentice B O Y named James Hoy, near 18 years old. about 5 feet 8 inches high, fair complexion, and hair tied behind. He took with him a brown jean coat, grey furtout, new fhoes, round felt hat, and many other articles of cloathing.——Whoever brings him back or confines him in gaol, fo that he be had again, fhall receive the above reward.

                                     JOHN FARRAN.
Philadelphia, June 26.   3fp

An advertisement offering a reward for a runaway apprentice.

And another, by a man, in 1769:

> Wants a Place, a Servant out of Employment, who
> can produce a very good character; understands to
> dress hair in the newest fashion; wait at table, and
> attend on horses; is capable to serve as valet de
> chambre, or as butler in a family; and would be very
> glad of being employed. Enquire of the printer.[22]

Newcomers to New York City from Europe also advertised for positions. Here is an example from the *Mercury* in 1767:

> Wants a Place. A Single young Man, from England,
> who is used to the Farming Business, and is willing
> to hire with any Gentleman Farmer, or to look after a
> Store, who can be recommended for his Sobriety, and
> Honesty. Enquire of the printer hereof.[23]

In Exchange for Ocean Passage

Another form of labor common to the colonies, indentured servitude, appeared at an early date. Evidence indicates that there were indentured servants among the Swedes in Delaware and later after the Dutch took over that colony. Under English rule, the Duke's Laws for New York dealt with the contracts—known as indentures—that established servitude, the duties of servants and masters, and procedures in the event an indentured servant ran away.

[22] Quoted in ibid.
[23] Quoted in ibid.

An indentured servant was a person whose transportation to the colonies had been paid for by someone else. In return, he or she agreed to work out the cost of the passage with labor for a term of from four to seven years. A child between the ages of five and ten had to serve until age twenty-one. Frequently a ship's captain paid the fare. Then, upon arrival in a colonial port, he sold the contract with the immigrant. Usually the price covered at least what the captain reckoned to be the cost of passage. Some people used the term "redemptionist" to describe indentured servants. The person "redeemed" his or her debt with labor.

The price varied. In Pennsylvania, in 1722, some Germans were sold as indentured servants for ten pounds apiece, to serve terms of five years. As the eighteenth century wore on, the price appears to have increased. After 1760 in Pennsylvania it was twenty-two or twenty-three pounds. In New York, one Mary Vander Ripe owed Joost Soy fifteen pounds. She elected to sell herself to him as an indentured servant for four years. The holder of a contract might sell it to another person for the remaining portion of a term. The unexpired term of an indenture contract might also be passed on in a will.

Poor and destitute Europeans, and those wishing to conserve what few funds they had, were the main source of indentures in the colonies. A number of people, no one knows how many, became indentured servants against their will. This was especially true of women and children, who were kidnapped and placed aboard a ship about to sail for America. The captain paid the kidnapper a fee and collected for the passage on the other side. In 1662 the mayor of Bristol, England, had this to say about the kinds of people who became indentured:

> Among those who repair to Bristol from all parts
> to be transported for servants to his Majesty's
> plantations beyond seas, some are husbands that have
> forsaken their wives, others wives who have
> abandoned their husbands; some are children and
> apprentices run away from their parents and masters;
> oftentimes unwary and credulous persons have been

tempted on board by men-stealers, and many that
have been pursued by hue-and-cry for robberies,
burglaries, or breaking prison, do thereby escape the
prosecution of law and justice.[24]

Prisons were an important source of servants. Thousands
of people imprisoned for political or religious dissent, and
those convicted of felonies or lesser crimes, were
"transported" during colonial times—sent across the ocean.
The majority seem to have gone to Maryland, Virginia, or
the island of Barbados in the West Indies. Apparently some
were shipped to New York. Although some convicts seem
to have arrived in Pennsylvania, the government there
consistently opposed the importation of prisoners as
contrary to sound public policy.

A number of people who accepted indentures were skilled
workers out of jobs or simply seeking to better themselves
in the New World. This is underscored by an ad which
appeared in the *New-York Mercury* in 1766 announcing the
arrival of persons to be sold as indentured servants:

Arrived in the *Franklin*, from Rotterdam, and to
be disposed of, sundry German Servants, vis. Four
Farmers, and their wives, one Sail Cloth, and figured
Linnen Weaver, one Potash Maker, and Family, One
Saltpeter and Gunpowder Maker, two single Women,
one of 30, and the other 23 years old.[25]

Here is a similar ad from the same paper eight years later:

Servants, Just Arrived from Scotland, To be sold on
Board the ship *Commerce*, Capt. Ferguson, lying at
the Ferry-stairs; among which are A number of
Weavers, Taylors, Blacksmiths, Nailors, Shoemakers,
Butchers, Sawyers, Wheel-Wrights, Hatters and
Spinsters [all of the above] From fourteen to

[24] Quoted in Abbot Emerson Smith, *Colonists in Bondage: White Servitude and Convict Labor in America, 1607–1776* (Chapel Hill: University of North Carolina Press, 1947), pp. 82–83.

[25] Quoted in McKee, *Labor in Colonial New York,* p. 105.

thirty-five years of age. For terms apply to Henry White, or said master on board.[26]

Sometimes entire families were advertised. A notice in the *New-York Post-Boy* in 1754 read:

To Be Sold, A German Servant Man, with his Wife and Son, of about Six Years old, who are to serve five Years, he is as compleat a Gardner as any in America; understands a Flower and Kitchen Garden to Perfection: Enquire of the Printers.[27]

Laws protected indentured servants from ill-treatment. In New York in 1695, for example, the widow Ann Sewell was hauled into court for keeping her servant Ann Parsons in chains, feeding her only bread and water for weeks at a time, and beating her. The widow Sewell protested that her servant had "highly offended her" and that she had not realized that any of her actions were illegal. The court ended the indenture and ordered Ann Sewell to pay the court costs.

Legislation also protected masters and mistresses from such tendencies on the part of servants as laziness and disobedience, failure to perform properly, and running away. Runaways were particularly troublesome. Being white, an indentured servant could melt into the general population—something no slave could do unless he or she possessed unusually light skin. Moreover, most people were not inclined to meddle in another's business and therefore did not inquire too closely into a white person's background or status. Owners of runaways remained hopeful, however, judging from the fact that nearly every issue of colonial papers carried ads describing indentured servants who had fled. One in the *New-York Gazette* in 1756 concerned Nancy Perron, an Irish girl who had run away from the employ of James Willson, a stonecutter. The notice described Nancy as "fresh coloured, with black curl'd hair, is thick and well set, round fac'd and

---

[26] Quoted in ibid.
[27] Quoted in ibid., p. 107.

looks very impudent; Had on when she went away, a
striped Homespun Gown, and a blue and white Apron."[28]
An ad in the *New-York Mercury* in 1760 pictured Hester
Ashton, a runaway, in this fashion: "She is about 19 Years of
Age, pretty likely Face, and a Ruddy Complexion,
remarkably strong made, is fat and clumsy.... It is
imagined she went off with some of the Train of Artillery
[soldiers]."[29] Another ad in the *Gazette* in 1765 had this
to say about George Fisher, a runaway bookbinder:

> [He is] between 25 and 26 Years of Age, about five
> feet five inches high, very thick, stoops much, and
> has a down Look; he is a little pock marked, has
> a scar on one of his Temples, is much addicted to
> Liquor, very talkative when drunk and remarkably
> stupid. He had on and carried away with him, several
> good white linen Shirts, a snuff colored Cloth Coat,
> and a suit of light colored Sagathy, other good
> wearing apparel, a new half cut Bob Wig and a Set of
> Silver Buckles.[30]

The runaway problem was scarcely confined to New York. A
notice in the Philadelphia *American Weekly Mercury* in
1720 said:

> Run away about Two Years ago from Cecil County
> in Maryland, Nicholas Collings, small statue, bushy
> Hair almost Grey: A Shoemaker by Trade. Whoever
> secures him, and gives Notice thereof to Mr. Abel van
> Burkeloo of the said County, shall have Ten Shillings
> Reward.[31]

Not everyone hesitated to question a person's status, of
course. Benjamin Franklin related that, on his way to
Philadelphia, "I made so miserable a figure that I was
suspected of being some runaway indentured servant, and

[28] Quoted in ibid., p. 108.
[29] Quoted in ibid.
[30] Quoted in ibid.
[31] Quoted in Cheesman A. Herrick, *White Servitude in Pennsylvania:
Indentured and Redemption Labor in Colony and Commonwealth* (Philadelphia: John Joseph McVey, 1926), p. 225.

was in danger of being taken up on that suspicion."[32] He was questioned more than once about being a runaway after his arrival in Philadelphia.

When runaways were apprehended, the finder usually placed an ad in a newspaper, such as this one in the *Pennsylvania Gazette* in 1760:

> Taken up and committed to Lancaster gaol, one Henry Reigdurff, lately advertised for running away from one John Chamber, of Birmingham Township, Chester County: These are to require of said John Chamber, or others whom it may concern, to come and take him out and pay the charges to the gaoler.[33]

Once the time of service was up, an indentured servant was free to do as he or she pleased. As to what occupations they pursued, Governor Henry Moore of New York, writing to the Lords of Trade in 1767, thought that

> the genius of the People in a Country where everyone can have Land to work upon leads them so naturally into Agriculture, that it prevails over every other occupation. There can be no stronger Instances of this, than in the servants Imported from Europe of different Trades; as soon as the time stipulated in their Indentures is expired, they immediately quit their masters, and get a small tract of Land, in settling which for the first three or four years they lead miserable lives, and in the most abject Poverty; but all this is patiently borne and submitted to with the greatest cheerfulness, the Satisfaction of being Land holders smooths every difficulty, and makes them prefer this manner of living to that comfortable subsistence which they could procure for themselves and their families by working at the Trades in which they were brought up.[34]

[32] Quoted in ibid.
[33] Quoted in ibid., p. 220.
[34] Quoted in McKee, *Labor in Colonial New York*, pp. 112–13.

Brown Brothers

The first slaves brought to the English colonies in North America arrived aboard this Dutch man-of-war in 1619.

The possibility of their running away made white indentured servants somewhat unreliable laborers. That was one reason why a number of people in the Middle Colonies preferred black slaves.

Slavery's Beginning

The evidence is sketchy, but apparently whites enslaved some Indians in New York at an early date. Yet settlers there, as in other English colonies, soon discovered that the Indian personality tended to break down in bondage, making enslaved Indians poor workers. Governor Edmund Andros prohibited Indian slavery in New York in 1679.

In 1626 the first black slaves, eleven in all, arrived in the Middle Colonies, landed at New Amsterdam. Slaves were in great demand in New Netherland and some of the cargoes placed ashore in later years were large. Three hundred slaves were reported to have arrived on Manhattan in 1664, the year Hollanders surrendered their colony to the English.

After the English took over, both colonial and home governments cooperated to promote and expand the slave trade. A census in 1698 showed 2,170 blacks in New York, most of them slaves, out of a total population of slightly more than 18,000. By 1746 the black population in the colony, through additional imports and natural increase, had reached 9,000. By 1771 New York's population stood at 168,007. Of these, 19,883 were black and the great majority of them were slaves.

Owing to economics, slavery in northern colonies was somewhat different from that in the South. Contrary to the southern experience, there was, in the North, little demand for large gangs of laborers. An unknown number of New York farmers used slaves, but in most cases only small numbers were needed, and then only during such times as the harvest season. In New York City slaves were in demand as common laborers, but there also was a market for the services of such skilled craftsmen as weavers, shoemakers, coopers, and so on, trades which slaves probably learned from their owners. Not only might they help in a master's business, but skilled slaves could also be hired out. A good many slaves were also hired out as laborers and servants.

Most slave owners possessed only a few slaves. A partial New York census in 1755 revealed that 2,456 adult slaves belonged to 1,137 owners. Only seven masters surveyed owned more than ten. Large land owners, of course, tended to be the largest slave holders. Lewis Morris, for example, at his death possessed a total of sixty-six slaves. Frederick Philipse owned forty. A descendant, Adolph Philipse, who died in 1749, left nineteen slaves as part of his estate.

George Washington, followed through the streets of Philadelphia by his personal slave.

Brown Brothers

Taxes, Prices, and Hiring Out

Almost from the beginning of English rule, the New York government taxed imported slaves. Those brought directly from Africa came in at a lower rate than those from elsewhere. And the duty tended to go up during the colonial period. In 1702, for example, it was fifteen shillings on a black imported from Africa and twice that on blacks from other sources. By 1762 the duty had climbed to two pounds per slave from Africa, four pounds on slaves from other places. One reason for the differences in duties lay in the fact that other colonies tended to deport slaves who had been convicted of crimes or were otherwise undesirable. New Yorkers saw danger from such slaves in their midst. An additional benefit with respect to the African source lay in the fact that slaves obtained there could be paid for in goods.

Those purchased elsewhere were usually exchanged for hard money.

Newspapers regularly carried notices of the arrival of slave vessels at New York wharfs. Some ships belonged to local slave traders like John Courtland, a merchant, whose brig *Mattey* engaged in the trade. Others were owned by Rhode Islanders and men from other colonies. Still others belonged to the Royal African Company, a powerful English slave-trading organization. The newspaper ads described a ship's content but seldom mentioned price. That was a matter for negotiation at the point of sale.

Prices varied according to age, sex, health, skills, and demand. As the eighteenth century progressed, both sale and rental prices for slaves tended to go up. By the end of the colonial period, the price of a desirable male had reached the neighborhood of one hundred pounds. In 1695 an ordinary laborer could be hired for five pounds a year. By 1725 the owner of the same kind of slave could command twenty pounds annually. The rental price of skilled slaves had reached sixty pounds a year by 1760. Slave wages—or rents—were usually about half the cost of free white labor, although the cost of housing, food, and clothing for a slave had to be added to the total.

Competition from slaves did not please white laborers. Lieutenant Governor George Clarke, speaking to the New York assembly in 1737, reported protests from white coopers:

> The artificers complain and with too much reason of
> the pernicious custom of breeding slaves to trades
> whereby the honest and industrious tradesmen are
> reduced to poverty for want of employ, and many of
> them forced to leave us to seek their living in other
> countries.[35]

Precisely how economically beneficial slavery was in the northern colonies is difficult to say. Judging from the fact that slave imports continued steadily over the years, the institution must have been profitable, or at least many

[35]Quoted in ibid., p. 127.

people thought it was. It was undoubtedly cheaper to own a slave house servant, whom one did not have to pay, than to hire a free person who would demand wages. In either case the cost of room and board would be the same. On the other hand, it was usually a losing proposition for a small farmer to own slaves for whom, in season and out, he would have to furnish room and board. Perhaps the person who owned slaves and hired them out benefited more than most. This probably was especially true in instances where the cost of room and board was paid by the person renting. The value of this form of capital decreased with age, however. A young slave usually commanded a better price for sale or hire than an older one.

Young blacks below the age of thirty were the most prized, especially if they were skilled. Children had little or no value. Females of child-bearing age were not desirable, especially in the city. Not only might there be non-productive mouths to feed, but also most city houses contained insufficient space for the offspring that female slaves might bear.

In the North more than in the South, slavery hindered the development and maintenance of black family ties. The housing problem was one reason for this. Another reason was that each member of a couple might work for a different master. When a serious attachment was formed, it was frequently difficult for the couple to spend much time together. Some masters arranged for visits after working hours. Others gave husbands and wives extra time off. And some upheld black families, even refusing to sell married slaves unless the buyer agreed to keep them—and any children—together. But on the whole, slave family life was unstable, extremely difficult to establish and maintain.

Converting Slaves to Christianity

Believing that Christianity would lend a stabilizing influence, New York authorities supported the idea of converting slaves. In this endeavor, the Society for the Propagation of the Gospel in Foreign Parts, an Anglican organization, played a leading role. Missionaries of the society worked among blacks in New York City and in surrounding communities. Besides religion, they also taught some slaves to read and write in evening classes. In 1760 the society opened a school for blacks in New York City. There missionaries taught reading, writing, and arithmetic, and gave girls sewing lessons.

Slave holders generally frowned on these missionary activities. They were suspicious of any outside influence on their chattels. If slaves were to be converted to Christianity, many owners preferred to do it themselves. They were particularly opposed to any Quaker or Baptist influence, for these groups upheld the equality of all humankind.

Slaves themselves displayed little enthusiasm for Christianity, at least in New York. It was reported that after ten years of missionary activity, only one slave in ten in New York City had embraced the Christian religion. During a fifty-six year period, only fifty-three slaves accepted baptism in Huntington. The record in Rye township was one out of a hundred baptized after ten years of effort. On the whole, slaves failed to see how Christianity improved their lot in life. And the morality that the missionaries preached hardly fit the slaves' situation.

Regulation and Resistance

Slaves were private property, and within broad limits an owner could do with them as he pleased. Murder was prohibited, as was cruel and unusual punishment. Yet in New York there appears to be no record of a master's being prosecuted for killing a slave, even though such deaths occurred. Flogging was the common punishment for slaves who committed offenses, as it was for whites who broke the law. New Yorkers seem to have held strong feelings against physical brutality, and public opinion acted as a damper on excessive punishment. Slaves were not branded. And some masters sold unruly slaves into another colony rather than take strong disciplinary action, wishing to avoid expressions of public distaste.

Authorities and the general white public, however, possessed greater concern for order and safety than for slave-master relationships. The presence of a large black population created tension, and with it fear, especially in New York City. Laws limited slave gatherings with respect to numbers and occasions. Curfews were established. Slaves frequently were punished more severely than whites for the same offense. Assault against a white was especially serious; murder, particularly of a white person, was even more so. In

1707, for murdering members of a white Long Island family, two slaves were sentenced to death by torture. During much of the colonial period, slaves convicted of murder were hung in chains until they died—a slow and miserable death. Burning at the stake, another common sentence for murder, was at least faster. Slaves convicted of killing other slaves were sentenced to the same punishments.

Many slaves in New York resisted their status. Although a slave might steal for any one of a number of reasons, for some theft was a gesture of defiance. Others deliberately performed shoddy work. Others just loafed on the job. Hundreds—no one knows how many—escaped bondage by running away. And, although it was probably rare, some slaves fled in groups, as this notice in the *New-York Post-Boy* in 1748 attests:

> Ran away from John Pell, of the Manor of Pelham, a Negro Wench [girl] named Bell, a Boy named Janneau, a Girl named Tamer, another named Dinah, and another named Isabel; also a Negro man named Lewis.[36]

It was more common for men to try to escape than women, and children seldom did. Running away was dangerous business. In any colony questions might be asked. Those who stowed away on ships in New York harbor probably fared better. Perhaps blacks who escaped to live with Indians made out best of all. Although allied wth the English, even the Iroquois took in runaways and refused to turn them over. Some escaping blacks stayed with Indians on their way to Canada. Many runaways were returned. Some, unable for whatever reason to make it on their own, came back voluntarily. A runaway who returned could expect a flogging.

The Uprising of 1712

In at least one instance, some New York blacks resisted slavery with guns.

Despite laws concerning gatherings, it was not difficult for slaves to meet in New York City as part of their daily lives

---

[36] Quoted in ibid., p. 138.

and employment. And one group of slaves, all recently imported from Africa, formed a plan in the spring of 1712. Shortly after midnight on the morning of April 7, twenty-four slaves gathered in an orchard on the northern outskirts of the comunity on Manhattan. They had firearms, swords, hatchets, and knives. One of them, a man named Coffee, set fire to a building. As whites came running to it, the blacks opened fire. They killed five and wounded six. Soldiers were called out, but before they appeared the whites managed to organize themselves and drove the slaves into the woods. Sentries were then posted to prevent their escape from the island.

Their worst fears realized, New Yorkers panicked. Men were put under arms and additional militia came in from Long Island. But no further exchange of fire occurred. The slaves were without food and shelter. Some committed suicide, and the rest finally gave themselves up. Authorities arrested a total of seventy blacks who had taken part in the uprising or were suspected of having some connection with it.

Two weeks later, trials began in a special court convened by Governor Robert Hunter. White panic inspired reliance on flimsy evidence in many cases, and a number of slaves were convicted unjustly. Governor Hunter intervened to dismiss some cases. Had he not done so, the number of deaths would have been far higher. Altogether, twenty-one blacks were put to death. Some were burned at the stake. Others were broken on the rack. Still others hanged in chains to die slowly. The result of the uprising was a general tightening of laws designed to control slaves.

The 1741 Affair

A more bizarre incident occurred in 1741. In February of that year someone burglarized Robert Hogg's tobacco shop. Several gold coins were missing. Hogg suggested that Christopher Wilson, a white sailor known to associate with slaves, might have had something to do with it. Wilson denied this, but he said that he had seen two blacks he knew with a hatful of coins in a tavern owned by John Hughson. The authorities arrested them.

Mary Burton, an indentured servant of Hughson, now came forward. She hinted that she knew something about the burglary and, upon questioning, implicated Hughson, his wife Sarah, their daughter Sarah, and a young woman who lived at the tavern with them, Peggy Kerry. They were all arrested. Mary Burton later said that Hughson was the ringleader.

Then a rapid succession of fires broke out. As one was extinguished, a new one flared up. And, because they seemed to be enjoying the whites' confusion, slaves became suspected arsonists. City authorities offered one hundred pounds for information leading to arrest and conviction. At this point Mary Burton said that the Hughson group, along with two blacks named Quack and Cuffee, had plotted to burn the city. Public relief at the possibility of having the crimes solved squashed any doubt about Mary Burton's word. The Hughson party was already in jail. And apparently no one wondered how only two people could have set so many fires so quickly in several parts of the city.

But the authorities were determined to clear up the matter. When Quack and Cuffee went on trial, no lawyer would defend them. They were quickly convicted, mainly on Mary Burton's testimony, and sentenced to be burned alive. As the two were led to the stakes around which wood had been piled, they broke down. They backed up Mary Burton, naming Hughson as the leader in the plot. This did not save them. Quack and Cuffee were executed.

Attention now shifted to the Hughson group. Again Mary Burton performed as the chief witness, reinforced by the word of one Arthur Price, a convicted felon. Although evidence from such a person was not admissible in court, the prosecution overcame that barrier and all were convicted. Hughson, his wife, and Peggy Kerry were hanged. Authorities offered Sarah Hughson, the daughter, a chance to cooperate with the prosecution, for the affair was not over yet.

Mary Burton was not finished. And so wrought up was the entire city population that she had no trouble convincing people as she dragged in names of blacks and whites whom she named as conspirators. Some of the accused, promised easy treatment if they too named names, did so gladly. And as additional slaves were convicted and executed, New York City jails overflowed.

Now the whole thing took another twist. Spaniards in Florida frequently crossed over into Georgia to inspire slaves and Indians to revolt. Distraught, Governor James Oglethorpe of that colony wrote to all governors urging them to be on the alert for Spaniards in their midst. He warned that Spain might send priests in disguise to New York to plot the destruction of the city. This alarm sucked the strong anti-Catholic feeling in New York colony into the whirlwind of rumor, fear, and panic. And an alleged priest was found as Mary Burton put the finger on one John Ury.

Ury had arrived in New York shortly before. He claimed to be a member of the Anglican ministry. But he knew Latin well, and he taught it as an assistant to a schoolmaster. He also loved to dispute over theology. And to New Yorkers, it seemed plain that a person who knew Latin and argued about theology had to be a Catholic priest. Denouncing Ury, Mary Burton named him the real leader of the conspiracy against the city. No one, it seems, reminded her that she had originally cast John Hughson in that role.

John Ury did a fair job of defending himself, but he was up against a biased judge and jury. Mary Burton testified. So did others she had accused and who had promised to cooperate in exchange for leniency. One of them was Sarah Hughson. Despite his strong defense, the jury required only fifteen minutes to convict Ury. He was hanged.

By this time fourteen slaves had been burned at the stake. Eighteen had been hanged. Seventy-two had been sent out of the colony. Still another fifty remained in jail. It gradually occurred to slave owners that a lot of valuable property had been lost or, imprisoned, lay useless to them. As a rule, in the event of slave executions, owners were compensated at public expense. But since this usually amounted to no more than twenty to thirty pounds, it hardly covered the value of an able-bodied slave. New York slave holders moved to quiet the city before more trials and executions occurred.

Mary Burton helped quell the panic too, although she probably did not mean to. Reflections on her great power to convince apparently unhinged her completely from reality, and the names of alleged conspirators now passing her lips reached into the highest and most respected circles of the city. Even those who had believed her before could not stomach Mary Burton's latest accusations. The authorities could not afford to entertain the possibility that they had been wrong, but neither could they permit miscarriages of justice to continue. Insisting that past actions had been necessary and just, they let the whole matter drop. Bold and brassy to the end, Mary Burton then applied for the reward that had been offered for exposing the conspirators. With their reputations at stake, feeling they had no choice, the authorities handed over the hundred pounds.

Freedom for Some

One path to freedom lay in manumission, the voluntary act of an owner releasing a slave from bondage. How many slaves in New York received manumission is anyone's guess. The number seems to have increased toward the end of the colonial period as the ideas of freedom, equality, and the rights of man were more frequently discussed. Probably the most common means of manumission was to include it in one's will. This bound the heirs to honor the stipulation, making it impossible for them to sell a person so freed.

Manumission was not always a simple matter. In many cases an owner had to post bond—a sum of money—against a former slave's becoming a public charge. Following the uprising in 1712, reflecting a fear of all blacks whether freed or slave, the New York assembly raised the manumission bond to two hundred pounds. This almost stopped manumission entirely and, following protests, in 1717 the assembly lowered the bond to a nominal figure.

Some slaves arranged with their masters to work during their spare time to earn money. They then saved their pay and eventually bought their freedom. How many, again, no one knows.

Freedom, whether through manumission or purchase, was not always a comfortable status. A black anywhere was always open to questioning. He or she had to be able to prove freed status. And instances of freed blacks being returned to slavery were not rare.

Slavery's Growth and Decline in Pennsylvania

The first shipload of slaves for Pennsylvania, 150 in all, landed at Philadelphia in 1684. Quakers and others eager for help in clearing trees and brush and erecting dwellings quickly purchased them. A trickle of slaves apparently continued to enter Philadelphia over the next few decades. The flow seems to have grown stronger after the import duty was reduced in 1729.

For many years, Philadelphians and other Pennsylvanians seem to have preferred indentured servants to slaves. This may have been because the supply was good— would-be indentured servants came in droves, especially between 1732 and 1754. The beginning of the French and Indian War brought change, however. There was less merchant shipping, and consequently less immigration. More important, the British drafted indentured servants into the army, perhaps as many as two thousand from Pennsylvania. This created a labor shortage and stimulated increased slave importation. During the 1740's and early 1750's, perhaps twenty to thirty slaves a year were brought in. But the number jumped to about a hundred in 1759, and in 1762 around five hundred arrived. Head tax lists in Philadelphia during the 1760's indicate that there were nearly a thousand black slaves in the city, and the lists include only those between twelve and fifty years of age. Adding those younger and older may have increased the total to fifteen hundred.

In Pennsylvania, as in other colonies, the fairly well-to-do owned most of the slaves. Twenty-eight of the 905 taxable slaves in Philadelphia in 1767 belonged to persons in the bottom quarter of the population with respect to wealth. Persons worth sixty pounds or more possessed nearly half the slaves. Benjamin Franklin, Joseph Galloway, and Edward Shippen were in this group. Artisans of all kinds, some farmers, and some ship owners held slaves too. Ship owners sometimes used slaves as sailors. A number of people rented slaves out by the day, month, or year.

As in New York, the killing of a slave in Pennsylvania was considered murder. But, according to a European observer in 1750,

Joseph Galloway.

There is not however an example here of a white man's having been executed on this account. A few years ago it happened that a master killed his slave; his friends and even the magistrates secretly advised him to leave the country, as otherwise they could not avoid taking him prisoner, and then he would be condemned to die according to the laws of the country, without any hopes of saving him. This lenity [lenience] was employed towards him, that the Negroes might not have the satisfaction of seeing a master executed for killing his slave; for this would lead them to all sorts of dangerous designs against their masters, and to value themselves too much.[37]

Beginning in the 1760's, the number of slaves in Pennsylvania declined. One reason was a virtual halt in the slave trade. This was due partly to a diminishing supply of slaves from Africa and partly to increases in the Pennsylvania import head tax. Another reason was the slaves' low birth rate or high infant mortality rate in the colony, or both, which created an excess of deaths over births. The low birth rate may have resulted from the fact that most slave holders owned only one adult slave. Few male and female slaves lived together or were able to associate with each other.

An Abolition Movement

Another reason for the decline of slavery in Pennsylvania was growing opposition to the institution. From the beginning, few Germans owned slaves, and this cut across religious lines—Quaker, Mennonite, Amish, and members of other sects. Dr. Benjamin Rush noted that the Germans, "as a general thing, [never] had colored servants or slaves."[38] Another observer pointed out that "slaves in Pennsylvania never were as numerous in proportion to the white population as in New York and New Jersey. To our German population this is certainly attributable—wherever they or their numerous descendants located they preferred *their own*

---

[37] Peter Kalm, "Travels into North America," in John Pinkerton, ed., *A General Collection of the Best and Most Interesting Voyages and Travels in All Parts of the World* (London: Longman, Hurst, Rees, Orme, and Brown, 1812), vol. 13, p. 501.

[38] Quoted in Edward Raymond Turner, *The Negro in Pennsylvania: Slavery—Servitude—Freedom, 1639-1861* (Washington, D.C.: American Historical Society, 1911), p. 68, fn. 13.

labor to that of Negro slaves."[39] Religious scruples aside, thrifty Germans considered slave labor too expensive. In 1724, there were 2,692 German taxpayers in Bucks County, representing 61% of the county's tax-paying population. Of this group, 44 held 62 slaves. Persons of other nationalities held 92. In York County, 27 Germans out of a total of 3,993 owned 44 slaves.

Quakers were another factor. From the beginning, a number of them owned slaves and some even engaged in the trade. Although this was directly contrary to Quaker sentiments about freedom and equality, those connected with slavery apparently learned to live with it. The first protest against the institution in Pennsylvania came from German Quakers in Germantown in 1688. At a monthly meeting that year, they drew up a document calling attention to the disparity between upholding freedom of conscience while denying blacks freedom of body. From their point of view, slavery and Quaker beliefs were simply not compatible.

George Keith, recognized earlier as the leader of a dissenting body of Quakers, also opposed slavery as contrary to Christian beliefs. And at a meeting of Friends in Philadelphia in 1693, the notion prevailed that one should purchase slaves only to free them. Another meeting three years later resolved to discourage further slave imports. Anti-slavery sentiment gradually grew stronger. At the yearly meeting in 1713, and at subsequent gatherings, Quakers were advised against participating in the slave trade or encouraging it by buying slaves. And it appears that after 1730 Quakers had abandoned activity in the trade.

John Woolman was the outstanding anti-slavery advocate of his time. Born in New Jersey in 1720, Woolman traced his American ancestry back to a John Woolman, a Quaker, who had come to the colonies from England in 1678. After some education in a village school and at home, the younger John Woolman became a teacher. Later he worked as a bookkeeper and clerk in a store, and still later he apprenticed himself to a tailor. But his great interest was religion, and in his late twenties Woolman became an itinerant preacher. A

[39] Quoted in ibid.

journey into Virginia in 1746 fanned the anti-slavery sentiment which had been smoldering within him. "I Saw in the
Southern Provinces," Woolman wrote,

> so many Vices and Corruptions, increased by this
> trade and this way of life, that it appeared to me as a
> dark gloominess hanging over the Land and though
> now many willingly run into it, yet in future the
> Consequence will be grievous to posterity. I express it
> as it hath appeared to me, not at once, nor twice, but
> as a matter fixed on my mind.[40]

Woolman's experience stimulated him to write an essay in
two parts, "Some Considerations on the Keeping of
Negroes." The first part appeared in 1746; he wrote the
second between 1754 and 1760. Woolman stated this
belief: "While we have no right to keep men as Servants
for Term of Life, but that of superior Power; to do this,
with Design by their Labour to profit ourselves and our
Families, I believe is wrong." He concluded, however,
that "I do not believe that all who have kept Slaves, have
therefore been chargeable with Guilt. If their Motives
thereto were free from Selfishness, and their Slaves
content, they were a Sort of Freemen; which I believe hath
sometimes been the Case."[41] Woolman was keenly per-
ceptive about slavery, placing his finger firmly on the root
of the institution and the legacy it would bequeath:

> Placing on Men the ignominious Title, SLAVE,
> dressing them in uncomely Garments, keeping them to
> servile Labour, in which they are often dirty, tends
> gradually to fix a Notion in the Mind, that they are a
> Sort of People below us in Nature, and leads us to
> consider them as such in all our Conclusions about
> them. And, moreover, a Person which in our Esteem is
> mean and contemptible, if their Language or
> Behaviour toward us is unseemly to disrespectful, it

[40]Amelia Mott Gummere, ed., *The Journal and Essays of John Woolman* (New York: Macmillan, 1922), p. 167.
    [41]Ibid., pp. 351–52.

excites Wrath more powerfully than the like Conduct
in one we accounted our Equal or Superior: and where
this happens to be the Case, it disqualifies for candid
Judgment; for it is unfit for a Person to sit as Judge in
a Case where his own personal Resentments are stirred
up; and, as Members of Society in a well framed
Government, we are mutually dependent. Present
Interest incites to Duty, and makes each Man attentive
to the Convenience of others: but he whose Will is a
Law to others, and can enforce Obedience by
Punishment; he whose Wants are supplied without
feeling any Obligation to make equal Returns to his
Benefactor, his irregular Appetites find an open Field
for Motion, and he is in Danger of growing hard, and
inattentive to their Convenience who labour for his
Support; and so loses that Disposition in which alone
Men are fit to govern. . . .

Through the Force of long Custom, it appears
needful to speak in Relation to Colour. Suppose a
white Child, born of Parents of the meanest Sort, who
died and left him an Infant, falls into the Hands of a
Person who endeavours to keep him a Slave, some
Men would account him an unjust Man in doing so,
who yet appear easy while many Black People, of
honest Lives and good Abilities, are enslaved in a
Manner more shocking than the Case here supposed.
This is owing chiefly to the Idea of Slavery being
connected with the Black Colour, and Liberty with the
White: and where false Ideas are twisted into our
Minds, it is with difficulty we get fairly disentangled.

. . . Selfishness being indulged, clouds the
Understanding; and where selfish Men, for a Long
Time, proceed on their Way without Opposition, the
Deceivableness of Unrighteousness gets so rooted in
their Intellects, that a candid Examination of Things
relating to Self-interest is prevented; and in this
Circumstance, some who would not agree to make a
Slave of a Person whose Colour is like their own,
appear easy in making Slaves of others of a different
Colour, though their Understandings and Morals are
equal to the Generality of Men of their own Colour.

The Colour of a Man avails nothing in Matters of
Right and Equity. Consider Colour in Relations to
Treaties; by such, Disputes betwixt Nations are
sometimes settled. And should the Father of us all so
dispose Things, that Treaties with black Men should
sometimes be necessary, how then would it appear
amongst the Princes and Ambassadors, to insist on the
Prerogative of the white Colour?

Whence is it that Men, who believe in a righteous
Omnipotent Being, to whom all Nations stand equally
related, and are equally accountable, remain so easy in
it; but for that the Idea of *Negroes* and Slaves are so
interwoven in the Mind, that they do not discuss this
Matter with that Candour and Freedom of Thought,
which the Case justly calls for?[42]

Anthony Benezet was another anti-slavery spokesman.
Born in 1713 into a Huguenot—French Protestant—family,
Benezet later joined the Society of Friends. He arrived in
Philadelphia in 1731 and became attracted to anti-slavery
sentiment about 1750. Benezet wrote frequently about
slavery and the slave trade, and he urged the institution's
abolition.

The work of Woolman, Benezet, and others who opposed
slavery undoubtedly influenced Pennsylvania Quakers. In
1754, Friends condemned the institution at their annual
meeting. They urged that their fellows who persisted in
owning slaves be denied membership in the Society. Four
years later the yearly meeting advised that all Quakers who
owned slaves should manumit them or leave the Society.
Woolman was appointed to visit Quaker slave holders to
try to persuade them.

Overall slave numbers in Pennsylvania gradually diminished. And in 1780 the assembly voted slavery's gradual
abolition. The end, however, did not come until the former
colony was well into statehood, owing to challenges to the
law and to the Pennsylvania constitution of 1790.

[42] Ibid., pp. 363, 366–67.

In New Jersey

New Jersey records contain few references to slavery in the seventeenth century. In one document of 1680, Colonel Richard Morris of Shrewsbury was said to have had sixty or more slaves working in his "mill and plantation."

Eighteenth-century records indicate that the English government encouraged the slave trade in New Jersey, as in other colonies. But at the same time, a 1714 New Jersey law laid a ten-pound import duty on slaves. The law, however, expired seven years later and the assembly apparently enacted no further legislation on the subject.

The Perth Amboy customs house reported no slave imports between 1698 and 1717, and only 115 between 1717 and 1726. This record implies an inaccurate picture of slavery in New Jersey. Census data of 1790 showed New Jersey with 11,423 slaves and 4,402 free blacks, out of a total population of 184,139. The proportion of slaves to total population in New Jersey then was the same as in New York, about 6%. New York possessed a population of 340,120, among which were 4,654 free blacks and 21,324 slaves.

Pennsylvania posted the best record at the time. It had a population of 434,373, which included 3,737 slaves and 6,537 free blacks. Records on Delaware are sketchy. One account dated in 1770 indicates 2,996 blacks there, and it is probably safe to assume that half of them, if not more than half, were slaves.

Schooling in New York and Pennsylvania

The Middle Colonies probably held more slaves than those in New England, but otherwise the slavery picture in the Middle Colonies was much the same as farther north. The schooling situation, however, was different. Unlike the New England colonies, those between were not noted for an emphasis on public education. There were schools, to be sure, but most of them were financed and operated by private means.

The Dutch established a dozen communities, and eleven of them had at least one school. These were sponsored and at first controlled by the Dutch West India Company, which also paid teachers' wages. The first school opened in 1638. During the final years of Dutch rule, Peter Stuyvesant tried to obtain more public support for the schools. But the leaders in each community refused to do more than provide a building for the school and a house for teacher. In 1650, when New Amsterdam had a population of about 4,000, the community held 7 schools. By 1689, when the population had reached 13,500, there were 11 schools in New York City.

"There is scarcely any one thing," William Penn wrote in 1679, "that so much needs the wisdom of the nation in the contrivance of a new law, as the 'education of our youth,' whether we consider the piety or prudence of our manners, the good life, or just policy of the government."[43] And in 1683 the Pennsylvania government required parents and guardians of children to "cause such to be instructed in reading and writing, so that they may be able to read the Scriptures and to write by the time they attain to twelve years of age."[44]

Little was done to establish public schools in Pennsylvania for several decades, though. Religious groups, Quakers included, offered the formal schooling that existed. This was especially the case among the Germans. They preferred private to public schooling. For one thing, the Pennsylvania Dutch were wary of all governmental activities. In addition, they wished to keep their culture as intact as possible. The curriculum in most German schools was limited. The rules and regulations of a school at Tulpehocken in 1744 were typical:

> The text book for the study of language [German] is the Primer and Reader issued by the University of Jena.
> Advanced readers are to use the Bible.
> Writing is to be taught.
> The reading of the same.
> As much arithmetic is to be taught as is.necessary for a Plantage Mann [farm manager].[45]

[43] Quoted in Lawrence A. Cremin, *American Education: The Colonial Experience, 1607–1783* (New York: Harper & Row, 1970), p. 306.

[44] Quoted in ibid., p. 125.

[45] Quoted in J. W. Early, "A Bit of Early School History," In *Proceedings of the Bucks County Historical Society* (Doylestown, Pa.: Bucks County Historical Society, 1898–1904), n.p.

The biggest educational controversy in colonial Pennsylvania centered on the Germans. As Pennsylvania Dutch
immigration continued and families grew, colonists of
English descent feared that Pennsylvania would become
predominantly German, to the disadvantage of the English-
speakers. Some wished to ban printing in German and the
importation of German books. Others wanted, in addition, a
law permitting only English-speaking colonists to vote.
Benjamin Franklin, a liberal on most issues, was one of those
concerned about German influence. And it was a minister
who wished to provide schooling for poor German children
who came up with a plan under which schools were
established for the main purpose of weaning Germans from
their un-English ways.

The Reverend Michael Schlatter, a Hollander who came
to Pennsylvania in 1746, proposed the establishment of
charity schools. He raised money for that purpose in the
Netherlands, and news of the scheme eventually crossed the
English Channel to London. There William Smith, soon to
become an Anglican minister, saw pro-English possibilities
in the plan. "By a common education of English and German
youth at the same schools," Smith wrote,

> acquaintances and connections will be formed, and
> deeply impressed upon them in their cheerful and open
> moments. The English language and a conformity of
> manners will be acquired, and they may be taught to
> feel the meaning and exult in the enjoyment of liberty,
> a home and social endearments. And when once these
> sacred names are understood and felt at the
> heart;—when once a few intermarriages are made
> between the chief families of the different nations in
> each country, which will naturally follow from school
> acquaintances, and the acquisition of a common
> language, no arts of our enemies will be able to divide
> them in their affection; and all the narrow distinctions
> of extraction, etc., will be forgot—forever forgot—in
> higher interests.[46]

---

[46]Quoted in Cremin, *American Education*, pp. 262–63.

Benjamin Franklin became a member of the board of trustees for the schools. He also contributed twenty-five pounds by deducting that amount from the price of a printing press the trustees purchased from him for the schools' use. Some schools opened early in 1755, and by 1759 eight were operating, all in such Pennsylvania Dutch communities as Lancaster, York, and Reading. More than four hundred pupils attended them.

The Pennsylvania Dutch were not enthusiastic. Christopher Saur, who published a German newspaper, was downright hostile. Saur saw the hand of Anglicans in the scheme, and he denounced the schools for trying to lure German children from their heritage. Saur was influential. By 1764 the schools, which at their peak attracted only about seven hundred pupils, were closed.

Besides supporting the establishment of charity schools, Benjamin Franklin figured in yet another educational effort. He believed in practical education. And in his *Proposals Relating to the Education of Youth in Pennsylvania,* published in 1749, Franklin suggested that pupils might be taught

> everything that is useful, and everything that is ornamental; but art is long, and their time is short. It is therefore proposed that they learn those things that are likely to be most useful and most ornamental, regard being had to the several professions for which they are intended.[47]

To carry out his ideas, Franklin persuaded about fifty men to contribute to the founding of an academy, and he became president of the board of trustees. The College, Academy, and Charitable School of Philadelphia began operating in January, 1751.

From Franklin's point of view, the school was a failure. It eventually emphasized classical studies, such as Latin, over more immediately useful subjects. Under the leadership of William Smith the school became, for its time, a kind of institution of higher learning. It offered languages, mathematics, sciences and, after 1765, medical training. It was the beginning of the University of Pennsylvania.

[47] Quoted in ibid., pp. 375–76.

The Middle Colonies had two other colleges. In New York, under the leadership of Samuel Johnson, a colleague of William Smith, King's College opened its doors in 1754. It offered the same curriculum as the College of Philadelphia, and introduced a medical course in 1767. King's College later became Columbia University. Presbyterians founded the third institution, the College of New Jersey, which went into operation in May, 1747. Located at first at Elizabethtown, the college moved to Princeton a decade later.

King's College in New York was established with funds raised through lotteries, beginning in 1746. Seventeen hundred dollars were raised that way in five years, and in 1754 the college opened its doors to eight students and one president-instructor.

SUGGESTED READINGS

Birmingham, Stephen. *The Grandees: The Story of America's Sephardic Elite.* Harper & Row.

Bridenbaugh, Carl. *Cities in Revolt: Urban Life in America, 1743–1776.* Oxford University Press, Galaxy Books.

Bridenbaugh, Carl. *Cities in the Wilderness: The First Century of Urban Life in America, 1625–1742.* Oxford University Press, Galaxy Books.

Bridenbaugh, Carl. *The Colonial Craftsman.* University of Chicago Press, Phoenix Books.

Illick, Joseph E. *Colonial Pennsylvania: A History.* Charles Scribner's Sons.

Lemon, James T. *The Best Poor Man's Country: A Geographic Survey of Early Southeastern Pennsylvania.* W.W. Norton.

Stroudt, John J. *Sunbonnets and Shoofly Pies: Pennsylvania Dutch Cultural History.* A.S. Barnes.

Woolman, John. *The Journal of John Woolman.* Seabury Press, Clarion Books.

A view of Philadelphia's Second Street, looking north from Market Street, with Christ Church in the foreground.

4

TRAVELER, TRADER,

MERCHANT, CHIEF

By the middle of the eighteenth century, the Atlantic seaboard had been solidly occupied. In some areas settlements extended more than a hundred miles inland. Each colony had its own legislature, each its own thriving economy. Only periodically did England pay the colonies as a whole much attention. A new nationality had developed, and a new nation was about to emerge.

One European visitor, a Swedish gentleman named Peter Kalm, was in a unique position to observe the colonies at mid-century. And the account he left of his travels is worth examining at some length.

Travels in the Middle Colonies

Peter Kalm was born in 1715 in the province of Angermanland, Sweden. He attended Abo Academy in Finland (then a part of Sweden) with the intention of becoming a minister. But he found zoology and botany more interesting, and at Uppsala University in Sweden he became the pupil of Carl von Linné—better known by the Latin version of his name, Linnaeus. Linnaeus was the foremost naturalist of the time, and under his guidance Kalm began a scientific career.

In 1745, Kalm was elected to the Swedish Royal Academy of Sciences. Two years later he became professor of agriculture at Abo. That same year, 1747, he was offered an opportunity to travel to America to make a scientific survey. He arrived in Philadelphia on September 15, 1748.

Kalm's major purpose was to observe, describe, and collect American plants and animals. But Kalm had a keen and far-roving eye, and his impressions of human society give an interesting picture of numerous aspects of eighteenth-century colonial life in America. About Philadelphia he wrote:

> The streets are regular, fine, and most of them are fifty foot, English measure, broad. Arch-street measures sixty-six feet in breadth, and Market-street, or the principal street where the market is kept, near a hundred. Those which run longitudinally, or from north to south are seven, exclusive of a little one, which runs along the river, to the south of the market, and is called Water-street. The lanes which go across, and were intended to reach from the Delaware to the Skulkill [Schuylkill], are eight in number. They do not go quite from east to west, but deviate a little from that direction. All the streets except two which are nearest to the river, run in a straight line, and make right angles at the intersections; some are paved, others are not, and it seems less necessary, since the ground is sandy, and therefore soon absorbs the wet. But in most of the streets is a pavement of flags [flagstones], a fathom or more broad, laid before the houses, and posts put on the outside three or four fathom asunder. Under the roofs are gutters which are carefully connected with pipes, and by this means, those who walk under them when it rains, or when the snow melts, need not fear being wet by the dropping from the roofs.
>
> The houses make a good appearance, are frequently several stories high, and built either of bricks or of stone; but the former are more commonly used, since bricks are made before the town, and are well burnt. The stone which has been employed in the building of other houses is a mixture of black or grey glimmer, running in undulated veins, and of a loose, and quite small grained limestone, which runs scattered between the bendings of the other veins, and are of a grey color, excepting here and there some single grains of sand of a paler hue. The glimmer makes the greatest part of the stone, but the mixture is sometimes of another kind. . . . This stone is now got in great quantities in the country, is easily cut,

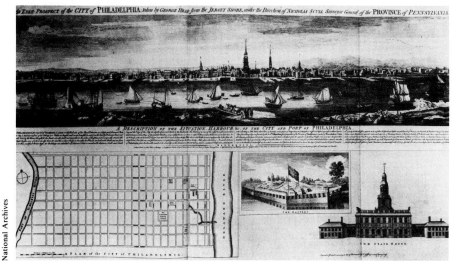

National Archives

This page from an old book shows, at the top, the harbor of Philadelphia as seen from the New Jersey shore. The State House (Independence Hall) is shown at the far right, and the Battery appears in the center insert. The city plan at the left shows how precisely the streets were laid out in checkerboard fashion, a design copied by many other American cities. Describing Philadelphia, Penn wrote, "Of all the many places I have seen in the world, I remember not one better seated."

and has the good quality of not attracting the moisture in a wet season. Very good lime is burnt every where hereabouts for masonry.

The houses are covered with shingles. The wood for this purpose is taken from ... a tree which Swedes here call the white juniper tree, and the English, the white cedar. Swamps and morasses formerly were full of them, but at present these trees are for the greatest part cut down, and no attempt has as yet been made to plant new ones. The wood is very light, rots less than any other in this country, and for that reason is exceeding good for roofs, for it is not too heavy for the walls, and will serve for forty to fifty years together.... Several people have already in late years begun to make roofs of tiles.[1]

[1]Peter Kalm, "Travels into North America," in John Pinkerton, ed., *A General Collection of the Best and Most Interesting Voyages and Travels in All Parts of the World* (London: Longman, Hurst, Rees, Orme, and Brown, 1812), vol. 13, pp. 387–88.

Brown Brothers

This Quaker meeting house, built around 1736, is typical of much of the architecture of eighteenth-century Philadelphia, with its shingle roof and stone walls.

Peter Kalm was struck by the number and variety of churches in Philadelphia, seeing them as an index to the city's religious mixture. Besides the two Friends' meeting houses, the city contained both an old and a new Presbyterian church, a German Lutheran church, and an Anglican church. In addition, there were churches to serve the Old German Reformed, the New Reformed, the Anabaptists, the Roman Catholics, the Swedish, and the Moravians. He went on:

Those of the English church, the New-lights, the Quakers, and the Germans of the reformed religion, have each of them their burying-places on one side out of town, and not near their churches, though the first of these sometimes make an exception. All the others bury their dead in their church-yards, and the Moravian Brethren bury where they can. The Negroes are buried in a particular place out of town. . . .

The town hall, or the place where the assemblies are held, is situated in the western part of the town; it is a fine large building, having a tower with a bell in the middle, and is the greatest ornament to the town. The deputies [assemblymen] of each province meet in it commonly every October, or even more frequently, if circumstances require it, in order to consider of the welfare of the country, and to hold their parliaments . . . in miniature. There they revise the old laws, and make new ones.

On one side of this building stands the library, which was first begun in the year 1742, on a public spirited plan, formed and put in execution by the learned Mr. Franklin; for he persuaded first the most substantial people in the town to pay forty shillings at the outset, and afterwards annually ten shillings, all in Pennsylvania currency, towards purchasing all kinds of useful books. The subscribers are entitled to make use of the books. Other people are likewise at liberty to borrow them for a certain time, but must leave a pledge [deposit], and pay eight pence a week for a folio volume, six pence for a quarto, and four pence for all others of a smaller size. As soon as the time allowed a person for the perusal of the volume is elapsed, it must be returned, or he is fined. The money arising in this manner is employed for the salary of the librarian, and for purchasing new books . . . The subscribers were so kind to me, as to order the librarian, during my stay here, to lend me every book which I should want, without requiring any payment. The library was open every Saturday from four to eight o'clock in the afternoon. Besides the books, several mathematical and physical instruments, and a large collection of natural curiosities, were to be seen in it. Several little libraries were founded in the town on the same footing or nearly with this.

The courthouse stands in the middle of Market-street, to the west of the market; it is a fine building, with a little tower in which there is a bell. Below and round about this building the market is properly kept every week.

The building of the academy is in the western part of the town. . . . The youths are here only taught

those things which they learn in our common schools;
but in time, such lectures are intended to be read
here as are usual in real universities.

At the close of the last war [King George's], a
redoubt [fort] was erected here, on the south side of
the town, near the river, to prevent the French and
Spanish privateers from landing. But this was done
after a very strong debate. For the Quakers opposed
all fortifications, as contrary to the tenets of their
religion, which allow not Christians to make war,
either offensive or defensive, but direct them to place
their trust in the Almighty alone. Several papers
were then handed about for and against the opinion.
But the enemy's privateers having taken several
vessels belonging to the town, in the river, many
of the Quakers, if not all of them, found it reasonable
to forward the building of the fortification as much
as possible, at least by a supply of money.[2]

Philadelphia, Kalm noted, thrived on coastal and international trade. The city's trade, he wrote, "may be compre-
hended from the number of ships which annually arrive at
and sail from this town. . . . The ships coming and going in
one year, are to be reckoned from the twenty-fifth of March
of that year to the twenty-fifth of March of the next":

The Year	Ships arrived	Ships sailed
1735	199	212
1740	307	208
1741	292	309
1744	229	271
1745	280	301
1746	273	293

The town not only furnishes most of the
inhabitants of Pensylvania with the goods which they
want, but numbers of the inhabitants of New Jersey
come every day and carry on a great trade.

[2] Ibid., p. 391.

The town has two great fairs every year; one in
May, and the other in November, both on the
sixteenth days of those two months. But besides
these fairs, there are every week two market days,
viz. Wednesday and Saturday. On those days the
country people in Pensylvania and New Jersey bring
to town a quantity of victuals, and other productions
of the country, and this is a great advantage to the
town. . . . You are sure to meet with every produce
of the season, which the country affords, on the
market-days. But on other days they are in vain
sought for. . . .

I have not been able to find the exact number of
the inhabitants of Philadelphia. In the year 1746,
they were reckoned above ten thousand, and since
that time their number is incredibly increased. Neither
can it be made out from the bills of mortality
[records of deaths], since they are not kept regularly
in all the churches. . . .

From these bills of mortality it also appears, that
the diseases which are the most fatal, are
consumptions, fevers, convulsions, pleurisies,
haemorrhages, and dropsies.

The number of those that are born cannot be
determined, since in many churches no order is
observed with regard to this affair. The Quakers, who
are the most numerous in this town, never baptize
their children, though they take a pretty exact account
of all who are born among them.

It is likewise impossible to guess at the number
of inhabitants from the dead, because the town gets
such great supplies annually from other countries.
In the summer of the year 1749, near twelve
thousand Germans came over to Philadelphia, many
of whom staid in that town. In the same year, the
houses in Philadelphia were counted, and found to
be two thousand and twenty-six in number.

The town is now quite filled with inhabitants,
which in regard to their country, religion, and trade,
are very different from each other. You meet with
excellent masters in all trades, and many things are

made here full as well as in England. Yet no manufactures, especially for making fine cloth, are established. Perhaps the reason is, that it can be got with so little difficulty from England, and that the breed of sheep which is brought over, degenerates in process of time, and affords but a coarse wool.

Here is great plenty of provisions, and their prices are very moderate. There are no examples of an extraordinary dearth [shortage].

Every one who acknowledges God to be the creator, preserver, and ruler of all things, and teaches or undertakes nothing against the state, or against the common peace, is at liberty to settle, stay, and carry on his trade here, be his religious principles ever so strange. No one is here molested on account of the erroneous principles of the doctrine which he follows, if he does not exceed the above-mentioned bounds. And he is so well secured by the laws in his person and property, and enjoys such liberties, that a citizen of Philadelphia may in a manner be said to live in his house like a king.

On a careful consideration of what I have already said, it will be easy to conceive how this city should rise so suddenly from nothing, into such grandeur and perfection, without supposing any powerful monarch's contributing to it, either by punishing the wicked, or by giving great supplies in money; and yet its fine appearance, good regulations, agreeable situation, natural advantages, trade, riches and power, are by no means inferior to those of any, even of the most ancient towns in Europe. It has not been necessary to force people to come and settle here; on the contrary, foreigners of different languages have left their country, houses, property, and relations, and ventured over wide and stormy seas, in order to come hither. Other countries, which have been peopled for a long space of time, complain of the small number of their inhabitants. But Pensylvania, which was no better than a desart in the year 1681, and hardly contained five hundred people [excluding Indians], now vies with several kingdoms in Europe in number of inhabitants. It has received numbers of people, which other countries to their infinite loss, have either neglected or expelled.[3]

The Swedish visitor was equally impressed with the Pennsylvania countryside:

A log house built during the colonial period in Lancaster County, Pennsylvania.

> As we went on in the wood, we continually saw, at moderate distances, little fields which had been cleared of the wood. Each of these was a farm. These farms were commonly very pretty, and a walk of trees frequently led from them to the high-road. The houses were all built of brick, or of the stone which is here commonly met with. Every countryman, even though he were the poorest peasant, had an orchard with apples, peaches, chestnuts, walnuts, cherries, quinces, and such fruits, and sometimes we saw the vines climbing along them. The vallies were frequently provided with little brooks that contained a crystal stream. The corn [wheat] on the sides of the road, was almost all mown, and no other grain besides maize and buckwheat was standing. The former was to be met with near each farm, in greater or lesser quantities; it grew very well and to a great length, the stalks being from six to ten feet high, and covered with fine green leaves. Buckwheat likewise was not very uncommon, and in some places the people were beginning to reap it. . . .

A half-timbered house—wooden beams with plaster in between—built in Lancaster County during colonial times. Half-timbering was a common style of building among the county's German settlers.

After a ride of six English miles, we came to Germantown; this town has only one street, but is near two English miles long. It is for the greatest part inhabited by Germans, who from time to time come from their country to North America, and settle here, because they enjoy such privileges, as they are not possessed of any where else. Most of the inhabitants are manufacturers, and make almost every thing in such quantity and perfection, that

---

[3] Ibid., pp. 394–97.

in a short time this province will want very little
from England, its mother country. Most of the
houses were built of the stone which is mixed with
glimmer, and found every where towards Philadelphia,
but is more scarce further on. Several houses
however were made of brick. They were commonly
two stories high, and sometimes higher. . . .

Many of the roofs were made in such a manner
that they could be walked upon, having a balustrade
round them. Many of the upper stories had balconies
before them, from whence the people had a prospect
into the street. The windows, even those in the
third story, had shutters. Each house had a fine
garden. The town had three churches, one for the
Lutherans, another for the Reformed Protestants, and
the third for the Quakers. The inhabitants were so
numerous, that the street was always full. The
Baptists have likewise a meeting house.[4]

Kalm later visited Wilmington, Delaware, "a little town,
about thirty English miles southwest from Philadelphia."

It was founded in the year 1733. Part of it stands
upon the grounds belonging to the Swedish church,
which annually receives certain rents, out of which
they pay the minister's salary, and employ the rest
for other uses. The houses are built of stone, and
look very pretty; yet they are not built close
together, but large open places are left between them.
The Quakers have a meeting-house in this town.
The Swedish church . . . is half a mile out of
town eastwards. The parsonage is under the same roof
with the church. A little river called Christina-kill
passes by the town, and from thence falls into
the Delaware. By following its banks, one goes
three miles before one reaches the Delaware. The
river is said to be sufficiently deep, so that the
greatest vessel may come quite up to the town;
for at its mouth or juncture with the Delaware it

4Ibid., p. 406.

This large Quaker meeting house was similar to the dwellings
described by Peter Kalm in his account of travels through the
Pennsylvania countryside. It had three stories and a balcony wide
enough to be walked upon. The porch, which became a common
feature of later colonial homes, was introduced by the colonists and
may have evolved from the stoops of the Dutch houses in New
Netherland.

is shallowest, and yet its depth even there, when
the water is lowest, is from two fathoms to two
and a half. But as you go higher, its depth
encreases to three, three and a half, and even four
fathoms. The largest ships therefore may safely,
and with their full cargoes, come to and from the
town with the tide. From Wilmington you have a
fine prospect of a great part of the river Delaware,
and the ships sailing on it. On both sides of the
river Christina-kill, almost from the place where
the redoubt is built to its juncture with the Delaware,
are low meadows, which afford a great quantity of
hay to the inhabitants. The town carries on a
considerable trade, and would have been more
enlarged if Philadelphia and Newcastle, which are
both towns of a more ancient date, were no so near
on both sides of it.[5]

[5] Ibid., pp. 427–28.

National Archives

The road from Philadelphia to New York in 1766. Roads during colonial times were primitive by any standards, and rivers served as the main routes for transporting goods. Travel by stagecoach became an adventure: the roads were dusty and dry in the summer and fall and almost impassable because of mud or snow in the winter and spring. Large streams had to be forded; there were numerous mud-holes and wash-outs. By 1756 there was a through stage between Philadelphia and New York, a journey that took three days, traveling eighteen hours a day.

After returning to Philadelphia, Kalm set out on a journey to New York.

About noon we arrived at New Brunswick, a pretty little town in the province of New Jersey, in a valley on the west side of the river Rareton; on account of its low situation it cannot be seen (coming from Pensylvania) before you get to the top of the hill, which is quite close up to it: the town extends north and south along the river.

... One of the streets it almost entirely inhabited by Dutchmen, who came hither from Albany, and for that reason they call it Albany-street. These Dutch only keep company among themselves, and seldom or ever go amongst the other inhabitants, living as it were quite separate from them. New Brunswick

belongs to New Jersey; however the greatest part,
or rather all its trade is to New York, which
is about forty English miles distant; to that place
they send corn, flour in great quantities, bread,
several other necessaries, a great quantity of linseed,
boards, timber, wooden vessels, and all sorts of
carpenter's work. Several small yachts are every
day going backwards and forwards between these
two towns. The inhabitants likewise get a considerable
profit from the travelers who every hour pass through
on the high road. . . .

  Elizabeth-town is a small town, about twenty
English miles distant from New Brunswick: we arrived
there immediately after sun setting. Its houses are
mostly scattered, but well built, and generally of
boards, with a roof of shingles, and walls covered
with the same. There were likewise some stone
buildings. . . .[6]

  From Elizabethtown, Peter Kalm took a ferry over to
Staten Island, then another ferry to Manhattan. Oysters
caught his attention first.

  The merchants here buy up great quantities of
oysters about this time, pickle them . . . and send
them to the West Indies: by which they frequently
make a considerable profit: for the oysters which
cost them five shillings of their currency, they
commonly sell for a pistole, or about six times as
much as they gave for them; and sometimes they
get even more: the oysters which are thus pickled
have a very fine flavor. . . .

  It is likewise a common rule here, that oysters
are best in those months, which have an *r* in their
name, such as September, October, &c.; but that they
are not so good in other months; however there
are poor people who live all the year long upon
nothing but oysters with bread.[7]

6 Ibid., pp. 450–51.
7 Ibid., p. 453.

National Archives

This colonial tavern, the Indian Queen, was a regular stop for stagecoaches. Because of the delays, difficulties, and discomforts of coach travel, numerous taverns along the way were not only necessary but welcome breaks in the long, jolting journey.

In describing the city of New York, Kalm noted that the streets "do not run so straight as those of Philadelphia, and have sometimes considerable bendings: however they are very spacious and well-built, and most of them are paved, except in high places, where it has been found useless."

In the chief streets there are trees planted, which in summer gave them a fine appearance, and during the excessive heat at that time, afford a cooling shade: I found it extremely pleasant to walk in the town, for it seemed quite like a garden. . . .

Most of the houses are built of bricks, and are generally strong and neat, and several stories high. Some had, according to the old architecture, turned the gable-end towards the streets; but the new houses were altered in this respect. Many of the houses had a balcony on the roof, on which the people used to sit in the evenings in the summer season; and from thence they had a pleasant view of a great part of the town, and likewise of part of the adjacent water, and of the opposite shore.[8]

[8] Ibid., p. 456.

New York, like Philadelphia, was known for its religious diversity. Kalm noted two Dutch Reformed churches, an Anglican church, a Presbyterian church, a German Lutheran church, a German Reformed church, a French Protestant church, a Quaker meeting house, and a Jewish synagogue.

The intense commercial life of the city interested Kalm especially. He remarked on the excellence of the port of New York and the year-round open water. "New York," he wrote,

The North Dutch Church on Fulton Street, New York.

probably carries on a more extensive commerce than any town in the English North American provinces; at least it may be said to equal them: Boston and Philadelphia however come very near up to it. The trade of New York extends to many places; and it is said they send more ships from thence to London than they do from Philadelphia. They export to that capital all the various sorts of skins which they buy of the Indians, sugar, logwood, and other dying woods, rum, mahogany, and many other goods which are the produce of the West Indies; together with all the specie [coin] which they get in the course of trade. Every year they build several ships here, which are sent to London, and there sold; and of late years they have shipped a quantity of iron to England. In return for these, they import from London stuffs [cloth], and every other article of English growth or manufacture, together with all sorts of foreign goods. England, and especially London, profits immensely by its trade with the American colonies; for not only New York, but likewise all the other English towns on the continent, import so many articles from England, that all their specie, together with the goods which they get in other countries, must altogether go to Old England, in order to pay the amount, to which they are however insufficient. From hence it appears how much a well-regulated colony contributes to the increase and welfare of its mother country.

New York sends many ships to the West Indies, with flour, corn, biscuit, timber, tuns [barrels], boards, flesh [meat], fish, butter, and other

Franklin Delano Roosevelt Library

Fulton Street in Brooklyn, New York, 1746, is seen in this engraving by Charles B. Hall.

provisions; together with some of the few fruits
that grow here. Many ships go to Boston in New
England, with corn and flour; and take in exchange,
flesh, butter, timber, different sorts of fish, and
other articles, which they carry further to the West
Indies. They now and then take rum from thence,
which is distilled there in great quantities, and sell
it here with a considerable advantage. Sometimes they
send yachts with goods from New York to
Philadelphia, and at other times yachts are sent from
Philadelphia to New York, which is only done, as
appears from the gazettes, because certain articles
are cheaper at one place than at the other. They
send ships to Ireland every year, laden with all kinds
of West India goods, but especially with linseed,
which is reaped in this province. . . .

Most of the wine, which is drunk here and in the
other colonies, is brought from the isle of Madeira,
and is very strong and fiery.

No manufactures of note have as yet been
established here; at present they get all
manufactured goods, such as woollen and linen cloth,

&c. from England, and especially from London. . . .

I cannot make a just estimate of the ships that annually come to this town or sail from it. But I have found, by the Pensylvania gazettes, that from the first of December in 1729, to the fifth of December in the next year, two hundred and eleven ships entered the port of New York, and two hundred and twenty-two cleared it; and since that time there has been a great increase of trade here. . . .

City Hall on Wall Street in New York, about 1700.

An assembly of deputies, from all the particular districts of the province of New York, is held at New York once or twice every year. . . .

At the above assembly the old laws are reviewed and amended, and new ones are made; and the regulation and circulation of coin, together with all other affairs of that kind, are there determined. For it is to be observed, that each English colony in North America is independent of the other, and that each has its proper laws and coin, and may be looked upon in several lights as a state by itself. . . .[9]

After a return to Philadelphia, Kalm soon journeyed once again into New Jersey, visiting a community he called Raccoon (it was probably Rancocas) which was made up mainly of Swedes. There he made a keen observation concerning the size of colonial families:

It does not seem difficult to find out the reasons why the people multiply more here than in Europe. As soon as a person is old enough, he may marry in these provinces, without any fear of poverty; for there is such a tract of good ground yet uncultivated, that a new-married man can, without difficulty, get a spot of ground, where he may sufficiently subsist with his wife and children. The taxes are very low, and he need not be under any concern on their account. The liberties he enjoys are so great, that he considers himself as a prince in his possessions.[10]

[9] Ibid., pp. 458–60.
[10] Ibid., p. 504.

Leaving Philadelphia once again, Kalm moved north to Albany, then to Niagara, and finally into Canada. He described Albany as a town in which the houses "are very neat, and partly built of stones covered with shingles of the white pine. Some are slated with tiles from Holland, because the clay of this neighborhood is not reckoned fit for tiles."[11] He noted that most of the people were of Dutch descent, and that merchants were the kingpins of Albany society. And he observed certain differences between the Dutch of Albany and the English residents of other towns:

> The inhabitants of Albany are much more sparing than the English. The meat which is served up is often insufficient to satisfy the stomach, and the [punch] bowl does not circulate so freely as among the English. The women are perfectly well acquainted with economy; they rise early, go to sleep very late, and are almost over-nice and cleanly in regard to the floor, which is frequently scoured several times in the week. The servants in the town are chiefly Negroes. Some of the inhabitants wear their own hair, but it is very short, without a bag or queue, which are looked upon as the characteristics of Frenchmen; and as I wore my hair in a bag the first day I came here . . . I was surrounded with children, who called me Frenchman, and some of the boldest offered to pull at my French dress.
>
> Their meat, and manner of dressing it, is very different from that of the English. Their breakfast is tea, commonly without milk. About thirty or forty years ago, tea was unknown to them, and they breakfasted either upon bread and butter, or bread and milk. They never put sugar into the cup, but take a small bit of it into their mouths while they drink. Along with the tea they eat bread and butter, with slices of hung beef. Coffee is not usual here; they breakfast generally about seven. Their dinner is butter-milk and bread, to which they sometimes add sugar, then it is a delicious dish for them; or fresh milk and bread; or boiled or

A colonial woman churning butter.

[11] Ibid., p. 584.

roasted flesh. They sometimes make use of butter-milk
instead of fresh milk, to boil a thin kind of porridge
with, which tastes very sour, but not disagreeable
in hot weather. To each dinner they have a great
salad, prepared with abundance of vinegar, and very
little or no oil. They frequently eat butter-milk,
bread, and salad, one mouthful after another. Their
supper is generally bread and butter, and milk and
bread. They sometimes eat cheese at breakfast and
at dinner; it is not in slices, but scraped or
rasped, so as to resemble coarse flour, which they
pretend adds to the good taste of cheese. They
commonly drink very small beer, or pure water.[12]

With reference to the Indians, or "old Americans" as he
called them, Kalm made this observation while in eastern
Pennsylvania and New Jersey:

For this account may perhaps meet with readers, who,
like many people of my acquaintance, may be of
opinion that all North America was almost wholly
inhabited by savage or heathen nations, and they
may be astonished that I do not mention them
more frequently in my account. Others may perhaps
imagine, that when I mention in my journal that
the country is much cultivated, that in several places
houses of stone or wood are built, round which
are corn-fields, gardens, and orchards, that I am
speaking of the property of the Indians; to
undeceive them, I here give the following
[explanation]. The country, especially all along the
coasts, in the English colonies, is inhabited by
Europeans, who in some places are already so
numerous that few parts of Europe are more
populous. The Indians have sold the country to the
Europeans, and have retired further up: in most
parts you may travel twenty Swedish miles, or about
a hundred and twenty English miles from the sea-shore
before you reach the first habitations of the Indians:
and it is very possible for a person to have been
at Philadelphia and other towns on the seashore

[12]Ibid., pp. 587–88.

for half a year together without so much as seeing an Indian. . . .[13]

Peter Kalm was mostly right. In eastern Pennsylvania only a few pockets of Indians remained. A remnant of Delaware occupied one of them.

Teedyuscung, Delaware King

An Indian of western Pennsylvania in the 1700's.

Before the Europeans arrived, perhaps eight thousand Delaware Indians resided in southern New York, eastern Pennsylvania, and western New Jersey. They lived in villages, depending on agriculture, hunting and fishing, and gathering.

The Europeans named these Indians after the Delaware River, which in turn derived its name from Thomas West, Lord De La Warr, governor of the Jamestown settlement in Virginia in 1610–1611. But the members of the tribe called themselves Lenni Lenape, a name that meant the "real people" or "original people," as did the names of some other tribes. The group's first contacts with Europeans came early in the seventeenth century and were probably with Dutch fur traders.

Teedyuscung himself was born about 1700, somewhat to the east of the settlement of Trenton. By then the Delaware of New Jersey had had nearly a century of contact with whites, and their traditional ways had all but vanished. They had come to depend on trade with whites for such essentials as clothing, blankets, hatchets, hoes, and kettles, for which they exchanged furs. The Delaware still planted corn, and other vegetables like squash and beans, but game was scarcer now. And such white diseases as smallpox had reduced the tribe's numbers considerably. Teedyuscung mastered English, although he never learned to read. To earn a living, he learned the craft of making baskets and brooms, selling his wares to whites. Those whites with whom he associated called him Honest John. Teedyuscung also learned to like rum and brandy.

For the New Jersey Delaware, life among whites became increasingly uncomfortable. About 1730 a band of them, Teedyuscung included, crossed the Delaware River to an

[13] Ibid., p. 449.

area in eastern Pennsylvania along the Lehigh River. Here, so far, no whites had come. The Indians more or less returned to a traditional way of life among the other Delaware who occupied the Lehigh River region.

Part of the area where the New Jersey Delaware settled was near the Forks—the area that became involved in the Walking Purchase of 1737. White settlement of the region soon began in earnest.

Throughout his life, Teedyuscung had been caught between his own and a foreign culture. As the region of the Forks filled with settlers, he decided in the late 1740's to throw in his lot with the whites. He moved to the town of Gnadenhutten, just north of present-day Bethlehem, to be a convert to Christianity. Teedyuscung became a Moravian.

The Moravians were a German Protestant sect, having broken with Roman Catholicism in 1467, before the time of Martin Luther. Persecution in Europe later drove many of them to America, and they found the religious climate of Pennsylvania congenial. To some extent the Moravians' beliefs were like those of the Quakers, and in Pennsylvania they lived a communal life. They were also earnest missionaries to the Indians. Upon baptizing Teedyuscung, Moravian missionaries renamed him Gideon. His wife also received baptism and a new name, Elisabeth.

Before long, however, the cloak of Christianity began to itch. In 1754 Teedyuscung left Gnadenhutten and the Moravians to heed a call from the Iroquois to settle with the other Delaware in the Wyoming Valley, along the north branch of the Susquehanna River.

The Wyoming Valley, where it was said that grass grew tall enough to hide a man on horseback, seemed a paradise. It was an area crucial to the Iroquois, for whoever commanded the valley also commanded movement toward their lands in New York. The Iroquois had learned of the formation of the Susquehanna Company in Connecticut, a group which planned to purchase land in the valley and send settlers there. The Iroquois hoped to prevent this by filling the valley with Delaware, over whom they exercised control.

In 1754, with war brewing between the French and English, the Albany Congress met to discuss intercolonial defense measures. Teedyuscung attended along with a delegation of Indians from the Wyoming Valley. He played no significant role there. At about the same time, some members of the Iroquois group sold land along the Susquehanna River to the Susquehanna Company. This act would later open the door to white settlement, even though the Iroquois Confederacy disallowed the sale.

Teedyuscung's presence at the Albany Congress suggests that he expected to maintain his friendship with the English colonists. Yet nothing came from Philadelphia—no communication, no guns or other supplies. And as far as he could tell from news gathered here and there, the French were winning the battles. A number of Delaware along the Susquehanna moved west to join fellow tribesmen and the French. The group remaining in the Wyoming Valley sent a message to Philadelphia: "We pray Brother Onas [an Indian term for the Pennsylvania government] & the people of Pennsylvania not to leave us in the lurch, but to supply us with necessaries to enable us to fight the French."[14] But the assembly was involved in a bitter quarrel over defense and who should pay for it. It gave no attention to the Delaware of the Wyoming Valley. Instead those Indians learned, in a roundabout way, that they had been accused of murdering settlers and that Pennsylvanians were planning to march on them.

In the meantime, in November, 1755, a band of pro-French Munsee Indians attacked the Moravian settlement of Gnadenhutten, killing ten whites. Other raids by pro-French Indians west of the Wyoming region resulted in about fifty deaths and the taking of more than a dozen white prisoners.

A Frenchman with a group of Indians in the Wyoming Valley.

Still the Wyoming Indians heard nothing from Philadelphia. Finally, growing increasingly edgy, and encouraged by some Seneca who had gone over to the French, they went on the warpath themselves. Led by Teedyuscung, the Delaware raided isolated farms north of the Kittatinny Mountains, killing several settlers and carrying others off. The band then retired north to the Indian village of Tioga, along the New York border, to spend the winter.

[14] Quoted in Anthony F. C. Wallace, *King of the Delawares: Teedyuscung, 1700–1763* (Philadelphia: University of Pennsylvania Press, 1949), p. 69.

Until this time Teedyuscung had not stood high in tribal affairs. Now, suddenly, he had demonstrated skill in leading a war party and ability as a warrior. He had achieved the status of sachem, and thereafter he would be a leading spokesman for the eastern Pennsylvania Delaware in dealings with the whites. Teedyuscung led no more war parties, but he directed others. In fact, the two hundred or so Delaware Indians on the Susquehanna, along with the seven hundred who had moved to Ohio, accounted for the deaths of some two hundred settlers in Pennsylvania during the winter of 1755–1756. Hardly an Indian village was without its white scalps and prisoners.

Pennsylvania declared war on the Delaware in 1756. The Iroquois, as allies of the English, then moved to quiet the Delaware and re-establish peace. Teedyuscung finally agreed to meet, pleased that the whites and the Iroquois regarded him highly as a Delaware leader. Grossly inflating his importance, he now considered himself the king of ten nations, the Iroquois included. He so presented himself at peace talks at Easton, near the Forks of the Delaware River. That Teedyuscung had such a following, especially among the Iroquois, was not true. But the whites were impressed with him and eager to halt the killings.

Teedyuscung and his band met with Pennsylvania representatives again at Easton late in 1756. Here Quakers interfered. Wishing to embarrass the government, and especially the Penn family, Quakers persuaded Teedyuscung to bring up the Walking Purchase of 1737. He was to label it a fraud, and Quakers convinced him that he should make a redress of grievances over the purchase a condition of peace. Fraudulent the purchase may have been, but it was far in the past and many things had changed. Bringing up the issue simply sent the treaty proceedings into an uproar. No permanent peace was made at that time, although the turmoil at Easton finally quieted. Pennsylvanians sent Teedyuscung and his Delaware off with about four hundred pounds worth of trade goods as gifts.

In the summer of 1757 Teedyuscung and his people met with whites once more at Easton. Again Teedyuscung dwelled on the Walking Purchase, and some of his followers finally rebelled. "Why did you bring us down?" one of them demanded.

National Archives

The aftermath of an Indian attack on a frontier settlement is depicted in this painting.

We thought we came down to make Peace with our Brethren the English, but you continue to quarrel about the Land affair which is Dirt, a Dispute we did not hear of till now. I desire you to enter upon the Business we came down for, which is Peace. We have been here these Twenty Days, and have heard nothing but scolding and disputing about Lands. Settle the Peace, and let all these Disputes stand till after.[15]

Realizing that he was in danger of losing his influence, Teedyuscung abruptly dropped the subject of the Walking Purchase. A treaty was drafted, and a great banquet was held. Trade was to be reopened with the Delaware, who badly needed the goods it would bring them.

In the spring of 1758, Teedyuscung helped make peace between the Pennsylvanians and the Ohio Delaware. This further increased his stature, although his leadership was probably not the deciding factor. At the time the war was

[15]Quoted in ibid., pp. 158–59.

beginning to swing against the French, and they had less than ever to offer their Indian allies.

Teedyuscung's life after that was mostly downhill. A classic example of an Indian caught between two cultures, Teedyuscung seems to have admired whites. He wished to be like them. This proved impossible—and the more he tried, the more influence he lost with his own people. Teedyuscung persuaded Pennsylvania authorities to build ten or twelve cabins in the Wyoming Valley as the nucleus of a Delaware town, or reservation. The Iroquois objected to his direct dealings with whites. They considered both the valley and the Delaware to be under their jurisdiction. Teedyuscung finally had to reaffirm that the Delaware were subject to the Iroquois—that the Iroquois were their "uncles"—in order to remain in his town.

But the Susquehanna Company was the greater threat. In September, 1762, more than a hundred settlers from Connecticut arrived in the Wyoming Valley. They brought livestock and seed grain with them, and they proceeded to erect blockhouses and cabins. An Iroquois delegation warned the settlers out, but within a few weeks Connecticut parties were back in even larger force. Teedyuscung did not know what to do. The Pennsylvania government took no action, relying on the government in England to halt the movement of people from Connecticut.

On the night of April 19, 1763, Teedyuscung burned to death in his cabin in his town in the Wyoming Valley. Almost at the same time, twenty surrounding cabins burst into flame. The survivors fled in terror. And newcoming families from Connecticut found the valley deserted of Indians. No one knew who had touched off the fires in Teedyuscung's town, or who might have caused them to be set.

One of Teedyuscung's sons, known as Captain Bull, thought he knew. He led a band of Delaware in revenge. The Indians massacred the Connecticut settlers in the valley. And before their capture, Captain Bull and his band killed more than fifty additional whites.

More Connecticut settlers came to the Wyoming Valley. In 1772, the last of the Delaware anywhere along the Susquehanna River were forced to move.

National Archives

Settlers in the trans-Appalachian region often built blockhouses as protection from Indian attack. As can be seen from the restored building in the photograph, the blockhouse was easily defensible, with its heavy timbers, it walls pierced with rifle slits, its projecting upper story, and its small, stoutly shuttered windows.

Trader, Diplomat, and Speculator

George Croghan knew Teedyuscung. As an Indian agent in Pennsylvania, Croghan was acquainted with hundreds of Indians and had many dealings with them.

No one knows when Croghan was born. Famine in Ireland appears to have driven him to America in 1741, when he was a young man. He soon became engaged in the Indian trade on the western Pennsylvania frontier.

Croghan probably learned the trade from Peter Tostee, who obtained his goods from the Philadelphia merchant, Edward Shippen. Croghan's first move into Indian country beyond the Allegheny Mountains seems to have been in the summer of 1742. The following year he was in business for himself, and he had purchased a plot of land in the settlement of Lancaster. In the winter of 1744–1745, Croghan traded for furs in the area of present-day Cleveland.

King George's War temporarily interrupted his trading activities. In the spring of 1745 he lost the entire season's gain—including forty-eight horseloads of deer skins and four hundred pounds of beaver pelts—to a band of Shawnee led by Frenchmen. Croghan survived, however, and he was able to add to his land holdings. He purchased several hundred acres along the Susquehanna near Harrisburg.

Despite the war and his loss, Croghan prospered in the trade. One of his thriving stations was at the forks of the Allegheny and Monongahela rivers, where Fort Duquesne was later built. He was so well respected among the Onondaga that they confirmed his title to two hundred thousand acres of land in that vicinity. His relations with such Ohio tribes as the Miami, Twightwee, and Wyandot were equally good. Croghan's activities in the Ohio country helped establish and maintain direct English contacts with these and other Indians. The Pennsylvania council called him "the most considerable Indian trader." The French felt differently. Wrote Sir William Johnson, Indian agent in New York:

> The French at De Troit and thereabouts have offered
> and given some Indians great presents to go and
> take or destroy one Mr. Croghan and Lawry, two
> of the chief men who trade from Pennsylvania, and
> have the most influence on all Indians living
> thereabouts of any that ever went among them, or in
> all likelihood ever may.[16]

Croghan possessed what some considered shortcomings. He drank too much. He liked to dress richly and live the good life. He tended to be overly optimistic, and he was not at all cautious about running up debts to obtain trade goods or to buy land. Frequently he contracted new debts to pay off old ones.

---

[16]Quoted in Nicholas B. Wainwright, *George Croghan, Wilderness Diplomat* (Chapel Hill: University of North Carolina Press, 1959), p. 36.

Library of Congress

Major George Croghan.

In 1751 Indian goods were in surplus and so were furs, bringing low prices on the London market. Croghan was in well over his head and his creditors demanded payment. He had to sell his household furnishings, his four black slaves, and his stock of trade goods to get by. But he still owned land, and western Indians owed him pelts for various favors. Croghan remained optimistic, but he took the precaution of disappearing into Indian country for a time.

Croghan later entered the service of Virginia and became one of Washington's advisers on Indian affairs at Fort Necessity. But Croghan failed to fulfill his rash promise to Virginia's governor, Robert Dinwiddie, that he would deliver flour to Washington and his men. Moreover, he proved unable to win the Shawnee and other Indians to the English side. As the French and Indian War came on, the tide in the west was running too strongly in favor of the French. And for his failure with the flour and the Shawnee, Croghan was blamed in part for the debacle at Fort Necessity which forced Washington's surrender there. But Croghan suffered too as the war crippled his trading activity. He lost about sixteen thousand pounds' worth of trade goods to the Indians and the French, and several of his employees were killed or captured.

George Croghan spent the remainder of 1754 at the trading post at Aughwick, on Aughwick Creek to the west of Carlisle, Pennsylvania. There he tried to hold what Indians he could to English allegiance while the Indians waited in vain for Pennsylvania to do something about frontier defense. In the spring of 1755, Governor Robert Hunter Morris of Pennsylvania ordered Croghan to muster as many Indians as possible to join General Braddock's expedition at Fort Cumberland. In the end only eight Indians volunteered. The French influence on the frontier was near its zenith, and it rose still higher after Braddock's force met disastrous defeat.

Because of his frontier knowledge and familiarity with Indians, Croghan was still valuable to Pennsylvania. And he had a stroke of luck when friends persuaded his creditors to petition the assembly to relieve him from arrest for debt for ten years. The assembly agreed. In addition, the colonial government placed Croghan in charge of constructing forts that were authorized by the assembly in 1756. He was also to try to re-establish peaceful relations with the Indians. But, as happened so often, Croghan overspent when buying presents for the Indians and providing for his own comforts. He was soon in trouble with the commissioners appointed to oversee defense and Indian expenditures, and in the spring of 1756 he resigned in anger. Croghan then went to New York, where he became a deputy to Sir William Johnson, the superintendent of Indian affairs for the northern colonies.

After Croghan successfully negotiated with the Iroquois, retaining their loyalty to the English, Johnson sent him back to Pennsylvania. There he was to mediate with Teedyuscung who, encouraged by anti-Penn Quakers, was charging fraud in connection with the Walking Purchase.

Croghan had a great deal of difficulty with Teedyuscung. But, with the aid of Teedyuscung's followers who wanted peace, he finally persuaded the Delaware leader to accept terms. Croghan then returned to New York. At about this time, toward the end of 1757, he married (or at least began living with) a daughter of Nickas, a Mohawk sachem. Earlier Croghan may have had a white wife; evidence on the matter is obscure.

Back again in Pennsylvania, Croghan participated in yet another conference with Teedyuscung, in the fall of 1758. Pennsylvania's governor, William Denny, was especially impressed by Croghan's success in holding the Delaware in line. "Mr. Croghan has exerted himself on all occasions for the good of His Majesty's service, and it required his peculiar address to manage the Indians, and counteract the designs of a wretched and restless faction [the Quakers]."[17] Denny and the assembly agreed that the success at Easton that year contributed to the French evacuation of Fort Duquesne and the English takeover there. By the end of 1759, the site—renamed Fort Pitt— was the center of a thriving English fur trade. Croghan later helped establish the English trade at Detroit, after that fort fell to the English forces.

During the winter of 1762–1763, Croghan resided on his estate, Croghan's Hall, near Fort Pitt. He lavishly entertained army officers, traders, and various passers-by. He also made some land sales to bring in money.

Rumors of an impending Indian war now grew stronger. And in June, 1763, upon arriving in Philadelphia, Croghan received news of an uprising of western tribes under Pontiac, an Ottawa. Indians again raided white settlements, and during the conflict they destroyed Croghan's Hall, which was later rebuilt. Pontiac's Rebellion was put down by November, but those few months of frontier fighting were ghastly, with atrocities committed by both sides.

As an Indian agent, Croghan was forbidden to engage in the fur trade. Although he did not honor this prohibition strictly, he did devote more and more of his attention to land speculation. By this means, given shrewdness, some political connections, and just plain luck, a person could acquire wealth.

[17] Quoted in ibid., p. 150.

Frontier settlers clearing the land. Often these settlers purchased their land from a speculator for what seemed a reasonable price, even though it was more than the cost would have been at a nearby general land office.

On the surface, land speculation was fairly simple. It involved acquiring title to land for little or no outlay, waiting for settlement to develop, and then selling for whatever the market would bring. But there were pitfalls. Indian and other titles were not always clear, nor always approved by government officials. In some cases the same land might be conveyed to more than one buyer. Settlement might not develop as anticipated, owing to Indian trouble or other problems. Land speculation did bring wealth to some. For others, it proved an ideal means of losing their shirts.

After October, 1763, would-be speculators faced an additional problem. In that month the English government issued a proclamation forbidding settlement by whites in most of the vast region newly won from France—the region west of the Appalachian Mountains. Furthermore, the proclamation prohibited land purchases from Indians anywhere in the colonies, whether east or west of the settlement line. Under the proclamation, the trans-Appalachian region was to be reserved for exclusive occupancy by the Indians, and it was to be administered directly by the English-appointed military commander-in-chief for the colonies. English officials believed, correctly, that resentment over unfair land dealings was one of the main causes of Indian restiveness. The Proclamation of 1763 was intended to protect the Indians and the colonists from each other, and to prevent any more costly uprisings like Pontiac's Rebellion.

Still, Croghan did not despair. With land speculation on his mind, he sailed to London in December, 1763. Through lobbying, he sought to persuade the English government to modify its policy in several important respects. First, he hoped the English would confirm titles to land obtained from Indians before the proclamation went into effect. Specifically, he wanted crown approval of the two hundred thousand acres he had received from the Iroquois in New York. Second, he and his partners in the fur trade hoped to get compensation—preferably in the form of land grants—for business losses they had suffered as a result of Indian troubles. And finally, as the shock of Pontiac's Rebellion wore off, he hoped to get the rich land of the Ohio Valley exempted from the ban on trans-Appalachian settlement. The idea of a fourteenth colony, in the West, had been broached in England in 1763, and Croghan discussed that possibility with a British official, Lord Halifax, during his stay in England.

Although British officials seemed receptive to his ideas, matters proceeded slowly. Croghan could do little more than plant seeds of thought before returning to America in the fall of 1764. He landed at New York City. After conferring with Johnson in northern New York, Croghan went on to Philadelphia.

There, in November, 1764, he purchased land—largely on credit—for what would become another estate, Monckton Hall. Turning then to western schemes, Croghan contacted General Thomas Gage, who was headquartered in New York as commander-in-chief of the British forces in the colonies. He convinced Gage that he was the man to reopen trade beyond the forks of the Ohio. Using credit Gage established for him—and overspending—Croghan purchased trade goods and set out for Fort Pitt.

General Thomas Gage.

National Archives

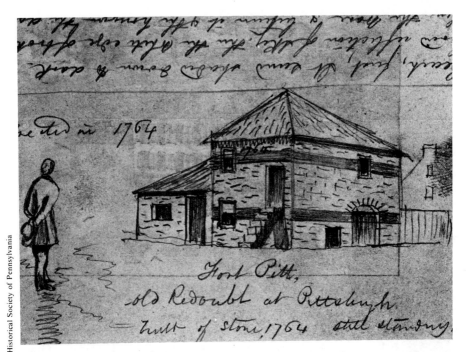

Historical Society of Pennsylvania

A sketch of Fort Pitt, which was built of stone in 1764 and which remained a British stronghold in Indian territory long after many other forts on the frontier had fallen to the French and Indians.

By this time the frontier was quieting. In May, 1765, Croghan gathered more than five hundred Indians at Fort Pitt to affirm a general peace. He then set out down the Ohio River with the goods he had purchased as presents to cement Indian relations and to look over what he fondly hoped would be the site of a new colony.

Peace was not yet firm with all the Indians of the Ohio Valley. A band of eighty Kickapoo and Mascouten attacked Croghan's party near the Wabash River. Before they were driven off, several whites had been killed and Croghan himself had been felled with a tomahawk wound in the head. The Shawnee and other tribes eventually quieted the hostiles and Pontiac, meeting with Croghan, agreed that the English should take over French forts in the region. Breaking the final Indian alliance with the French was

Croghan's contribution and, as he later wrote, "I got the stroke of a hatchett on the head, but my scull being pretty thick, the hatchett would not enter, so you may see a thick scull is of service on some occasions."

Croghan went on to Detroit, and then by way of the Great Lakes to northern New York to meet once again with Johnson. During their visit, they discussed the establishment of a colony in the West. From Johnson's residence Croghan journeyed to New York City to report on his recent western expedition to General Gage. After that he returned to Philadelphia.

Plans for settlement and a new colony in the Ohio Valley involved, besides Croghan, such interested parties as Benjamin Franklin and his son William, Sir William Johnson, and some officials in the British government and other Englishmen. At the nucleus of the plan was a land company that at various times went by different names. It was first the Indiana Company, organized in 1765, shortly after Croghan returned from England. Then, in March, 1766, subscribers to the plan drew up "Articles of Agreement" for the Illinois Company. In December, 1769, the speculators concerned reorganized as the Grand Ohio Company. Regardless of company name, the whole plan turned on a grant from the British government and the sale of land to westward moving settlers. The colony to be established would be called Vandalia, in honor of Queen Charlotte, wife of George III, who was said to be a descendant of the Vandals of ancient Germany.

Sir William Johnson.

In the spring of 1766, Croghan was off to the West once again with presents for Indians. This time he and his party traveled down the Ohio to where it joins the Mississippi. The group then moved about a hundred miles upstream on that river to Fort Chartres. There Croghan made another Indian treaty.

He then came down with malaria and spent some time in New Orleans regaining his health. In December, 1767, Croghan sailed from there to New York. And by this time his dreams of riches as a result of western settlement seemed closer to reality.

In the four years since Pontiac's Rebellion, the English government had already made a number of modifications in the Proclamation of 1763. Then, in the spring of 1768, officials announced that the settlement line would be moved west if land could be honorably obtained from Indians. In November that year, Sir William Johnson concluded the Treaty of Fort Stanwix with the Iroquois. The treaty transferred extensive lands to the British crown. At the same time, and more important from Croghan's point of view, Johnson arranged for the company in which they had an interest to secure a large tract of land south of the Ohio River. Vandalia, it seemed, was at last to take shape. All that remained was for company agents in England to obtain confirmation of the land grant and a charter authorizing the establishment of the new colony.

While awaiting further developments in the western plan, Croghan, with some associates, obtained thousands of acres of land in northern New York around Lake Otsego. He sold off some of the land and began the erection of yet a third estate, Croghan's Forest. He bought fine furniture for his mansion with its six fireplaces, and stocked his farm with cows, oxen, and sheep. Here, he thought, he would live out his days, soon to be supported in comfort by income from Vandalia.

Meanwhile, Croghan's financial affairs were a mess. He had not been above inflating the value of land to obtain a mortgage. He had on occasion given mortgages on the same land twice. Debts to some of his Pennsylvania creditors went back many years, and some creditors brought lawsuits against him. Like most speculators, though, he remained eternally optimistic, hoping for the big break that would bring lasting fortune. Others had won wealth through land speculation. Croghan was sure that he would too.

He did not. The efforts of the company's agents in London were blocked by agents of the Ohio Company, a group of wealthy Virginians who claimed that the Ohio Valley had been included in Virginia's original charter and therefore that company had the right to develop land in the West. Ohio Company agents lobbied fiercely against Vandalia among British government officials. There was still some hope for a new colony, but it was clear that a long fight for political influence lay ahead. Despite Ohio Company efforts, the British government did approve the Vandalia grant in August, 1772. But bureaucracies operated slowly then, as they do now. The paperwork was not completed by the outbreak of the War for Independence, and the war spelled an end to Vandalia.

And so Croghan's career continued its downward slide. Most of his New York holdings went to satisfy creditors. The building of fortifications at Philadelphia later destroyed Monckton Hall. Croghan had to sell much of his land around Fort Pitt, and he was disappointed that George Washington, whom he entertained at Croghan's Hall, declined to buy. His credit dwindled to nothing, and he spent the war years in obscurity.

As a speculator, George Croghan had at times been devious. He sometimes lied about land values and sources and certainty of credit. He was frequently able to persuade creditors and sometimes even government officials to support his schemes because they were eager for fortunes too. Among those who had backed him at one time or another were Benjamin Franklin; Franklin's son William, governor of New Jersey; Thomas Penn, governor of Pennsylvania; Sir William Johnson, superintendent of Indian affairs; and Joseph Galloway, a man high in Pennsylvania political circles. Croghan had made great contributions as a colonial diplomat among the Indians. But he had also gambled heavily for high stakes. And he went down with a reputation for dishonesty and sharp dealing. Too often he had overplayed his hand and "out-schemed" himself.

George Croghan died in Philadelphia, in poverty, on August 31, 1782. His personal belongings were valued at fifty pounds, thirteen shillings, and six pence. They included a pair of shoes worth ten shillings; a coat, two jackets, and a pair of pants valued at two pounds; and "1 Old Antediluvian coach or Waggon with Harness," worth three pounds. Croghan had dreamed great dreams. Few of them were realized.

A Prominent Family

During George Croghan's first year in the fur trade, Edward Shippen, a Philadelphia merchant, supplied both Croghan and his tutor, Peter Tostee, with Indian goods. Shippen, officially Edward Shippen III, was a third-generation member of a well-known and well-to-do Pennsylvania family.

The American branch of the Shippen family had begun with old Edward, who had been born in England in 1639 and arrived in Boston in 1668. There he soon prospered

Edward Shippen III.

as a merchant and bought land. He also became a Quaker, a move which proved not to his advantage in the Puritan capital of Massachusetts. Quaker persecution in Boston died down after Mary Dyer's execution in the 1660's, but it revived a decade later. In August, 1677, Shippen himself was twice publicly whipped for attending Quaker meetings. This did not dampen his faith. The persecution finally eased off, and his business continued to prosper.

Old Edward Shippen was of stubborn, hearty stock. He married Elizabeth Lybrand in 1671, when he was thirty-nine. This wife bore eight children in seventeen years. Upon her death in 1688, Shippen married again, this time the widow Rebekah Richardson. She bore him one child, who did not survive. When Rebekah died in 1706, with what some observers considered unseemly haste, Shippen again remarried, taking another widow, Esther James. Two children came of this marriage, and one lived beyond childhood. Altogether, only four of Edward Shippen's children lived to maturity.

Shippen remained in Boston for twenty-six years, but because he was a Quaker he never became a member of the inner political, commercial, and social group. In 1694, having established many business connections in the Quaker city, he decided to move to Philadelphia. He did even better as a merchant there than in Boston, and he acquired even more land.

Edward III, offspring of Edward Shippen's son Joseph, was born in 1703. When he was still in his teens, his father apprenticed him to James Logan, secretary to William Penn and prominent in his own right in politics and commerce, in order that the boy might learn the fur trade. After Edward became familiar with the business and was assured of an income, he married his stepsister, Sarah Plumley, whose mother had married Joseph Shippen following the death of Edward's mother. At the time of his marriage, Edward was twenty-two.

Shippen might not have gone so far so fast in business had James Logan not suffered his fall on the ice in 1728. This accident kept Logan in bed for three months before he was able to hobble around on crutches. In the meantime, Shippen took on more and more responsibility, and Logan made him a junior partner. Shippen lived for a time in Logan's house on his estate, Stenton, and with Logan's backing he was elected to the Philadelphia city council in 1732 at the age of twenty-nine.

Like most fur trade merchants, Logan and Shippen were middlemen. They bought trade goods—knives, axes, cloth, and so on—from English merchants, frequently on credit. They then either advanced the goods to traders or exchanged them for furs. As the furs came in, Logan and Shippen sent them to England, partly to pay their bills and partly to sell for profit. Shippen spent much of his time here and there on the frontier trying to track down traders who had not settled their accounts. And, at Logan's urging, he frequently hauled them into court for non-payment.

James Logan was a tough taskmaster, and his crippled condition contributed to his ill humor. He frequently scolded his young partner for not paying close enough attention to the business. "Indeed you have ... exceedingly disappointed me," Logan wrote to Shippen on one occasion. "The Account of Powder I find has been so confusedly kept I can make nothing of it." At another point Logan became concerned about a debt: "I think thou hast been inexcusably negligent," he said in a letter to Shippen. "If thou couldst not goe thyself [to collect], some other methods might have been taken, & thus not let a whole year pass without knowing the least little about it."[18]

Still, Edward III advanced steadily. In the 1730's he purchased land in western Pennsylvania, near Lancaster, to establish an estate, Shippensburg. He rented portions of it to tenants. Later he bought land in Philadelphia County and acquired an interest in additional land which held a copper mine, although the copper never paid off. In 1744 he won election as mayor of Philadelphia. By then, on his own, he was receiving annual shipments of goods from England valued at nearly two thousand pounds, and business was good. Shippen could note in 1744 that "we live in a very flourishing Province of about 60 years [in age], Our City containing at least 1,500 Houses and 15,000 Inhabitants & they are trading toil every Year upwards of 300 vessels which are Loaded with our wheat, flour, bisket, Tobacco, staves, Beef Pork [and many kinds of furs]."[19]

Edward Shippen's brother, Joseph II, was also a merchant, and the two of them frequently made joint ventures. In the 1740's they acquired the *Charming Catherine*, which

---

[18] Quoted in Randolph Shipley Klein, *Portrait of an Early American Family* (Philadelphia: University of Pennsylvania Press, 1975), p. 154.

[19] Quoted in ibid., p. 61.

sailed between Philadelphia, the islands of Antigua and Saint Christopher in the West Indies, and London. Edward Shippen's interests broadened beyond the fur trade as he began to deal at wholesale in cloth and other dry goods, and in grain which he shipped to London.

He also continued to invest in real estate. In one deal he acquired a whole Philadelphia city block for a little more than £2,000. Later Shippen bought two tenements—rental properties—for £420. At about the same time he purchased more than three thousand acres in Bucks and Chester counties. He felt prosperous enough to send his elder son, Edward IV, to study law in London. The other son, Joseph III, went to the College of New Jersey, the institution that later became Princeton University.

Toward the end of the 1740's, Edward Shippen became involved in a scandal. His wife had died in 1735, at the age of twenty-nine. After several years had passed Shippen remarried, taking Mary Gray Howland, a widow, for his second wife. Her husband, John Howland, had gone off to Barbados in the West Indies some years before and had not been heard from since. He was presumed dead. But in August, 1747, a few weeks after the Shippen-Howland wedding, news arrived that John Howland was alive and well in Barbados. If true, this made Shippen's new wife a bigamist and Edward III an adulterer. At that time, in Pennsylvania, bigamy was punishable by thirty-nine lashes on the bare back and life imprisonment. Until the matter was cleared up, Edward and Mary agreed not to share a bed, and later she went to live with her parents.

The news became public in 1750 and Mary seems to have borne the brunt of gossip and criticism, but the Shippen family rallied around the couple. Shippen's brother-in-law, Charles Willing, mayor of Philadelphia, promised that if Howland returned he would be barred from entering the city. Governor James Hamilton, brother-in-law of one of Shippen's cousins, also promised to protect the couple.

John Howland never appeared, but nevertheless a grand jury convened and indicted Mary. In the meantime, efforts were made to learn whether or not Howland really was alive. At last, Charles Willing heard from his business agent in Barbados that the man indeed was dead. A memorial service was held, and Mary returned to live with Edward.

The scandal, or threat of one, had taken its toll. Shippen finally moved with his wife from Philadelphia to Shippensburg to get her out of the public eye. This, in fact, placed him nearer his fur trade interests. Also, while in Lancaster he could devote more time to his duties as clerk of the court and registrar of deeds, positions he had obtained in 1737 and 1745 respectively.

Edward Shippen III was a sober, serious, hard-working man, close with his resources and careful with his accounts. He frequently upheld the straight and narrow in letters to his sons. At one point he wrote to Edward IV: "Young married Men shou'd be very diligent, frugal & carefull, that they may not only be able always to support a Wife & a housefull of Children, but also to lay up a hundred or two pounds for every one of them when they go out into the wide world." He warned his sons not to "sit at table two or three hours tipling Wine and punch, which [renders them] unfit for any business." He pointed out that idle youths wasted their lives bowling and playing billiards and staying in taverns until late at night, at last to "stagger away home to Snore, Spue, and Groan." Furthermore, he said, "Avoid what the world calls pleasure. Pleasure is only for Crowned Heads and other great Men who have their Incomes sleeping and waking." He insisted that his son Joseph III, while in college, keep a careful account of money he received from his father. In 1749 the account ran on for ten pages and totaled only eight pounds, eight shillings, and one pence, but Edward III apparently thought the lesson worth it. He lectured Joseph III on his studies: "I would not have you neglect the School Knowledge, tho' you may never have occasion to use it, it may enable you to detect Falsehood when disguised as a syllogism." Joseph III promised his father, "You may depend upon it, Sir, I shall take your agreeable Advice in every particular."[20]

Edward Shippen IV became a lawyer and a land owner in his own right and was active in politics. Joseph III joined his father in business and later became a merchant on his own. He seemed at his happiest, though, as a militia officer in the French and Indian War. The daughter, Sarah, married James Burd, a Philadelphia merchant.

[20] Quoted in ibid., p. 89.

The family and those who married into it formed a vast network of power and influence in Pennsylvania affairs. If it was not the colony's or Philadelphia's first family, it was sufficiently close to it. During the late colonial period Shippens and their relatives were found on the Philadelphia city council and at posts in the colonial government nearly every year. Others were prominent judges, lawyers, and doctors.

Shippens were a prolific group. Old Edward fathered eleven children. Four reached maturity, five living one year or less. Edward II and Joseph II, Edward's sons, contributed five children who matured. Edward III fathered a total of seven, three of whom lived. Two were twin boys who died within their first year. His brother, Joseph II, had six children who survived. And his sister Anne, who married Charles Willing, had ten out of eleven children live to adulthood. Edward III's children, Sarah, Joseph III, and Edward IV, produced a total of twenty-nine children, of whom twenty-one reached maturity. One of Edward IV's daughters, Margaret, better known as Peggy, became the wife of Benedict Arnold. Altogether, through the fifth generation which extended beyond the middle of the nineteenth century, 232 descendants of the first Edward Shippen have been recorded.

A member of the conservative group, Edward Shippen III did not favor independence from Great Britain. On the other hand, he did not speak out strongly against it. He eventually lost his public offices and, toward the end of his long life, had to sell of some land holdings to pay debts and taxes.

Edward Shippen III was, by 1780, the patriarch of the family, and he had kept his particular branch closely knit about him. Mary Shippen died in 1778, and Edward III turned more and more to religion. He fell seriously ill in the spring of 1781. The end came in September of that year, when Shippen was seventy-eight. Wrote his son, Joseph III: "The Situation of my Mind, while at Lancaster was such, that I could not think of writing. . . . The loss I have sustained in the Death of an affectionate & good Father has been truly distressing."[21]

---

[21] Quoted in ibid., p. 198.

A New York Merchant and Land Owner

Robert Livingston came to New York in 1673. He established himself as a merchant, became a large land owner, and for many years was active in politics. He founded a commercial, land-owning, and political dynasty.

Robert Livingston.

Livingston was born in Scotland on December 12, 1654, the son of a Presbyterian minister. He was the family's fourteenth child, most of the others having died in childhood. Because there was no school in the small village of Ancrum, where he was born, Livingston was educated at home.

Scottish Presbyterians were in and out of trouble with the established Anglican Church of England, and in 1663 Livingston's father was exiled. He and his wife and their two youngest children, Elizabeth and Robert, left for Rotterdam, in Holland. Spending nine years in the Netherlands, Robert Livingston learned to read, write, and speak Dutch, a skill that would prove useful to him later.

Livingston's father died in 1672, and the eighteen-year-old youth accompanied his mother back to Scotland. No occupation there appealed to him, and so on April 28, 1673, he sailed for Massachusetts Bay Colony. His father's name was well known in Massachusetts, which, like Scotland, was a stronghold of dissenting Protestantism. John Hull, a Puritan merchant, befriended Livingston. The young man probably possessed a small inheritance from his father, and in addition Hull advanced him thirty-four pounds. Not lingering long in the Bay Colony, Livingston moved on to Albany, New York. There, owing to the predominant Dutch population, his language ability would help him become established in the fur trade, his first ambition.

At the time Albany held between five hundred and six hundred people. The settlement contained eighty or ninety houses, a Dutch Reformed church and a Lutheran church, and a number of commercial buildings. Life in Albany was centered on commerce, and merchants ruled the town.

Livingston purchased a town lot in the palisaded community, and soon thereafter he became secretary to Nicholas Van Rensselaer, who oversaw the huge patroonship the Dutch West India Company had granted his family. Livingston later was made secretary of the town of Albany and a member of the New York colonial board of Indian commissioners. And his activity in the fur trade soon returned a profit.

In 1679, Livingston married Alida Schuyler Van Rensselaer, his employer's widow, who was then in her early twenties. This allied him with two powerful New York colonial families. Moreover, his wife's sister Gertruyd had married into the Van Cortlandt family, giving Livingston another important connection. He had become acquainted with Governor Edmund Andros in 1678, and in 1680 Andros appointed Stephanus Van Cortlandt, Gertruyd's husband, to the governor's council.

Edmund Andros was an able military leader, but he generated hostility in Boston with his open support of the Church of England. The Bostonians were also outraged by his noisy, Sabbath-profaning soldiers, who were accused of teaching the people "to drink, blaspheme, curse, and damn."

Livingston's activity in the fur trade was much like that of Edward Shippen III. He furnished goods to traders, obtained furs, and shipped them to England. And his hunger for land equalled his zest for profit in the trade. He sought first to satisfy it by trying, through his wife's connections, to obtain control of part of the million-acre estate of Rensselaerswyck. After much legal wrangling, which persisted until 1685, he failed. He had, however, earlier received from Governor Andros the authority to purchase certain Indian lands, which he now acquired. Later, from Governor Thomas Dongan, Livingston obtained the right to buy several hundred thousand additional acres. He now held title to 2,600 acres of land along the Hudson River near Albany. Somehow, though, through what historians have concluded must have been shady dealings between Livingston and Dongan, Livingston Manor amounted to 160,000 acres when it was surveyed some years later.

In the meantime, while still involved in the fur trade, Livingston became a general merchant in Albany. In addition to gaining and strengthening ties with New York City merchants, he imported and sold such commodities as rum, brandy, molasses, flour, and sugar. And through selling goods and lending money, Livingston also became a creditor. By June, 1681, he carried three hundred and fifty pounds' worth of debts on his books, and on more than one occasion he took a debtor to court to collect. His appointment as subcollector of customs duties in Albany brought Livingston additional income—fifty pounds a year, later changed to five percent of all he collected—and additional time in court suing merchants who had failed to pay.

The establishment of the Dominion of New England in 1688 did not disturb Livingston or his fortunes. The advent of Jacob Leisler and his rule of New York did. To Livingston and other Albany merchants, Leisler was an impulsive fire-brand who might, if he gained control of the city, disrupt the fur trade and stir up trouble with the Iroquois. Conse-quently, Livingston and other Albany merchants established a convention made up of civil and military leaders. They raised money for defense, pledged allegiance to the new sovereigns, William and Mary, and kept control of Albany in their own hands. The Schenectady massacre of 1690, however, indicated how weak their defenses were. Livingston headed a delegation to Connecticut and Massa-chusetts to seek help. They failed to obtain it. And before the group could return, Livingston learned that fear of the French and their Indian allies had driven Albany merchants to surrender the city to three Leislerian commissions headed by Leisler's chief lieutenant and son-in-law, Jacob Mil-borne. Livingston decided that it would be the better part of wisdom to remain in Connecticut, which he did until Governor Henry Sloughter arrived in New York in 1691. Livingston was in New York City at the time of the Leislerian trials and the executions of Leisler and Milborne.

Livingston's Manor-house.

The Albany merchant was now thirty-six. He had four sons and a daughter, a large estate, and a sound reputation as a merchant and civic leader. When Governor Sloughter visited Albany in May, 1691, he stayed at the Livingston residence. He also granted Robert Livingston a contract to supply food—to victual—British troops in both Albany and New York.

This deal had its drawbacks, though, for Livingston experienced much difficulty in collecting money due him from the government, as did other victualers like Stephanus Van Cortlandt and Peter Schuyer. Livingston finally de-cided that he would have to go to London to get payment. He and his eldest son John sailed from New York on December 10, 1694.

Winter crossings were risky at best, and this one proved disastrous. Buffeted by heavy storms, the ship lost its rudder. Using makeshift gear, the captain and crew tried to steer for the West Indies. This failed, and as food and drink began to

A plan of the town of Albany, drawn in 1695. The plan reflects the settlers' fear of the Indians. As the plan shows, the town was surrounded by a wooden stockade (marked 10 on the plan); this could be entered through six gates (11), all of them guarded by blockhouses (7). The fort (1) stood at the top of the triangular town, while a "great gun" (9) commanded the frontage along the river.

dwindle, the ship became lost somewhere on the Atlantic. Near starvation, and by now at each other's throats after many weeks of such close and frustrating existence, passengers and crew at last sighted the coast of Portugal on April 25, 1695. Livingston and his son did not reach London until July 25.

Livingston found the English bureaucracy a wearisome and endless maze, extremely difficult to deal with. There was controversy over how much was owed him and how much interest he was due on his accounts. Livingston was shuttled from one person or office to another, and the wait for action seemed to go on forever. Finally, after a year had passed, a settlement was made granting Livingston a portion of what he thought he had coming, some of which was to be collected in New York. This proved unfortunate.

Political power in England was shifting away from the faction that had approved Governor Benjamin Fletcher's appointment in New York, and Fletcher's political star was fading. Livingston himself had had some harsh things to say about Fletcher and the way he ran the New York government. In his appearances before the Board of Trade, Livingston had blamed Fletcher for his troubles in collecting on his victualing and on his salary as secretary to the board of Indian commissioners. He charged Fletcher with diverting money for defense into his own pocket and with interfering in New York assembly business. Livingston hoped that this would aid his cause. But Fletcher still had his defenders in England, and news of Livingston's accusations preceded him across the Atlantic. Upon Livingston's arrival, Fletcher struck back. He stripped Livingston of his job in Indian affairs, as subcollector of customs, and as clerk of Albany. And payments due him were held up.

Robert Livingston remained in political limbo for two years, until the arrival of Richard Coote, earl of Bellomont, to replace Fletcher in 1698. At that point Livingston was returned to his victualing and to his role in Indian affairs, although he would still have trouble collecting on what was owed him. Bellomont also made Livingston a member of his council.

Livingston had been anti-Leisler, and Leislerians were now in control of the New York assembly. They connived to hold up payments to him for victualing, and they blocked repayment of money he had lent the government. Bellomont himself, probably as part of his desire to go along with the Leislerian faction, began to criticize Livingston and other victualers for supplying "sad provisions." Then, although he paid Livingston £470 on his victualing account, a few days afterward Bellomont removed Livingston from his post as subcollector of customs at Albany. In addition, Bellomont nullified some land grants Governor Fletcher had made, and it appeared that he might void even older ones, including some made to Livingston. Bellomont died before taking action, but the assembly—led by a Leislerian temporary governor—passed a law confiscating Livingston's lands. Livingston retreated to his manor for a time. He occupied himself in part with arranging the marriage of his son John to Mary Winthrop, only child of Fitz-John Winthrop, governor of Connecticut and a descendant of Massachusetts's leading family.

Under the next administration, that of Edward Hyde, Lord Cornbury, Robert Livingston fared better. Anti-Leislerians now controlled the assembly, and that body repealed the law taking over Livingston's acreage. All charges that Leislerians had brought against him for alleged financial manipulation and playing fast and loose with customs money were dropped. Cornbury did not press the assembly over Livingston's claims to money, however. It appears that the governor was too busy looking out for his own financial interests, and this preoccupation eventually led to his replacement as governor.

On June 2, 1702, Livingston sailed once again for England. There, at their request, he would represent the Iroquois before the government to ask for more defense effort against the French in Canada. He would also pursue complex claims for back pay as secretary to the Indian commissioners, for victualing, for interest, and for various expenses. He found the bureaucracy unchanged, as he indicated in a letter to his wife:

> The Earl of Peterborough took me in his coach and
> delivered my request to the Earl of Nottingham,
> Secretary of State, who immediately went to the
> Queen and had the matter referred to the Lord
> Godolphin, High Treasurer. The above mentioned Earl

took me along last Thursday to the Lord High Treasurer and spoke for me and gave him my request and the Queen's order, who has referred my affair to the Earl of Ranelagh and Mr. Blathwayt. What they will now do with it, time will tell. I do my very best every day to make friends, and save no trouble or expenses. What the result will be, God only knows.[22]

Livingston finally achieved most of his money goals, but his efforts long delayed him in England. He did not arrive back in New York until September 16, 1706.

A street in Albany, as it looked around 1700.

The War of the Spanish Succession—Queen Anne's War in the colonies—created many refugees in the Palatinate, a German province. More than two thousand refugees flocked to England. The English government planned to settle some of the Palatines in New York, where they would be put to work producing naval stores—tar, pitch, turpentine, and masts for ships—making use of the colony's resource of pine trees. New Yorkers around Albany, near where the Palatines were to locate, welcomed the idea. The Albany area would benefit from the additional items for export.

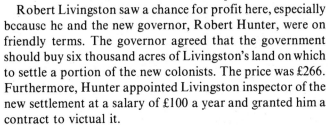

New York State Library

Robert Livingston saw a chance for profit here, especially because he and the new governor, Robert Hunter, were on friendly terms. The governor agreed that the government should buy six thousand acres of Livingston's land on which to settle a portion of the new colonists. The price was £266. Furthermore, Hunter appointed Livingston inspector of the new settlement at a salary of £100 a year and granted him a contract to victual it.

The Albany merchant went into debt buying supplies for the settlers and, as usual, he had trouble collecting from the government. In addition, the settlement plan ran into difficulty almost from the start. As commonly was the case in the colonies, new settlers were reluctant to work for someone else. The opportunities to own land and work for oneself were too great in America. The English government soon lost interest in the Palatine scheme, and by the end of 1712 it had been abandoned. As for Livingston, he had had a gristmill, a sawmill, a brewery, and a bakehouse erected on his

[22] Quoted in Lawrence H. Leder, *Robert Livingston, 1654–1728, and the Politics of Colonial New York* (Chapel Hill: University of North Carolina Press, 1961), pp. 189–90.

Hudson River estate to serve the Palatines. These could still bring a profit, and he possessed nearly £800 in merchandise to sell in the area. Later, the New York assembly voted Livingston £564 for his claims concerning the Palatine settlement, about one-fourth of the total amount.

According to Peter Kalm, who wrote about the region several decades later, many Palatines remained in the Albany area and obtained land. But, he went on,

> After they had lived there for some time, and had built houses and churches, and made corn-fields and meadows, their liberties and privileges were infringed, and, under several pretenses they were repeatedly deprived of parts of their land. This at last roused the Germans; they returned violence for violence, and beat those who thus robbed them of their possessions. But these proceedings were looked upon in a very bad light by the government; the most active people among the Germans being taken up, they were very roughly treated, and punished with the utmost rigor of the law. This, however, so far exasperated the rest that the greater part of them left their houses and fields, and went to settle in Pensylvania; there they were exceedingly well received, got a considerable tract of land, and were indulged in great privileges, which were given them for ever. The Germans, not satisfied with being themselves removed from New York, wrote to their relations and friends, and advised them, if ever they intended to come to America, not to go to New York, where the government had shewn itself so unequitable. This advice had such influence that the Germans, who afterwards went in great numbers to North America, constantly avoided New York, and always went to Pensylvania. It sometimes happened that they were forced to go on board such ships as were bound to New York; but they were scarce got on shore, when they hastened on to Pensylvania, in sight of all the inhabitants of New York.[23]

In 1716 Livingston won election to the assembly, and he later was elected speaker. Here, with the aid of the governor

[23] Kalm, "Travels into North America," p. 463.

and his friends, he was able to shepherd through debt bills in which he had a personal interest. He had presented an expense claim of £1,696 in connection with his second London trip, and the assembly agreed to settle for £1,484. At the same time, Livingston helped his youngest son Gilbert and a partner to obtain a contract to collect excise taxes. For this privilege the partners guaranteed £1,500 a year to the government, hoping their collections would exceed that. It proved a poor bargain; collections amounted to no more than £900 annually.

Robert Hunter, who had performed well in office, left for England in 1719. There he traded jobs with William Burnet, who was comptroller of customs in the English government. Burnet arrived to take over the New York governorship in 1720.

Still in the assembly, Livingston got on as well with Burnet as he had with Hunter. Over the opposition of other Albany merchants, he supported Burnet's plan to halt trade between them and the French. The assembly voted to make that trade illegal, which meant that merchants would have to rely on direct trade contacts with western Indians. Albany merchants eventually won, though, when the English government vetoed the law. Also owing to his friendship with Governor Burnet, Livingston won his son Philip's appointment as deputy secretary of Indian affairs.

By now Robert Livingston was well on in years. He had carved out a secure niche as influential merchant, land owner, legislator, and man of colonial affairs. The business risks he took, the debts he ran up, his difficulties in collecting money owed him—all were typical of the time. Livingston had done well, but he was tired. He wished retirement, and a prolonged illness finally ended his assembly speakership. His eldest son, John, had died in London some years before. After many years of illness, his wife Alida died in 1727. Robert Livingston himself died the following year, after having written a will dividing his possessions among his three remaining sons, and his two daughters.

A number of Livingston's descendants made special marks in American history. Philip (1716–1778), a grandson, was a signer of the Declaration of Independence. William (1723–1790) attended the Constitutional Convention, and became the first governor of the state of New Jersey. Robert

R. (1746–1813) had a most distinguished career. He was a member of the Continental Congress, helped write the Declaration, worked to win New York's ratification of the Constitution, administered the first presidential oath of office to George Washington in New York, and, as minister to France under President Thomas Jefferson, helped negotiate the Louisiana Purchase in 1803. He also aided Robert Fulton in the building of his steamboat, *Clermont,* which was named after a part of the estate which the first Robert Livingston had established on the Hudson and which he had willed to his son, Robert, Jr.

Surveyor-General, Sometimes Governor

The paths of Robert Livingston and his sons crossed the path of Cadwallader Colden on numerous occasions. Coming to New York in 1718, Colden devoted more than half a century to public service in the colony.

Cadwallader Colden was born in Scotland in 1688. He attended the University of Edinburgh, where he studied sciences and medicine. After further study at the University of London, at the suggestion of an aunt, he emigrated to Philadelphia in 1710 to establish a medical practice. Colden went back to England five years later, returning to Philadelphia within a year with a wife. Then, because building a comfortable living as a physician proved a slow process, in 1718 he accepted Governor Robert Hunter's invitation to become New York's surveyor-general.

Cadwallader Colden.

Colden's interest in science, botany in particular, persisted beyond his college days. He was acquainted with Edmund Halley, after whom Halley's Comet was named. One of Colden's papers concerning botanical research in America was read before the Royal Society of scientists in England. And Colden became friendly with Benjamin Franklin, owing in large part to mutual scientific interests, and corresponded with him after moving to New York. In that colony, Colden's interests broadened to include a study of the Iroquois, which he published in 1727 under the title *The History of the Five Nations Depending on the Province of New York.* William Bradford printed it.

Much of Colden's work as surveyor-general consisted of straightening out land claims. He went on surveying trips along the Mohawk Valley and in the Catskill Mountains.

Surveys he directed established firm borders between New York and Connecticut and fixed boundaries for New Hampshire and Massachusetts. The office of surveyor-general did not pay a high salary, but it did enable Colden to become familiar with areas of choice land, some of which he purchased for himself. He also received a sizeable land grant from the New York government, the estate lying partly in Ulster and partly in Orange County. There he erected a manor-house, Coldenham. The surveyor-general's social position rose when in 1738 his daughter Betty married Peter De Lancey, James De Lancey's brother.

A number of New York governors participated in land speculation and, as a political appointee, Colden cooperated with them by steering them on to favorable acquisitions. He worked on behalf of William Cosby as well as others, although he had some harsh words for Cosby in a history of New York that he published later. Colden was further involved in colonial politics because, as surveyor-general, he became a member of the governor's council.

The outbreak of King George's War in 1744 put an end to surveying for a time. This suited Colden, for he wished to devote more attention to his land and his private affairs. He did not even want to attend council meetings in New York when he could avoid it, preferring to remain at Coldenham. "The attendance on the Council," he wrote to Governor George Clinton,

Governor George Clinton.

Library of Congress

puts the Gentlemen who live in town to no extra expense & their number is sufficient. We in the country may therefore hope to be excused when there is no necessity but if it be tho't requisite that some of us who live in the country attend as Mr. Livingston [Robert, Jr.] did not attend last Session & has not in general given his attendance so often as I have done & has not the same excuse which I have, I hope my excuse may be preferr'd to his. I suppose that the Business of the Session is concerted [decided] before the meeting & when that is done as I take the business of the Council is little else beside formal because we have no parties nor disputes among us. Whenever my attendance shall be though of real use I shall very cheerfully give it but when it is not so I hope it will

not be insisted upon or that Mr. Livingston & I be so
far indulged as to give our attendance by turns. . . .[24]

Colden supported Governor Clinton's defense policy for
New York and his plans to invade Canada. His relationship
with Clinton gradually moved him to the opposite side of the
political fence from the James De Lancey faction. Upon
Clinton's recall in 1753, De Lancey became lieutenant
governor and then, after newly arrived Governor Danvers
Osborne's death, acting governor. Although Colden remained on the council, as one of Clinton's former supporters
he possessed little influence. But then in August, 1760, the
news of De Lancey's heart attack and death reached
Coldenham. As senior councillor, Colden now became
lieutenant governor and acting governor. He was seventy-
two years old, but still clear-headed and physically vigorous.
Colden would be lieutenant governor, and, periodically,
acting governor over the next thirteen years.

As Colden assumed the acting governorship, New
Yorkers were anticipating the end of the French and Indian
War, during which many had prospered. In New York City,
according to his biographer, Colden "found many changes
of a more obvious sort."

Wealth and luxury had increased to an astonishing
degree. The provincial gallants and ladies of fashion
could be as well turned out in Hanover Square and
Broad Street as in London itself; it was the fault of a
man's pocket or his taste did he not set his table with
delicacies from all parts of the world; house
furnishings and decorations of an elegance of which
the earlier inhabitants had never dreamed were
imported in quantities; and people of a literary sort
were no longer obliged to look to England and the
Continent for the inspiration of new books. Prices,
too, had steadily mounted. Provisions and other
necessities cost three times as much as they had a very
few years before.

[24] Quoted in Alice Mapelsden Keys, *Cadwallader Colden: A Representative Eighteenth-Century Official* (New York: Columbia University Press,
1906), p. 138.

Lower Market Street, New York, in an engraving by Charles B. Hall.

. . . In September came the news of the final surrender of Canada at Montreal. In November came Amherst himself to the booming of the guns of Fort George, when the city was brilliant with the British colours by day and illuminations by night, and when the mayor, aldermen, and commonalty conferred the freedom of their municipality on the victor, in the usual gold box and with an unusually patriotic address. Finally, before the winter set in, the news of the death of King George II and of the accession of George III lent that pictorial interest to political relations that such changes inspire. Hymns and anthems of thanksgiving were published in the newspapers; the overthrow of "the insulting Gaul" [France], the triumph of British mercy over British valor, and the fatherly care of the old king were all subjects for poetic congratulation; while one enthusiast went so far as to forecast the future and through many verses saw "Europe tremble at the name of George."

Public opinion was tinged with the same mild patriotism, and partly from this and partly from the caution of surprise, Colden's first assembly was comfortably uneventful.[25]

Owing to his long familiarity with the colony and its affairs, Colden was well equipped for the duties of the governorship. He played his hand cautiously, though. In exchange for the satisfactory salary that the assembly voted him, he approved paper money and tax bills similar to some he had opposed in the past. And, although James De Lancey could hardly have been counted a friend of Colden's, the acting governor went out of his way to praise the late governor's administration.

Cadwallader Colden continued as acting governor until the arrival of Governor Henry Moore in 1766. Then, following Moore's death in 1769, Colden assumed the office once again. He remained acting chief executive until John Murray, Lord Dunmore, arrived in New York as governor in 1770.

Interestingly enough, when Denmore assumed office, Colden found himself in a similar position to that of Rip Van Dam when William Cosby had taken over. Dunmore demanded half the salary Colden had received as acting governor. Colden hired a lawyer to defend him, and Dunmore himself heard the case. Public opinion had rallied behind Colden, and although Dunmore apparently had previously decided to find the case in his own favor, he ultimately asked the New York supreme court for an opinion instead. The justices leaned in favor of the defendant, and Dunmore dropped the matter.

In 1771 Lord Dunmore left to become governor of Virginia and was succeeded by William Tryon. Then, in the spring of 1774, Tryon returned to England, leaving Colden acting governor once more.

Cadwallader Colden's times as New York's chief executive in the 1760's and 1770's coincided with growing restiveness among the colonists over British trade and tax policies. The New York assembly voiced its opinion on the matter in this fashion, in a document addressed to Colden:

[25] Ibid., pp. 264–65, 267–68.

When his [Majesty's] Service requires it, we shall ever be ready to exert ourselves, with Loyalty, Fidelity, and Zeal, and as we have always complied in the most dutiful manner with every Requisition made by his Directions; We with all Humility hope, that his Majesty, who, and whose Ancestors have long been the Guardians of British Liberty will so protect us in our Rights, as to prevent our falling into the abject State of being forever hereafter incapable of doing what can merit either his Distinction or Approbation. Such must be the deplorable State of that Wretched people, who (being taxed by a Power subordinate to none and in a great Measure unacquainted with their circumstances) can call Nothing their own. This we speak with the greatest Deference to the Wisdom and Justice of the British Parliament, in which we confide. . . .

We hope, your Honour will join with us, in an Effort to secure that great Badge of English Liberty, of being taxed only with our Consent; to which, we conceive, all His Majesty's Subjects at home and abroad equally entitled, and also in pointing out to the Ministry, the many mischiefs arising from the Act, commonly called the Sugar Act, both to us and Great Britain.[26]

Colden himself had expressed his views earlier, in a letter to a son: "We have instances in History of Kingdoms well governed, under absolute monarchy; but it seems to me, that it is impossible that a people can be happy, under a Government formed on genuine independent principles."[27]

As lieutenant governor and acting governor, Colden remained steadfastly loyal to the British crown and supportive of the British government. This, as the next chapter notes, proved costly. After the War for Independence began in 1775, Colden no longer enjoyed political influence in New York. He died the following year, aged eighty-eight.

[26] Quoted in ibid., pp. 297–98.
[27] Quoted in ibid., p. 270.

SUGGESTED READINGS

Burnaby, Andrew, *Travels through the Middle Settlements in North America in the Years 1759 and 1760.* 2nd ed. Cornell University Press.

Cooper, James Fenimore. *The Deerslayer; The Last of the Mohicans; The Pathfinder.* 3 vols. New American Library, Signet Books.

Flexner, James Thomas. *Lord of the Mohawks: A Biography of Sir William Johnson.* Rev. ed. Little, Brown.

Jacobs, Wilbur R. *Wilderness Politics and Indian Gifts: The Northern Colonial Frontier, 1748–1763.* University of Nebraska Press, Bison Books.

Jacobs, William Jay. *Women in American History.* Glencoe.

Tolles, Frederick. *Meeting House and Counting House: The Quaker Merchants of Colonial Philadelphia, 1682–1763.* W. W. Norton, Norton Library.

Wright, Louis B. *Everyday Life in Colonial America.* G. P. Putnam's Sons.

Wright, Louis B., ed. *The Cultural Life of the American Colonies.* Harper & Row, Torchbooks.

The identity of those who participated in the Boston Tea Party was a closely guarded secret, but some of the participants are now known from clues in old diaries and letters. An observer, for example, noted lace showing under the disguise of one "Indian"—lace of a kind that only John Hancock was known to wear.

5

TOWARD WAR

FOR INDEPENDENCE

Discussing the French and their relationship to the English colonies, the Swedish naturalist Peter Kalm remarked:

> I have been told by Englishmen, and not only by such as were born in America, but even by such as came from Europe, that the English colonies in North America, in the space of thirty or forty years, would be able to form a state by themselves, entirely independent of Old England: but as the whole country which lies along the seashore is unguarded, and on the land side is harrassed by the French in times of war, these dangerous neighbours are sufficient to prevent the connection of the colonies with their mother country from being quite broken off. The English government has therefore sufficient reason to consider the French in North America as the best means of keeping the colonies in their due submission.[1]

Scarcely a decade after Kalm made this observation, the situation had changed completely. The French danger had passed. And the timetable for independence would prove much shorter than anyone then might have dared to imagine.

[1] Peter Kalm, "Travels into North America," in John Pinkerton, ed., *A General Collection of the Best and Most Interesting Voyages and Travels in All Parts of the World* (London: Longman, Hurst, Rees, Orme, and Brown, 1812), vol. 13, p. 461.

New Policies

With the French gone, English colonists felt secure. Some could bask in a glow of pride, knowing that they had helped end French rule in America. Furthermore, the mingling of militiamen from different colonies in battles against the French and Indians had planted seeds of mutual understanding that would eventually grow into a sense of unity. Colonial troops discovered that they all spoke the same language—however various the accents—and that they shared common problems, even common ideals. Moreover, the successful end to the war, while welcomed, created a set of headaches for the British government that would have serious consequences for the residents of all the colonies.

The global struggle for empire had carried a heavy cost. The British government was deeply in debt—by some one hundred and thirty million pounds. And victory over the French meant that the government would now have to provide for the administration and defense of a larger territory. The land between the Appalachian Mountains and the Mississippi River now was British, as was Canada to the north. Britain's main rivals in North America now were the Spanish, to whom the French had ceded their lands west of the Mississippi. Spain also held Florida to the south. And, as Pontiac's uprising attested, the Indian problem had not gone away.

To deal with that last problem, the British government in 1763 issued its proclamation concerning western settlement. Drawing a line along the Appalachians from western Georgia north to Lake Ontario, the government prohibited settlement beyond it to the west. The line cut off about half of present-day Pennsylvania and removed a portion of New York. It placed Forts Niagara and Pitt in the forbidden zone.

The British drew the Proclamation Line hastily, but it seemed reasonable to them to halt the westward flow of settlement until something could be done about the Indians and fur-trading interests, and about organizing the territory. The line was not meant to be permanent.

Colonists paid no attention to that fact. To them, the line represented an instrument of oppression. It denied them the right to move and take up land wherever they chose. Already there had been a trickle of pioneers across the mountains into Kentucky and Tennessee. Angry about the Proclamation Line, colonists simply ignored it. And the rivulet of westward-moving settlers became a stream.

Trade and Regulation

The Proclamation of 1763 proved to be no more than a pinprick, a short-lived pain that caused no serious injury to colonial interests. But British efforts to raise money to pay off war debts and to administer and defend the American colonial empire would create more sensitive sores.

Great Britain, like other European nations with colonies, operated under the economic system known as mercantilism. Essentially, this arrangement depended on various monopolies, and stipulated that colonies existed primarily to provide raw materials for the mother country and to act as markets for manufactured goods.

Americans did not, on the whole, fare badly under mercantilism. They had a ready and protected market in Britain for such items as resin and turpentine (needed on the wooden ships of the time), and for timber, tobacco, wheat, rice, and sugar. It was true that balances between raw materials shipped and finished goods received had to be cleared in hard money, which left that a scarce commodity in the colonies. It was true, too, that the colonies were deprived of the opportunity to develop manufactures for export under such laws as the Hat Act and the Woolen Act, although these prohibitions were frequently ignored. And it was also true that such navigation acts as those requiring shipping only in American or British ships to some extent hampered freedom of choice in trade. But if they complied with regulations concerning the origin of ships, colonials were fairly free to trade wherever in the world they pleased. And they did. Actually, probably only about twenty-five percent of all American products went to England. Parliament placed duties on some products imported into the colonies, of course. For example, a sixpence tax on molasses from the West Indies was levied in 1733.

The worst thing about mercantilism, it appears, was that it did restrict, regardless of the extent. It denied colonists complete freedom to buy, sell, ship, or manufacture to the goal of maximum profit.

But, at the same time, until 1763, trade and other acts had been enforced only now and then. And smuggling was fairly easy for those who wished to avoid duties and regulations entirely. For about a hundred and fifty years, Great Britain had been preoccupied with wars in Europe and elsewhere and with minding affairs at home. Change began after the French and Indian War, and it led to conflict.

The Molasses Tax

Parliament was mainly interested in having the colonies assume a portion of the expense of maintaining ten thousand British troops in America. This ran to more than £220,000 a year. As far as the British were concerned, the soldiers were there to protect the colonies from Indians and the Spanish. Colonists did not like the presence of troops, and the idea that they should help support these soldiers angered them further. They noted that the majority of the force was garrisoned cities, where danger from Spaniards and Indians was fairly remote. To the British, that simply begged the question.

As the first step toward its financial goal, in 1764 Parliament enacted a tax of seven pounds per ton on Madeira, a wine named after the island in the Mediterranean and highly popular in the colonies. It was felt that if colonists did not wish to pay a higher rate for Madeira, they could drink cheaper English wines, which would help British merchants. At the same time the British government took steps to tighten up customs collections. For one thing, it ordered appointed collectors to go to the colonies and perform their jobs, instead of remaining comfortably in England, collecting their salaries while farming out their tasks abroad. The government also planned to crack down on smuggling. And in 1764 Parliament passed the Sugar Act, reducing the duty on molasses from six to three pence a gallon. While this would seem beneficial to colonists, the duty was still about twice what it cost per gallon to smuggle molasses. The substance, made from sugar, was the main ingredient in the distillation of rum, a favorite colonial beverage, and it was therefore the basis of one of the more important colonial industries. Some molasses came from British sugar islands in the West Indies; about four-fifths arrived from French possessions in the Caribbean. Most important from the

The New-York Historical Society

The port of New York as seen by an unknown artist about 1756.

colonial point of view, the British government confessed that the molasses duty was not so much a means of regulating trade as a way to raise badly needed revenue. And a revenue tax was something new in the colonies.

Those in New York and other colonies concerned with the molasses trade protested vigorously. Income from the trade and from rum helped pay for manufactured goods imported from Britain. Enforcing the tax would ruin trade with the French West Indies. Unable to import molasses because of the duty, colonists would be unable to sell fish and other products to the French in the Caribbean. Moreover, the end of the French and Indian War had brought economic depression in America. Taxes simply made hard times worse. Finally, colonists disliked the idea that they would be taxed mainly for revenue purposes.

To retaliate, many colonists in New York City, Philadelphia, and elsewhere vowed to rely on American manufactures and goods. Members of Philadelphia's fire departments, for example, resolved to eat only lamb raised locally and to drink only domestic beer. And colonists produced many pamphlets and newspaper articles condemning the Sugar Act. Reaction against this legislation was mild, however, compared to that which greeted the Stamp Act the following year.

No Stamps Will Be Used

The Stamp Act ran on for about twenty-five pages, listing such items as playing cards, dice, pamphlets, and legal documents that would require a revenue stamp, and stating the amount of tax on each. The highest levy, ten pounds, was for a stamp to be placed on lawyers' licenses. A stamp tax had existed for some time in England and it was not considered onerous. Certainly, from the British point of view, it seemed just. But the Stamp Act raised a real ruckus in the colonies.

Interestingly enough, New York had passed a stamp tax of its own in 1756 to help raise money during the French and Indian War, and so had Massachusetts. Few people had objected to it, although it was dropped in New York when the fighting ended because it brought in little money. Almost to a man, however, American colonists opposed the British Stamp Act of 1765.

Americans, like people everywhere and at any time, felt overtaxed. They paid what were to them heavy local taxes to support their governments and services. As a rule, only consumers could complain about customs duties. Merchants added these to wholesale and then to retail prices. In addition, these were indirect taxes and, most people apparently agreed, mainly meant to regulate trade. The stamp tax, however, fell directly on numerous groups of people. Unlike a customs duty, it was difficult to pass on. Merchants and working people, lawyers and newspaper owners, and many others would have to pay it. Also, it was a revenue-only tax, and it had been passed without colonial consultation.

Numerous colonial legislatures passed resolutions against the Stamp Act. Then in June, 1765, James Otis of Massachusetts called for cooperative colonial action against it. He proposed that representatives meet in a congress to protest the act on behalf of all the colonies.

Twenty-seven delegates from various colonies attended the Stamp Act Congress, which convened in New York City Hall in October, 1765. They produced four documents. One was a declaration of rights and grievances. Another was a petition to the king. The third and fourth were petitions to the House of Lords and the House of Commons—the two

In this British cartoon, colonists are shown pouring tea down the throat of a customs official, John Malcolm, who has already been tarred and feathered.

houses of Parliament. The Stamp Act Congress declared, in essence, that Americans could be taxed only by their own representatives, and they had none in Parliament. Therefore only colonial legislatures could levy taxes. The petitions called for the Stamp Act's repeal. Britain ignored the Stamp Act Congress.

Several months passed before stamps could be printed, loaded, and shipped to America. This gave colonists a chance to organize against the act with weapons more effective than petitions. In Boston, Andrew Oliver was named stamp distributor. And on August 14 a mob demonstrated against him. It hanged Oliver in effigy, burned one of his buildings, and ransacked his residence. Oliver resigned his

The Stamp Act riots in Boston. The sign reads, "The Folly of
England and the Ruin of America." In the background, Andrew
Oliver, the stamp distributor, is being hung in effigy.

office. Hearing the news from Boston, James McEvers, who
had been appointed distributor in New York, wrote to the
acting governor, Cadwallader Colden:

> Since the Late Riott at Boston & the Inflammatory
> Papers lately printed in the Colonies, People of this
> City are so Incens'd against me as a Distributor of
> Stamps for this Province that I find it will be
> Attended with the greatest Risque of my Person and
> Fortune, to attempt & indeed impossible for me to
> execute the Office to Prevent the same Cruel Fate
> Mr. Oliver met with at Boston . . . from the
> Information I have had that if I Attempted it, my
> House would have been Pillag'd, my Person
> Abused.[2]

Following Oliver's lead, McEvers resigned. The *New-York
Mercury* praised him as "a great patriot."

[2]Quoted in Alexander C. Flick, ed., *History of the State of New York*
(New York: Columbia University Press, 1933), vol. 3, p. 193.

Nonetheless, a British ship bearing stamps arrived in New York. As the news spread, crowds gathered at the waterfront. The Sons of Liberty—a protest group made up mostly of workingmen—prepared for action. That night the Sons placed the following notice on the door of every public office in New York City:

Pro Patria

The first man that either distributes or makes use of stamped paper, let him take care of his house, person, and effects.

Vox Populi

"We Dare"[3]

Acting Governor Colden did not back down, but he did have the stamps removed to Fort George in the New York harbor for safekeeping. He meant to distribute the stamps, but it looked as if he would have to do it himself. McEvers did not want the job. Neither did anyone else.

The Sons of Liberty had set Friday, November 1, as a day for public demonstration. And on the appointed day the Sons, and many other people, were out. Here is how one historian described the action:

> In New York the uprising was terrific, for the population rushed together as one man—as Gage, the commander of Fort George said, "by thousands."
> The sailors flocked in from the vessels, the farmers from the country, and the shouts, and ringing of bells, and firing of cannon made the city fairly tremble. Colden was terrified at the storm that was raised, and took refuge in the fort. An old man, bent and bowed with the weight of eighty years, he tottered nervously to the shelter of its guns, and ordered up a detachment of marines from a ship of war in port, for his protection. In his indignation, he wanted to fire on the people, and the black muzzles of the cannon pointing on the town had an ominous look. Whether he had threatened to do so by a message, we do not know; at any rate, the people either suspected his determination

[3]Joel Tyler Headley, *The Great Riots of New York, 1712-1873* (New York: E. B. Treat, 1873), p. 49.

or got wind of it, for during the day an unknown person handed in at the fort-gate a note, telling him if he did, the people would hang him ... on a sign-post. He wisely forebore to give the order, for if he had not, his gray hairs would have streamed from a gibbet.

At length the day of turmoil wore away, and night came on, but with it came no dimunition of the excitement. Soon as it was dark, the "Sons of Liberty," numbering thousands, surged tumultuously up around the fort, and demanded that the stamps should be given up that they might be destroyed. Colden bluntly refused, when with loud, defiant shouts they left, and went up Broadway to "the field" [the present Central Park], where they erected a gibbet, and hanged on it Colden in effigy, and beside him a figure holding a boot; some said to represent the devil, others Lord Bute, of whom the *boot,* by a pun on his name, showed for whom the effigy was designed. [Lord Bute, former first lord of the treasury, was a close adviser of King George III.]

The demonstration now became a riot, and the Sons of Liberty degenerated into a mob. The feeling that had been confined to words all day must now have some outlet. A torchlight procession was formed, and the scaffold and images taken down, and borne on men's shoulders along Broadway toward the Battery. The glare of flaring lights on the buildings and faces of the excited crowd, the shouts and hurrahs that made night hideous, called out the entire population, which gazed in amazement on the strange, wild spectacle.

They boldly carried the scaffold and effigies to within a few feet of the gate of the fort, and knocked audaciously for admission. Isaac Sears was the leader of these "Sons of Liberty."

Finding themselves unable to gain admittance, they went to the Governor's carriage-house, and took out his elegant coach, and placing the two effigies in it, dragged it by hand around the streets by the light of torches, amid the jeers and shouts of the multitude. Becoming at last tired of this amusement, they returned towards the fort, and erected a second gallows, on which they hung the effigies the second time.

All this time the cannon, shotted and primed, lay silent on their carriages, while the soldiers from the ramparts looked wonderingly, idly on. General Gage did not dare to fire on the people, fearing they would sweep like an inundation over the ramparts, when he knew a general massacre would follow.

The mob now tore down the wooden fence that surrounded Bowling Green, and piling pickets and boards together, set them on fire. As the flames crackled and roared in the darkness, they pitched on the Governor's coach, with the scaffold and effigies; then hastening to his carriage-house again, and dragging out a one-horse chaise, two sleighs, and other vehicles, hauled them to the fire, and threw them on, making a conflagration that illumined the waters of the bay and the ships riding at anchor. This was a galling spectacle to the old Governor and the British officers, but they dared not interfere. . . .

Although Sears and other leaders of the Sons of Liberty tried to restrain the mob, their blood was now up, and they were bent on destruction. Having witnessed the conflagration of the Governor's carriages, they again marched up Broadway, and some one shouting "James' house," the crowd took up the shout, and passing out of the city streamed through the open country to where West Broadway now is, and near the corner of Anthony Street. This James was Major in the Royal Artillery, and had made himself obnoxious to the people by taking a conspicuous part in putting the fort into a state of defence. He had a beautiful residence here, which the mob completely gutted, broke up his elegant furniture, destroyed his library and works of art, and laid waste his ornamented grounds. They then dispersed, and the city became quiet.

The excitement was, however, not quelled—the people had not yet got hold of the stamps, which they were determined to have. Colden, having seen enough of the spirit of the "Sons of Liberty," was

afraid to risk another night, even in the fort, unless
it was in some way appeased; and so the day after
the riot, he had a large placard posted up, stating
that he should have nothing more to do with the
stamps, but would leave them with Sir Henry Moore,
the newly appointed Governor, then on his way from
England.

This, however, did not satisfy the Sons of Liberty:
they wanted the stamps themselves, and through
Sears, their leader, insisted on their being given up—
telling him very plainly that if he did not they would
storm the fort, and they were determined to do it.

The Common Council of the city now became
alarmed at the ungovernable, desperate spirit of the
mob, which seemed bent on blood, and begged the
Governor to let them be deposited in the City Hall.
To this he finally though reluctantly consented,
but the feeling in the city kept at fever heat, and
would remain so until the act itself was repealed.

Moore, the new Governor, soon arrived, and
assumed the reigns of government. The corporation
[city council] offered him [a document granting him]
the freedom of the city in a gold box, but he refused
to receive it, unless upon stamped paper. It was
evident he was determined to enforce the stamp act.
But on consulting with Colden and others, and
ascertaining the true state of things, he wisely
abandoned his purpose, and soon made it publicly
known. To appease the people still more, he
dismantled the fort, which was peculiarily obnoxious
to them from the threatening attitude it had
been made to assume. Still, the infamous act was
unrepealed, and the people refused to buy English
manufactures, and commerce languished.[4]

The New York Sons of Liberty had set up committees of
correspondence so that Sons in all the colonies could be
kept informed of actions. And in Philadelphia, as in New
York, flags flew at half mast to mourn the Stamp Act and
stamps. Stamps, however, were not distributed in Philadelphia any more than they were in Boston or New York.

[4]Ibid., pp. 50–53.

The Scene in Philadelphia

In Philadelphia, John Hughes was appointed stamp distributor upon the recommendation of Benjamin Franklin, who was in London at the time. As it turned out, Franklin did his friend no favor. Hughes soon began to hear suggestions that he resign his post. He also heard rumors that his house might be pulled down. His friends, including Joseph Galloway, rallied to his protection. Hughes wrote the following report during the night of September 16, 1765:

John Hughes was appointed stamp distributor in Philadelphia on Benjamin Franklin's recommendation.

> I for my Part am well arm'd with Fire-Arms, and am
> determin'd to stand a Siege. If I live till to-morrow
> I shall give you a further Account, but as it is now
> about 8 a Clock, I am on my Guard, and only write
> this between whiles, as every Noise or Bustle of the
> People calls me off.
> 9 a Clock.—Severall Friends that patroll between my
> House and the Coffee House, come in just now, and
> say, the Collection of Rabble begins to decrease
> visibly in the Streets, and the Appearance of Danger
> seems a good deal less than it did.
> 12 a Clock. There are now several Hundreds of our
> Friends about street, ready to suppress any Mob, if
> it should attempt to rise, and the Rabble is dispersing.
> Sept. 17. 5 in the morning—We are all yet in the
> Land of the Living, and our Property safe. Thank
> God.—[5]

That was not the end of Hughes's troubles, though. Stamps arrived in Philadelphia on October 5, along with Hughes's commission as distributor. Responding to the roll of drums, a mob began to gather. Benjamin Shoemaker, a Quaker and a city alderman, sought to turn the milling crowd back. According to Hughes, Shoemaker

> met with the Drummers, as they were allarming the
> City and took them to task, requiring to know by
> what authority they were endeavouring to raise a
> Mob, they answered if He would go to the State

[5]Quoted in Edmund S. and Helen M. Morgan, *The Stamp Act Crisis, Prologue to Revolution,* rev. ed. (New York: Macmillan, Collier Books, 1963), pp. 314–15.

The tax stamp issued by the British.

House, He might know. He than asked who ordered them to beat about Streets, they said they had their orders from the Coffee House [where mob leaders were headquartered]. ... Mr. Shoemaker then forbid them to proceed any farther, and said He would go immediately to the Mayor, and have them committed, they answered they could get the Mayor's orders when they pleased; But Mr. Shoemaker could not find the Mayor, nor any Officer to assist him, and therefore was obliged to desist, least He should draw the Mob upon Himself and Family and to have his house pulled down.[6]

At three that afternoon the mob surrounded the state house. Seven from among them called on Hughes for his resignation as stamp distributor. After an hour's argument, the seven agreed that Hughes need not resign; he had only to promise not to try to distribute stamps until more was heard from England. Hughes accepted that. And the following day he signed a statement declaring that he would not distribute stamps until they were distributed in other colonies. Later, as Hughes reported, he had an opportunity to twit his opponents:

> I sometimes tell some of our Warm Blades, that it is a piece of Inconsistency in them to call themselves Englishmen, Because Gentlemen say I, If you are Englishmen you must be bound by Acts of Parliament until that Parliament releases you, from that Obedience, which has not yet been done as I know of.
> To this they reply, our Charters have done it.
> Absolutely no Gentlemen, Your Charters are but the Declaration of the Kings that Granted them, and they cannot be Tortured to mean no more than that the Kings of Great Britain, would not arbitrarily and without Law raise money on the Subject in America, And this is all our forefathers seem to have asked, when they left Britain, and Indeed it is all the Kings of Great Britain can legally promise, for

[6]Quoted in ibid., pp. 315–16.

the King cannot Bar the Rights of the Lords and Commons, any more [than] they can his Prerogatives.

The Answer then is you are an Enemy to America, and ought to have your brains beat out. . . .

One Reason assign'd for not paying Obedience to this Act of Parliament, is that we have no Representatives in Parliament, I then say let us Petition for Representatives.

O no we will not agree to that, because we have Representatives of our own, and have always given money when we have been cald upon by the King or his Ministers, and if that will not do let us have a House of Commons in America to settle what shall be the Quota of each Colony when Money is wanted &c.

No Gentlemen you have foreclosed yourselves of that, for you have demonstrated your [propensity] to Rebellion to that Degree that it is my opinion the Ministry never can advise his Majesty to Unite you more than you now are, But if they know'd our Circumstances Rightly they wou'd devide us yet more, by forming New Colinies out of Virginia, and Perhaps some others that are already but too large.[7]

A colonist's version of the hated stamp.

Things were much the same in New Jersey. It was reported that William Coxe, the New Jersey stamp officer, was refused the rental of a house unless he would insure it against damage or being pulled down. Urged on by his friends, Coxe resigned in September, although Governor William Franklin was determined that the stamps would be distributed. They were not. And in December the New Jersey Sons of Liberty called on William Coxe at his home in Woodbridge. They asked him to reaffirm his resignation. Coxe did so, gladly, and toasts were drunk to the king, to him, and to "Confusion to every American Stamp Master unless he resigns his abhorred and detestable office."

Throughout the colonies, lawyers and judges resolved not to use the stamps. The doors of the halls of justice closed. Merchants refused to have anything to do with stamps. And they agreed to boycott British goods.

[7] Quoted in ibid., pp. 318–19.

British merchants and manufacturers eventually suffered from colonial non-importation agreements. In fact, the boycott hurt far more than the rioting had done. Business in England declined and workers lost their jobs. As the economic situation worsened, Englishmen joined Americans in demanding repeal of the act. And finally, after long and stormy debate, Parliament abolished the Stamp Act on March 18, 1766.

When news of repeal reached New York,

> the most unbounded joy was manifested. Bells were rung, cannon fired, and placards posted, calling on a meeting of the citizens the next day to take measures for celebrating properly the great event. At the appointed time, the people came together at Howard's Hotel, and forming a procession, marched gayly to "the field," and right where the City Hall now stands, then an open lot, a salute of twenty-one guns was fired. A grand dinner followed, at which the Sons of Liberty feasted and drank loyal toasts to his Majesty, and all went "merry as a marriage-bell." The city was illuminated, and bonfires turned the night into day. . . .[8]

But the debate over taxation had not ended. Parliament did not want to appear to be backing down entirely, and so on the same day it repealed the Stamp Act it also passed the Declaratory Act. In this act, Parliament declared that it had the right and the power to legislate for the colonies "in all cases whatsoever." Members of Parliament assumed that this meant, among other things, the power to levy taxes. Colonists would continue to disagree.

More Acts, More Responses

In 1764 Parliament had forbidden the further issuance of paper money in the colonies. The act was to be effective in New York in 1768, when the last notes of credit the assembly had issued would fall due for payment. Customs duties were to be collected in hard money only. This threatened to work a hardship in the colony, where coin

---

[8] Headley, *The Great Riots,* p. 53.

remained scarce. And it provided yet another grievance against Great Britain.

During the same year Parliament passed the Stamp Act, 1765, it also passed the Mutiny, or Quartering, Act. This required the colonists to furnish barracks, fuel, beds, candles, and some food supplies to British troops stationed in America. Because General Gage was headquartered in New York, that colony had the greatest number of troops to support.

The New York assembly refused to appropriate money to quarter soldiers. So the British government suspended the assembly, effective in 1767. Before that date was reached, however, the assembly reconsidered and passed the appropriations measure. This was not the end of the matter; it later became connected with the paper money issue.

After repealing the Stamp Act, Britain still needed revenue. And in 1767 Parliament passed the Townshend duties, laying taxes on imported paint, paper, glass, and tea. Another act passed at the same time authorized the use of writs of assistance—general search warrants—mainly as a means of curbing smuggling. Still another law set up an American Board of Customs Commissioners to oversee and tighten the collection of customs duties in all the colonies.

Following the enactment of the Townshend duties, John Dickinson came to the fore as an important advocate of American rights and liberties, ranking as a spokesman along with Samuel Adams and James Otis of Massachusetts.

John Dickinson.

Dickinson was born on November 8, 1732, at Croisa-doré, the family estate, in Talbot County, Maryland. In 1740 his father, Samuel Dickinson, moved the family to Kent County, Delaware, where he purchased a large estate. Young Dickinson was educated at home by a tutor until the age of eighteen, when he began to study law under John Moland of Philadelphia. In 1753 his father sent him to London for further legal study in the Middle Temple. He returned to Philadelphia to begin his law practice in 1757. In October, 1760, he was elected to the Delaware assembly, and two years later to the lawmaking body of Pennsylvania.

Dickinson wholeheartedly supported the colonial position on taxation. He attended the Stamp Act Congress in 1765, but he made a more important contribution two years later with his "Farmer's Letters." The *Pennsylvania Chronicle* published the first letter on December 2, 1767. Dickinson began, "I am a farmer," (which was not precisely true),

> settled, after a variety of fortunes, near the banks of the river Delaware, in the Province of Pennsylvania. I received a liberal education, and have been engaged in the busy scenes of life, but am now convinced that a man may be as happy without bustle as with it. Being generally master of my own time, I spend a good deal of it in my library, which I think the most valuable part of my small estate. I have acquired, I believe, a greater knowledge of history and of the laws and constitution of my country than is generally attained by men of my class.[9]

Dickinson then argued the colonies' case. As to the suspension of the New York assembly, for example, he said, "If an Assembly may be legally deprived in such a case of the privilege of legislation, why may it not with equal reason be deprived of every other privilege?"[10] As to the Townshend duties, he wrote:

> We must have paper and glass and tea, and we must by existing laws import them from England alone. Once admit that Great Britain may levy duties on articles of necessity, which we are forced by law to import from her, under the plea that such a proceeding is a commercial regulation, then she will not be restrained from levying what duties she thinks proper on all articles which she prohibits us to manufacture, as well as those required for daily use, which we must take from her."[11]

---

[9]Quoted in Charles J. Stillé, *The Life and Times of John Dickinson* (Philadelphia: J. B. Lippincott, 1891), pp. 82–83.

[10]Quoted in ibid., p. 83.

[11]Quoted in ibid., p. 84.

Finally, Dickinson asked: "For who are a free people?" He answered:

> Not those over whom government is reasonably and equitably exercised, but those who live under a government so constitutionally checked and controlled that proper provision is made against its ever being otherwise exercised.[12]

The "Farmer's Letters" were widely read, well received, and very influential. They helped reinforce observance of non-importation agreements and buttressed colonists' arguments against what they considered unjust taxation.

On the whole, colonists did not take kindly to the new taxes, nor did they like writs of assistance. Such writs, they argued, violated their rights as Englishmen. In New York, though, it appears that people paid the new duties with little if any protest during the first year. But the ban on paper money was having its effect as the economy slowed down. New Yorkers took two actions. First, in November, 1768, the legislature provided for the issuance of £120,000 in paper money. Second, merchants agreed to boycott British goods in protest against the Townshend duties, just as merchants in Philadelphia, Boston, and other ports had done. The value of imports into New York from Britain fell from £490,000 in 1768 to £75,900 in 1769. Yet merchants began to prosper once again as the paper money issue stimulated the economy and helped them clear their inventories.

New York's Sons of Liberty defending their "Liberty Pole." Poles or trees were set up in many towns to mark the meeting places of pro-revolutionary groups.

To reinforce New Yorkers' attitudes toward the Townshend duties, in 1769 the Sons of Liberty took to the streets again. They frequently expressed their feelings by erecting a "liberty pole," a symbol of defiance against the British. The New York Sons put up four, and British soldiers cut them down. In January, 1770, the Sons erected a fifth. This time they padded the base with iron to make it more difficult for the soldiers to dismantle. But after four days' work, on January 16 the redcoats had it down. Two days later, following a mass meeting, the Sons

[12] Quoted in ibid., p. 89.

of Liberty seized some soldiers and dragged them to the mayor's office. Their fellows moved out to rescue them, and the "Battle of Golden Hill" resulted. The fracas produced bruises and bloody noses aplenty, but there were no deaths, as there would be in the Boston Massacre which occurred a few months later.

Following renewed non-importation and a severe drop in British business, Parliament once again was forced to read the negative handwriting on the wall in the colonies. It repealed the Townshend duties, keeping only a sixpence tax on tea. Non-importation now ceased. Britain had disallowed the New York paper money issue of 1768. Now, in a change of mind, it allowed it.

The Tea Affair

The East India Company's offices in England.

Colonists refused to buy tea that was taxed, preferring the smuggled variety, most of which came from Holland. Noting this, the British government decided to try an end run, mainly to help the East India Company, which had a lot of tea on hand and was facing bankruptcy. In 1773, the government declared that henceforth there would be only a threepence tax on tea imported into America, a rather small levy. Furthermore, the government granted the East India Company a monopoly on the transport and sale of tea in the colonies, and the right to sell it directly to retailers. This would greatly benefit the company, for it was estimated that Americans drank some six million pounds of tea a year. Americans would benefit, even with the small tax, for the wholesale mark-up on tea would be lower than before. The only real losers were the merchants—the wholesalers—on both sides of the ocean.

The scheme seemed highly reasonable, but the British government failed to take into account the colonists' insistence on making a point about taxes. In pamphlets and in newspaper articles, New Yorkers and others denounced the tea tax and the monopoly idea as well. Merchants to whom the East India tea was to be consigned, who would act for the company, were asked if they would receive the shipments. They would not. Furthermore, the Sons of Liberty swung into action again, reviving their committees of correspondence to keep in touch on the tea

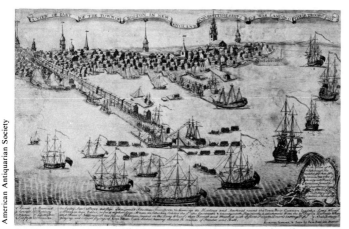

American Antiquarian Society

Paul Revere's engraving of the port of Boston in 1768 shows British troops debarking at Long Wharf to occupy the town and "rescue the government from the hands of a trained mob." Revere made and published the engraving to stir up anger over this British show of force.

question throughout the colonies. The New York assembly appointed its own committee of correspondence.

Late in December, 1773, dispatch rider Paul Revere arrived in New York after a swift trip from the north. He brought news of the Boston Tea Party, which had taken place on December 16. Thereupon some New York merchants wrote a letter to the captain of the ship *Nancy*, expected to arrive with tea, telling him that they would not accept his cargo. The letter was to be delivered upon the ship's arrival off Sandy Hook.

On April 18, the *Nancy* rode at anchor. The captain acknowledged the letter and asked permission to lay in supplies for the return voyage. This was granted, so long as he made no move to unload the 689 chests of tea aboard. But the captain tried once more, informing merchants that he was ready to deliver, and once again they refused to accept his tea.

Meanwhile the *London* arrived in port. Two Sons of Liberty went aboard to search for tea. They found none, and the ship was allowed to dock. Still suspicious, though, a "number of citizens" boarded the *London* and threatened to open every cask in a thorough search for tea. The captain then admitted that he had eighteen chests aboard, which enraged the crowd gathered along the wharf. And that night, a group of men boarded the *London*, found the tea, and dumped it overboard. That was New York's "tea-party"—milder than Boston's, but with identical sentiments attached.

The *London* set sail for England. The *Nancy*, its tea still undelivered, followed on April 23.

Responding to the Boston Tea Party, Parliament passed a number of laws which the colonists lumped together as the Intolerable Acts. Among them was one closing the port of Boston until the ruined tea was paid for. Another restricted town meetings. Still another reorganized the Massachusetts government, establishing, among other things, that council members be appointed rather than elected. These acts were aimed at Boston, but another, passed at the same time, posed a threat to other colonies.

The Quebec Act of 1774 guaranteed French Canadians the right to practice their Roman Catholic religion and to retain their own language, customs, and institutions. These institutions did not include trial by jury or representative assemblies such as the English colonists enjoyed. Even more alarming to the English colonists, the boundaries of Quebec province were widened far west and south to the Ohio and Mississippi rivers. The enforcement of the act would cut out land speculators and settlers from the rich Ohio Valley. It would open the way for what colonists considered a non-democratic government in an area all had considered American. It would end dreams of establishing communities in the region similar to those the colonists had become accustomed to, communities which enjoyed a large measure of self-government. Finally, to Protestants, the act meant encroachment by Roman Catholicism into an area judged to be ear-marked for Protestants. To those outside Massachusetts, which bore the brunt of the Intolerable Acts, the Quebec Act seemed the most onerous of all.

The Intolerable Acts furthered colonial unity. Flags throughout the colonies flew at half mast in sympathy and in support for Bostonians. Colonists gathered food and

The Public Archives of Canada

Americans viewed the Quebec Act of 1774 as the most oppressive of the Intolerable Acts, but the French in Canada felt differently and refused to align themselves with the patriots of the American Revolution. Pictured above are British troops parading on the grounds of the Governor's House in Quebec. Behind them are the Cathedral, Jesuits' College, and Recollect Friars' Church.

clothing to send to them. At the same time, Sons of Liberty in Massachusetts and elsewhere began storing arms, gunpowder, and ammunition. Militiamen began to drill. And on June 17, 1774, the Massachusetts House of Representatives called for an intercolonial meeting to consider courses of action. Delegates from every colony except Georgia gathered as the First Continental Congress met in Philadelphia on September 5. They met in the building later known as Independence Hall.

There delegates listened to a plan proposed by Joseph Galloway, a well-to-do and conservative Philadelphia lawyer. Galloway called for the establishment of a united American government with a legislature in which every colony would be represented. The government would have full power to legislate and to enforce its laws, and the power to veto any act of Parliament affecting the colonies. Parliament, in turn, could veto any American legislation.

Independence Hall, Philadelphia, where the Declaration of Independence, the Articles of Confederation, and the Constitution were signed. It presently houses the Liberty Bell.

Historical Society of Pennsylvania

A plan of government, however, was not uppermost in the delegates' minds at the time. Most of them wished to address themselves to rights and grievances.

The declaration issued by the First Continental Congress began by expressing loyalty to King George III. Then it denied the right of Parliament to legislate for the colonies or to levy taxes. Parliament could do no more than regulate trade. In addition, the Congress created an association to oversee non-importation, non-exportation, and non-consumption of British goods. It warned Parliament that a boycott of all trade with Britain would be in effect until all colonial grievances were redressed. The Congress then adjourned, recommending that another meet in the spring of 1775.

Parliament refused any concessions. Throughout the winter, Sons of Liberty and members of the association kept busy enforcing the trade boycott. Sometimes they resorted to tarring and feathering to make their point. Protest and boycott had brought down the Stamp Act and the Townshend duties. Force or threat of force had kept

English tea from American shores. But this time such measures failed to sway the British government.

Earlier, Benjamin Franklin had been sent to England as Pennsylvania's representative. He returned home a few days before the Second Continental Congress was to meet in May, 1775. The news he received upon landing heartened him. Franklin learned that on the night of April 18 British regulars had moved out from Boston to seize military stores in Concord. Minutemen had met them early the next day on Lexington Green. Shots had been fired. Next, from behind stone fences and trees, militiamen had harassed the redcoats as they marched back to Boston from Concord, killing and wounding many.

The seeds of revolution, which had been planted years before, had borne fruit: colonists had grown into Americans. The War for Independence was upon them.

SUGGESTED READINGS

Boorstin, Daniel J. *The Americans: The Colonial Experience.* Random House, Vintage Books.

Dickerson, Oliver M. *The Navigation Acts and the American Revolution.* University of Pennsylvania Press.

Kammen, Michael. *A Rope of Sand: The Colonial Agents, British Policies, and the American Revolution.* Random House, Vintage Books.

Maier, Pauline. *From Resistance to Revolution: Colonial Radicals and the Development of American Opposition to Britain.* Random House, Vintage Books.

Morgan, Edmund S. and Helen M. *The Stamp Act Crisis: Prologue to Revolution.* Macmillan, Collier Books.

Rossiter, Clinton. *The First American Revolution: The American Colonies on the Eve of Revolution.* Rev. ed. Harcourt Brace Jovanovich, Harvest Books.

Rushton, William Faulkner. *The Cajuns: From Acadia to Louisiana.* Farrar, Straus & Giroux.

BIBLIOGRAPHY

Chapter One

Acrelius, Israel. "Account of the Swedish Churches in New Sweden." In Albert Cook Myers, ed., *Narratives of Early Pennsylvania, West New Jersey and Delaware, 1630–1707*. New York: Charles Scribner's Sons, 1912.

Adams, Spencer L. *The Long House of the Iroquois*. 1944. Reprint ed. New York: AMS Press, 1977.

Andrews, Charles M. *Our Earliest Colonial Settlements: Their Diversities of Origin and Later Characteristics*. Ithaca, N.Y.: Cornell University Press, 1959.

Archdeacon, Thomas J. *New York City, 1664–1710: Conquest and Change*. Ithaca, N.Y.: Cornell University Press, 1976.

Beauchamp, William M. *Iroquois Folk Lore*. 1922. Reprint ed. New York: AMS Press, 1976.

Brodhead, John Romeyn. *History of the State of New York*. New York: Harper & Brothers, 1853.

Buranelli, Vincent. *The King and the Quaker*. Philadelphia: University of Pennsylvania Press, 1962.

Clarkson, Thomas. *Memoirs of the Private and Public Life of William Penn*. London: Longman, Hurst, Rees, Orme, and Brown, 1813.

Condon, Thomas J. *New York Beginnings: The Commercial Origins of New Netherland*. New York: New York University Press, 1968.

Dunn, Mary. *William Penn: Politics and Conscience*. Princeton, N.J.: Princeton University Press, 1967.

Endy, Melvin. *William Penn and Early Quakerism*. Princeton, N.J.: Princeton University Press, 1973.

Flick, Alexander C., ed. *History of the State of New York*. Vol. 1. New York: Columbia University Press, 1933.

Hunt, George T. *The Wars of the Iroquois: A Study in Intertribal Trade Relations*. Madison: University of Wisconsin Press, 1960.

Jameson, J. Franklin, ed. *Narratives of New Netherland, 1609–1664*. New York: Charles Scribner's Sons, 1909.

Kammen, Michael. *Colonial New York: A History*. New York: Charles Scribner's Sons, 1975.

Laet, Johan de. "New World." In J. Franklin Jameson, ed., *Narratives of New Netherland, 1609–1664*. New York: Charles Scribner's Sons, 1909.

Lodwick, Charles. "Letter to His Uncle." In *Collections of the New-York Historical Society for the Year 1849*. Vol. 2. New York: New-York Historical Society, 1849.

Lokken, Roy N. *David Lloyd: Colonial Lawmaker*. Seattle: University of Washington Press, 1959.

Megapolensis, Johannes, Jr. "A Short Account of the Mohawk Indians." In J. Franklin Jameson, ed., *Narratives of New Netherland, 1609–1664*. New York: Charles Scribner's Sons, 1909.

Meteren, Emanuel van. "On Hudson's Voyage." In J. Franklin Jameson, ed., *Narratives of New Netherland, 1609–1664*. New York: Charles Scribner's Sons, 1909.

Miller, John. *Description of the Province and City of New York . . . in the Year 1695*. London: T. Rodd, 1843.

Morison, Samuel Eliot. *The European Discovery of America: The Northern Voyages*. New York: Oxford University Press, 1971.

Myers, Albert Cook, ed. *Narratives of Early Pennsylvania, West New Jersey and Delaware, 1630–1707*. New York: Charles Scribner's Sons, 1912.

Myers, Albert Cook, ed. *William Penn's Own Account of the Lenni Lenape or Delaware Indians*. Rev. ed. Wallingford, Pa.: Middle Atlantic Press, 1970.

O'Callaghan, E. B., ed. *The Documentary History of the State of New-York*. Vol. 2. Albany: Weed, Parsons, 1849.

Parkman, Francis. *The Jesuits in North America in the Seventeenth Century*. Vol. 2. Boston: Little, Brown, 1899.

Penn, William. "Some Account of the Province of Pennsilvania" and "A Further Account of the Province of Pennsylvania." In Albert Cook Myers, ed., *Narratives of Early Pennsylvania, West New Jersey and Delaware, 1630–1707*. New York: Charles Scribner's Sons, 1912.

Reich, Jerome R. *Leisler's Rebellion: A Study of Democracy in New York, 1664–1720*. Chicago: University of Chicago Press, 1953.

Rising, Johan Clason. "Relation of the Surrender of New Sweden." In Albert Cook Myers, ed., *Narratives of Early Pennsylvania, West New Jersey and Delaware,*

1630–1707. New York: Charles Scribner's Sons, 1912.

Ritchie, Robert C. *The Duke's Province: A Study of New York Politics and Society, 1664–1691.* Chapel Hill: University of North Carolina Press, 1977.

Sanders, Thomas E., and Peek, Walter W. *Literature of the American Indian.* Encino, Calif.: Glencoe, 1973.

Smith, George L. *Religion and Trade in New Netherland: Dutch Origins and American Development.* Ithaca, N.Y.: Cornell University Press, 1973.

Tuckerman, Bayard. *Peter Stuyvesant.* New York: Dodd, Mead, 1893.

Weslager, Clinton A. *Dutch Explorers, Traders, and Settlers in the Delaware Valley.* Philadelphia: University of Pennsylvania Press, 1964.

Weslager, Clinton A. *The English on the Delaware: 1610–1682.* New Brunswick, N.J.: Rutgers University Press, 1967.

Wildes, Harry E. *William Penn.* New York: Macmillan, 1974.

Chapter Two

Armistead, Wilson. *Memoirs of James Logan.* 1851. Reprint ed. St. Clair Shores, Mich.: Scholarly Press, 1976.

Bonomi, Patricia. *Fractious People: Politics and Society in Colonial New York.* New York: Columbia University Press, 1971.

Buck, Solon J., and Buck, Elizabeth H. *The Planting of Civilization in Western Pennsylvania.* Pittsburgh: University of Pittsburgh Press, 1969.

Buranelli, Vincent, ed. *The Trial of Peter Zenger.* 1957. Reprint ed. Westport, Conn.: Greenwood Press, 1976.

Chidsey, Donald B. *The French and Indian War.* New York: Crown, 1969.

Colden, Cadwallader, "History of William Cosby's Administration as Governor of the Province of New York . . . through 1737." In *Collections of the New-York Historical Society for the Year 1935.* New York: New-York Historical Society, 1937.

Dunbar, John R., ed. *The Paxton Papers.* The Hague: Martinus Nijhoof, 1957.

Eckert, Allan W. *Wilderness Empire.* Boston: Little, Brown, 1969.

Franklin, Benjamin. *Autobiography and Other Writings.* Edited by Russel B. Nye. Boston: Houghton Mifflin, 1958.

Franklin, Benjamin. *Poor Richard's Almanac.* New York: David McKay, 1976.

Frost, William J. *The Quaker Family in Colonial America.* New York: St. Martin's Press, 1973.

Hutson, James H. *Pennsylvania Politics, 1746–1770: The Movement for Royal Government and Its Consequences.* Princeton, N.J.: Princeton University Press, 1972.

Kalm, Peter. "Travels into North America." In John Pinkerton, ed., *A General Collection of the Best and Most Interesting Voyages and Travels in All Parts of the World.* London: Longman, Hurst, Rees, Orme, and Brown, 1812.

Konkle, Burton A. *The Life of Andrew Hamilton, 1676–1741.* 1941. Reprint ed. New York: Arno Press, 1972.

Kopperman, Paul E. *Braddock at the Monongahela.* Pittsburgh: University of Pittsburgh Press, 1976.

McCardell, Lee. *The Ill-Starred General: Braddock of the Coldstream Guards.* Pittsburgh: University of Pittsburgh Press, 1962.

McCormick, Richard P. *New Jersey from Colony to State, 1609–1789.* 2nd ed. New Brunswick, N.J.: Rutgers University Press, 1970.

Parkman, Francis. *Montcalm and Wolfe.* New York: Macmillan, Collier Books, 1962.

Peckham, Howard H. *Colonial Wars, 1689–1762.* Chicago: University of Chicago Press, 1964.

Peckham, Howard H. *Pontiac and the Indian Uprising.* 2nd ed. 1961. Reprint ed. New York: Russell & Russell, 1970.

Pomfret, John E. *Colonial New Jersey: A History.* New York: Charles Scribner's Sons, 1973.

Reich, Jerome R. *Leisler's Rebellion: A Study of Democracy in New York, 1664–1720.* Chicago: University of Chicago Press, 1953.

Sharpless, Isaac. *Two Centuries of Pennsylvania History.* Philadelphia: J.B. Lippincott, 1900.

Tully, Alan. *William Penn's Legacy: Politics and Social Structure in Provincial Pennsylvania, 1726–1755.* Baltimore: Johns Hopkins University Press, 1978.

Uhler, Sherman P. *Pennsylvania's Indian Relations to*

1754. 1951. Reprint ed., New York: AMS Press, n.d.

Waitley, Douglas. *Roads of Destiny: The Trails That Shaped a Nation.* Washington, D.C.: Robert B. Luce, 1970.

Watson, John Fanning. *Annals of Philadelphia, and Pennsylvania in the Olden Time: Being a Collection of Memoirs, Anecdotes, and Incidents. . . .* Vol. 2. Philadelphia: E. S. Stuart, 1898.

Weslager, Clinton A. *The Delaware Indians: A History.* New Brunswick, N.J.: Rutgers University Press, 1972.

Whitehead, W. A., et al., eds. *Documents Relating to the Colonial History of the State of New Jersey.* Newark: *Daily Journal,* 1880–1886.

Chapter Three

Andrews, Charles M. *Colonial Folkways.* New Haven, Conn.: Yale University Press, 1921.

Birmingham, Stephen. *The Grandees: The Story of America's Sephardic Elite.* New York: Harper & Row, 1971.

Bridenbaugh, Carl. *Cities in Revolt: Urban Life in America, 1743–1776.* New York: Oxford University Press, Galaxy Books, 1970.

Bridenbaugh, Carl. *Cities in the Wilderness: The First Century of Urban Life in America, 1625–1742.* New York: Oxford University Press, Galaxy Books, 1971.

Bridenbaugh, Carl. *The Colonial Craftsman.* Chicago: University of Chicago Press, Phoenix Books, 1961.

Cremin, Lawrence A. *American Education: The Colonial Experience, 1607–1783.* New York: Harper & Row, 1970.

Early, J. W. "A Bit of Early School History." In *Proceedings of the Bucks County Historical Society.* Doylestown, Pa.: Bucks County Historical Society, 1898–1904.

Fletcher, Stevenson Whitcomb. *Pennsylvania Agriculture and Country Life, 1640–1840.* Harrisburg: Pennsylvania Historical and Museum Commission, 1950.

Frese, Joseph R., and Judd, Jacob. *Business Enterprise in Early New York.* Tarrytown, N. Y.: Sleepy Hollow Restorations, 1979.

Gummere, Amelia Mott, ed. *The Journal and Essays of John Woolman.* New York: Macmillan, 1922.

Herrick, Cheesman A. *White Servitude in Pennsylvania:*

Indentured and Redemption Labor in Colony and Commonwealth. Philadelphia: John Joseph McVey, 1926.

Horsmanden, Daniel. *The New York Conspiracy, or a History of the Negro Plot.* 1810. Reprint ed. Westport, Conn.: Negro Universities Press, n.d.

Illick, Joseph E. *Colonial Pennsylvania: A History.* New York: Charles Scribner's Sons, 1976.

Kalm, Peter. "Travels into North America." In John Pinkerton, ed., *A General Collection of the Best and Most Interesting Voyages and Travels in All Parts of the World.* London: Longman, Hurst, Rees, Orme, and Brown, 1812.

Klees, Frederic. *The Pennsylvania Dutch.* New York: Macmillan, 1950.

Kuhns, Oscar. *The German and Swiss Settlements of Colonial Pennsylvania: A Study of the So-Called Pennsylvania Dutch.* New York: Henry Holt, 1901.

Lemon, James T. *The Best Poor Man's Country: A Geographic Survey of Early Southeastern Pennsylvania.* New York: W. W. Norton, 1976.

McKee. Samuel, Jr. *Labor in Colonial New York, 1664–1776.* New York: Columbia University Press, 1935.

Marcus, Jacob R. *The Colonial American Jew: 1492–1776.* 3 vols. Detroit: Wayne State University Press, 1970.

Rothermund, Dietmar. *Layman's Progress: Denominations and Political Behavior in Colonial Pennsylvania.* Philadelphia: University of Pennsylvania Press, 1962.

Sharfman, I. Harold. *Jews on the Frontier: An Account of Jewish Pioneers and Settlers in Early America.* Chicago: Contemporary Books, 1977.

Smith, Abbot Emerson. *Colonists in Bondage: White Servitude and Convict Labor in America, 1607–1776.* Chapel Hill: University of North Carolina Press, 1947.

Stroudt, John J. *Sunbonnets and Shoofly Pies: Pennsylvania Dutch Cultural History.* Cranbury, N.J.: A. S. Barnes, 1973.

Turner, Edmund R. *The Negro in Pennsylvania: Slavery, Servitude, Freedom, 1639–1861.* 1911. Reprint ed. New York: Arno Press. 1969.

Chapter Four

Burnaby, Andrew. *Travels through the Middle Settlements in North America in the Years 1759 and 1760.*

2nd ed. Ithaca, N.Y.: Cornell University Press, 1960.

Chapman, Isaac. *The History of Wyoming Valley in Pennsylvania*. New Orleans: Polyanthos, 1975.

Colden, Cadwallader. *The History of the Five Indian Nations*. Ithaca, N.Y.: Cornell University Press, 1958.

Dexter, Elizabeth W. *Colonial Women of Affairs*. 2nd ed. Boston: Houghton Mifflin, 1931.

Flexner, James Thomas. *Lord of the Mohawks: A Biography of Sir William Johnson*. Rev. ed. Boston: Little, Brown, 1979.

Furnas, J. C. *The Americans: A Social History of the United States, 1587–1914*. New York: G. P. Putnam's Sons, 1969.

Gray, Elma E., and Gray, Leslie R. *Wilderness Christians: The Moravian Mission to the Delaware Indians*. 1956. Reprint ed. New York: Russell & Russell, 1973.

Hofstadter, Richard. *America at 1750*. New York: Random House, Vintage Books, 1973.

Jacobs, Wilbur R. *Wilderness Politics and Indian Gifts: The Northern Colonial Frontier, 1748–1763*. Lincoln: University of Nebraska Press, Bison Books, 1966.

Kalm, Peter. "Travels into North America." In John Pinkerton, ed., *A General Collection of the Best and Most Interesting Voyages and Travels in All Parts of the World*. London: Longman, Hurst, Rees, Orme, and Brown, 1812.

Keys, Alice Mapelsden. *Cadwallader Colden: A Representative Eighteenth-Century Official*. New York: Columbia University Press, 1906.

Klein, Randolph Shipley. *Portrait of an Early American Family*. Philadelphia: University of Pennsylvania Press, 1975.

Leder, Lawrence H. *Robert Livingston, 1654–1728, and the Politics of Colonial New York*. Chapel Hill: University of North Carolina Press, 1961.

Miller, John C. *First Frontier: Life in Colonial America*. New York: Dell, 1966.

Nammack, Georgiana, C. *Fraud, Politics, and the Dispossession of the Indians: The Iroquois Land Frontier in the Colonial Period*. Norman: University of Oklahoma Press, 1969.

Norton, Thomas E., and Frank, Robert. *The Fur Trade in Colonial New York, 1686–1776*. Madison: University of Wisconsin Press, 1974.

Pound, Arthur. *Johnson of the Mohawks.* New York: Macmillan, 1930.

Seymour, Flora W. *Indian Agents of the Old Frontier.* 1941. Reprint ed. New York: Octagon Books, 1973.

Sosin, Jack. *The Revolutionary Frontier, 1763–1783.* Albuquerque: University of New Mexico Press, 1974.

Tolles, Frederick. *Meeting House and Counting House: The Quaker Merchants of Colonial Philadelphia, 1682–1763.* New York: W. W. Norton, 1963.

Trent, William. *Journal of Captain William Trent from Logstown to Pickawilly,* A.D. *1752.* 1871. Reprint ed. New York: Arno Press, 1971.

Van Rensselaer, Mrs. John. *The Goede Vrouw of Mannahatin: At Home and in Society, 1609–1760.* 1898. Reprint ed. New York: Arno Press, 1972.

Volwiler, Albert T. *George Croghan and the Westward Movement, 1741–1782.* Cleveland: A. H. Clark, 1926.

Wainwright, Nicholas B. *George Croghan, Wilderness Diplomat.* Chapel Hill: University of North Carolina Press, 1959.

Wallace, Anthony F. C. *King of the Delawares: Teedyuscung, 1700–1763.* Philadelphia: University of Pennsylvania Press, 1949.

Wright, Louis B. *Everyday Life in Colonial America.* New York: G.P. Putnam's Sons, 1966.

Wright, Louis B., ed. *The Cultural Life of the American Colonies, 1607–1763.* New York: Harper & Row, 1957.

Chapter Five

Arbuckle, Robert. *John Nicholson, 1757–1800: Pennsylvania Speculator and Patriot.* University Park: Pennsylvania State University Press, 1975.

Bauman, Richard. *For the Reputation of Truth: Politics, Religion, and Conflict among the Pennsylvania Quakers, 1750–1800.* Baltimore: Johns Hopkins University Press, 1971.

Boorstin, Daniel J. *The Americans: The Colonial Experience.* New York: Random House, Vintage Books, 1958.

Bridenbaugh, Carl. *The Spirit of '76: The Growth of American Patriotism before Independence.* New York: Oxford University Press, 1975.

Dawson, Henry B. *The Sons of Liberty in New York*. 1859. Reprint ed. New York: Arno Press, n.d.

Decker, Malcolm. *The Brink of Revolution: New York in Crisis, 1765–1776*. New York: Argosy-Antiquarian, 1964.

DePauw, Linda G., and Hunt, K. Conover. *Remember the Ladies: Women in America, 1750–1815*. New York: Viking Press, 1976.

Dickerson, Oliver M. *The Navigation Acts and the American Revolution*. Philadelphia: University of Pennsylvania Press, 1974.

Flick, Alexander C., ed. *History of the State of New York*. Vol. 3. New York: Columbia University Press, 1933.

Hanna, William S. *Benjamin Franklin and Pennsylvania Politics*. Stanford, Calif.: Stanford University Press, 1964.

Harrington, Virginia. *The New York Merchant on the Eve of Revolution*. Magnolia, Mass.: Peter Smith, 1964.

Headley, Joel Tyler. *The Great Riots of New York, 1712–1873*. New York: E. B. Treat, 1873.

Illick, Joseph E., ed. *America and England, 1558–1776*. New York: Irvington, 1970.

Kalm, Peter. "Travels into North America." In John Pinkerton, ed., *A General Collection of the Best and Most Interesting Voyages and Travels in All Parts of the World*. London: Longman, Hurst, Rees, Orme, and Brown, 1812.

Kammen, Michael. *A Rope of Sand: The Colonial Agents, British Policies, and the American Revolution*. New York: Random House, Vintage Books, 1974.

Ketcham, Ralph. *From Colony to Country: The Revolution in American Thought, 1750–1820*. New York: Macmillan, 1974.

Lucas, Stephen, E. *Portents of Revolution: Rhetoric and Revolution in Philadelphia, 1765–1776*. Philadelphia: Temple University Press, 1976.

Maier, Pauline. *From Resistance to Revolution: Colonial Radicals and the Development of American Opposition to Britain, 1765–1776*. New York: Random House, Vintage Books, 1973.

Martin, James K. *Men in Rebellion: Governmental Leaders and the Coming of the American Revolution*. New Brunswick, N.J.: Rutgers University Press, 1973.

Morgan, Edmund S. and Helen M. *The Stamp Act Crisis: Prologue to Revolution.* Rev. ed. New York: Macmillan, Collier Books, 1963.

Pole, J. R. *Political Representation in England and the Origins of the American Republic.* Berkeley: University of California Press, 1971.

Rossiter, Clinton. *The First American Revolution: The American Colonies on the Eve of Independence.* Rev. ed. New York: Harcourt Brace Jovanovich, Harvest Books, 1956.

Rushton, William Faulkner. *The Cajuns: From Acadia to Louisiana.* New York: Farrar, Straus & Giroux, 1979.

Schlesinger, Arthur M. *The Colonial Merchants and the American Revolution, 1763–1776.* New York: Atheneum, 1968.

Stillé, Charles J. *The Life and Times of John Dickinson.* Philadelphia: J. B. Lippincott, 1891.

INDEX